THE TRANSFORMERS
INFILTRATION

IDWPUBLISHING.COM
SAN DIEGO, CA

THE TRANSFORMERS
INFILTRATION

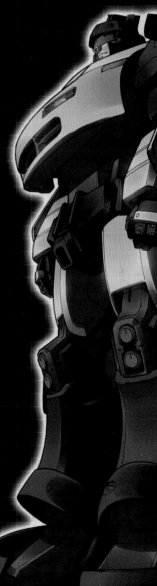

Written by
Simon Furman

Art by
E.J. Su

Colors by
John Rauch
With Josh Burcham, Aaron Myers,
Simon Bork, Mark Englert, Sunder Raj,
and Kevin Senft

Letters by
Robbie Robbins and Tom B. Long

Original Series Edited by
Chris Ryall and Dan Taylor

Collection Edited by
Aaron Myers

Book Design by
Neil Uyetake

ISBN10: 1-60010-010-0
ISBN13: 978-160010-010-9
09 08 07 06 1 2 3 4 5

www.IDWPUBLISHING.com

Licensed by: Hasbro Properties Group

IDW PUBLISHING IS:
Ted Adams, Co-President • Robbie Robbins, Co-President
Chris Ryall, Publisher/Editor-in-Chief • Kris Oprisko, Vice President
Neil Uyetake, Art Director • Dan Taylor, Editor
Aaron Myers, Editorial Assistant • Chance Boren, Editorial Assistant
Matthew Ruzicka, CPA, Controller • Alex Garner, Creative Director
Yumiko Miyano, Business Development • Rick Privman, Business Development

Special Thanks to Hasbro's Aaron Archer, Elizabeth Griffen, Richard Zambarano, and Amie Lozanski for their invaluable assistance.

THE TRANSFORMERS: INFILTRATION TPB. SEPTEMBER 2006. FIRST PRINTING. IDW Publishing, a division of Idea and Design Works, LLC. Editorial offices: 4411 Morena Blvd., Suite 106, San Diego, CA 92117.

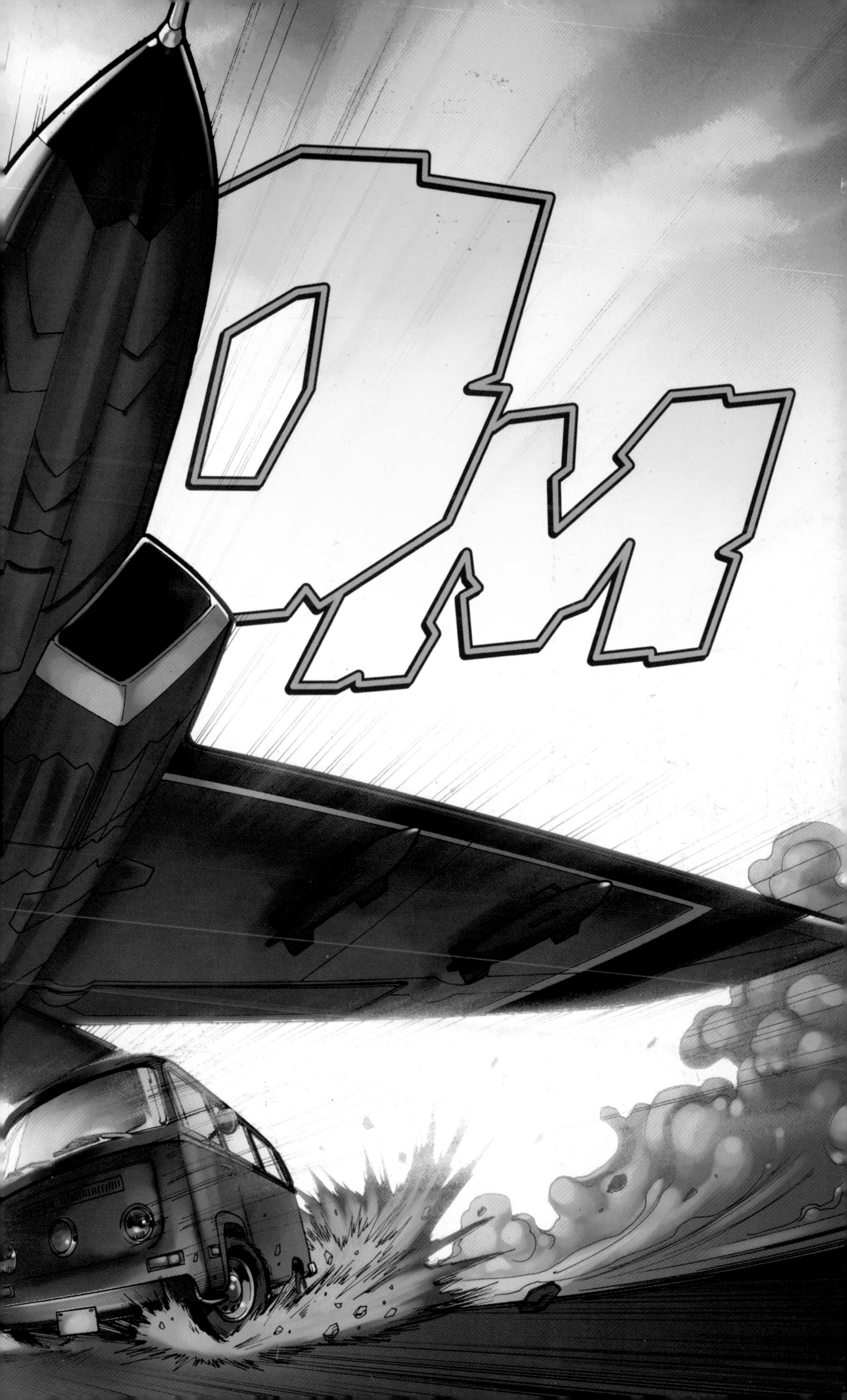

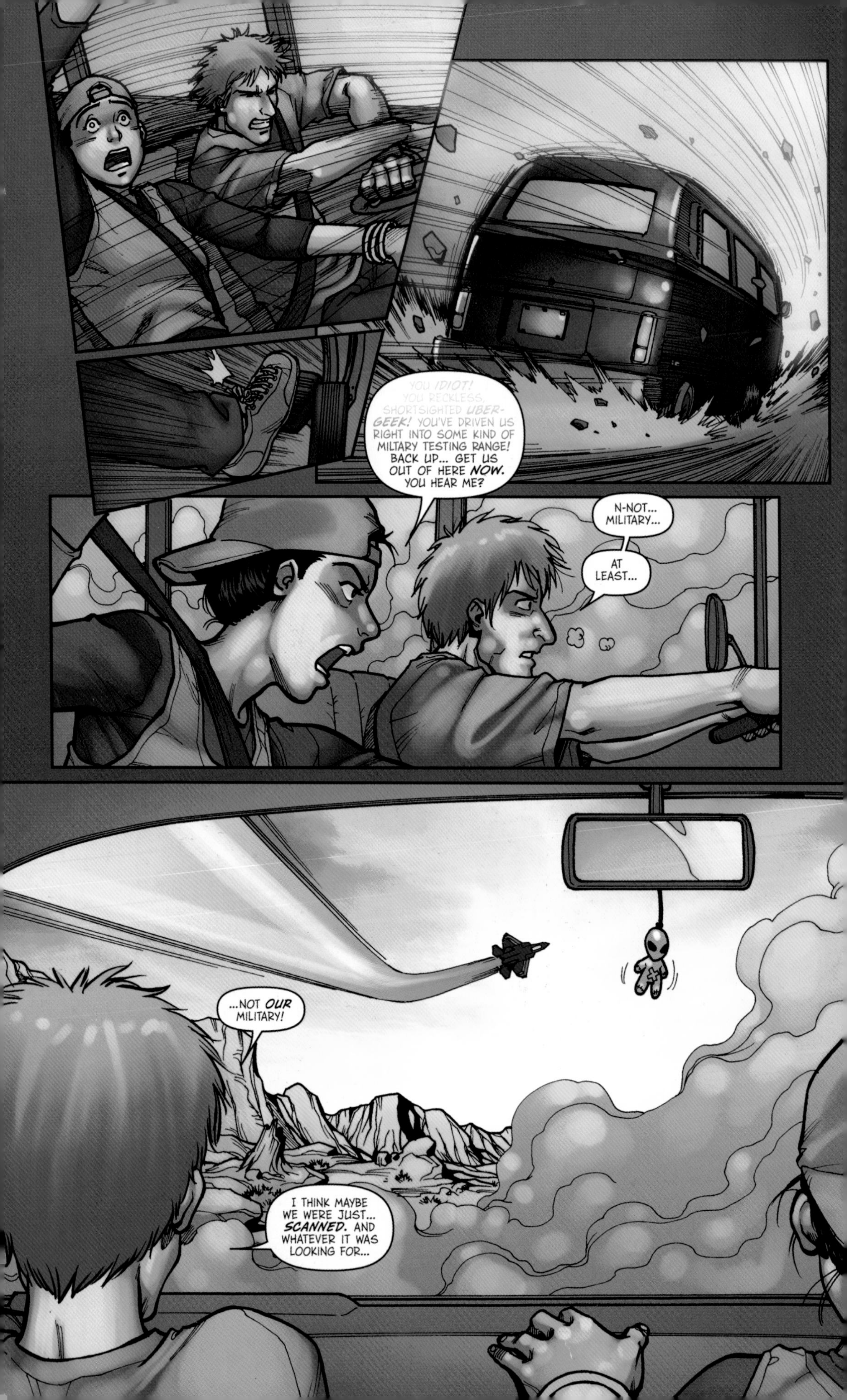
YOU IDIOT! YOU RECKLESS, SHORTSIGHTED UBER-GEEK! YOU'VE DRIVEN US RIGHT INTO SOME KIND OF MILTARY TESTING RANGE! BACK UP... GET US OUT OF HERE NOW. YOU HEAR ME?
N-NOT... MILITARY...
AT LEAST...
...NOT OUR MILITARY!
I THINK MAYBE WE WERE JUST... SCANNED. AND WHATEVER IT WAS LOOKING FOR...

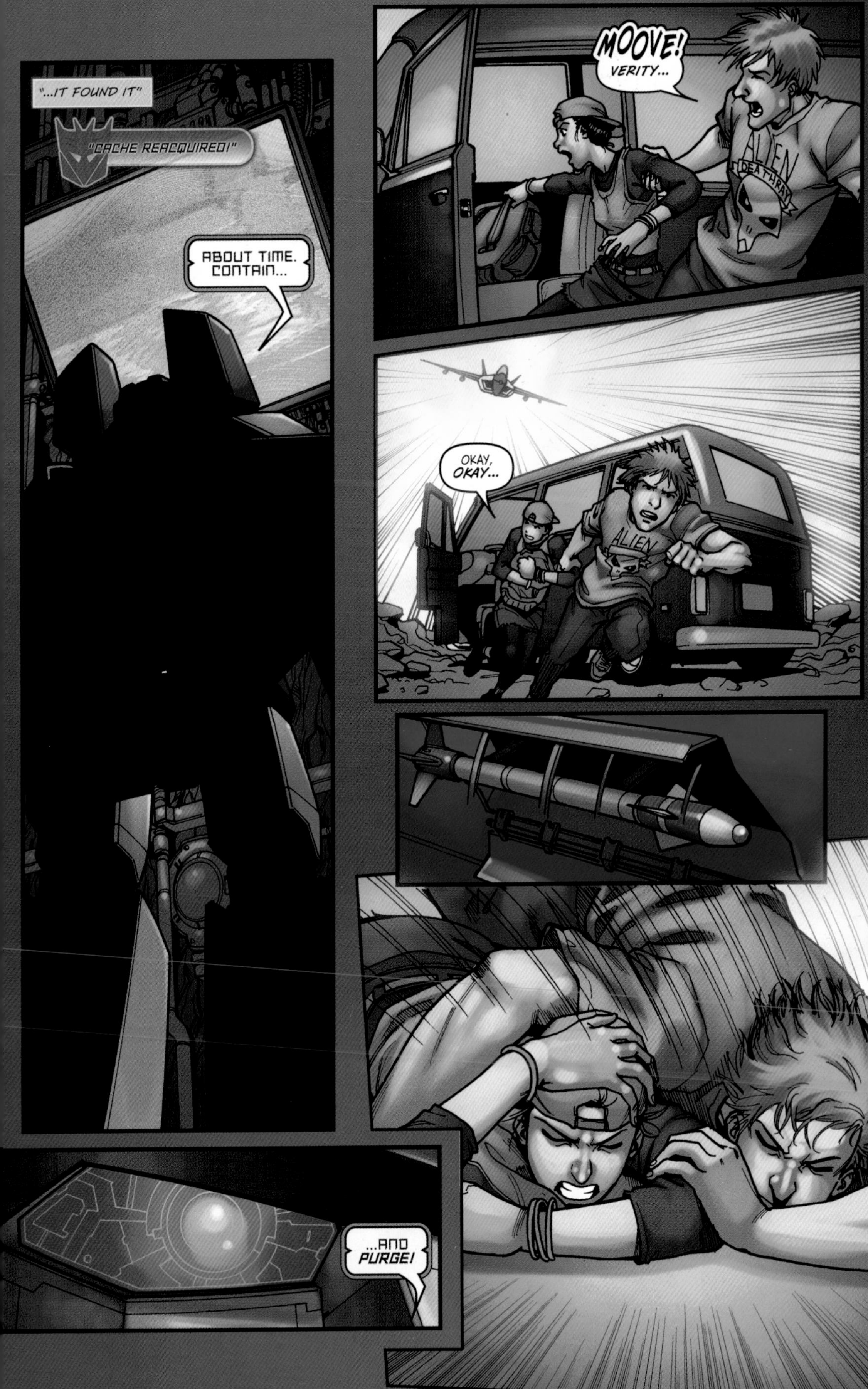
"...IT FOUND IT"
"CACHE REACQUIRED!"
ABOUT TIME. CONTAIN...
MOOVE! VERITY...
OKAY, OKAY...
...AND PURGE!

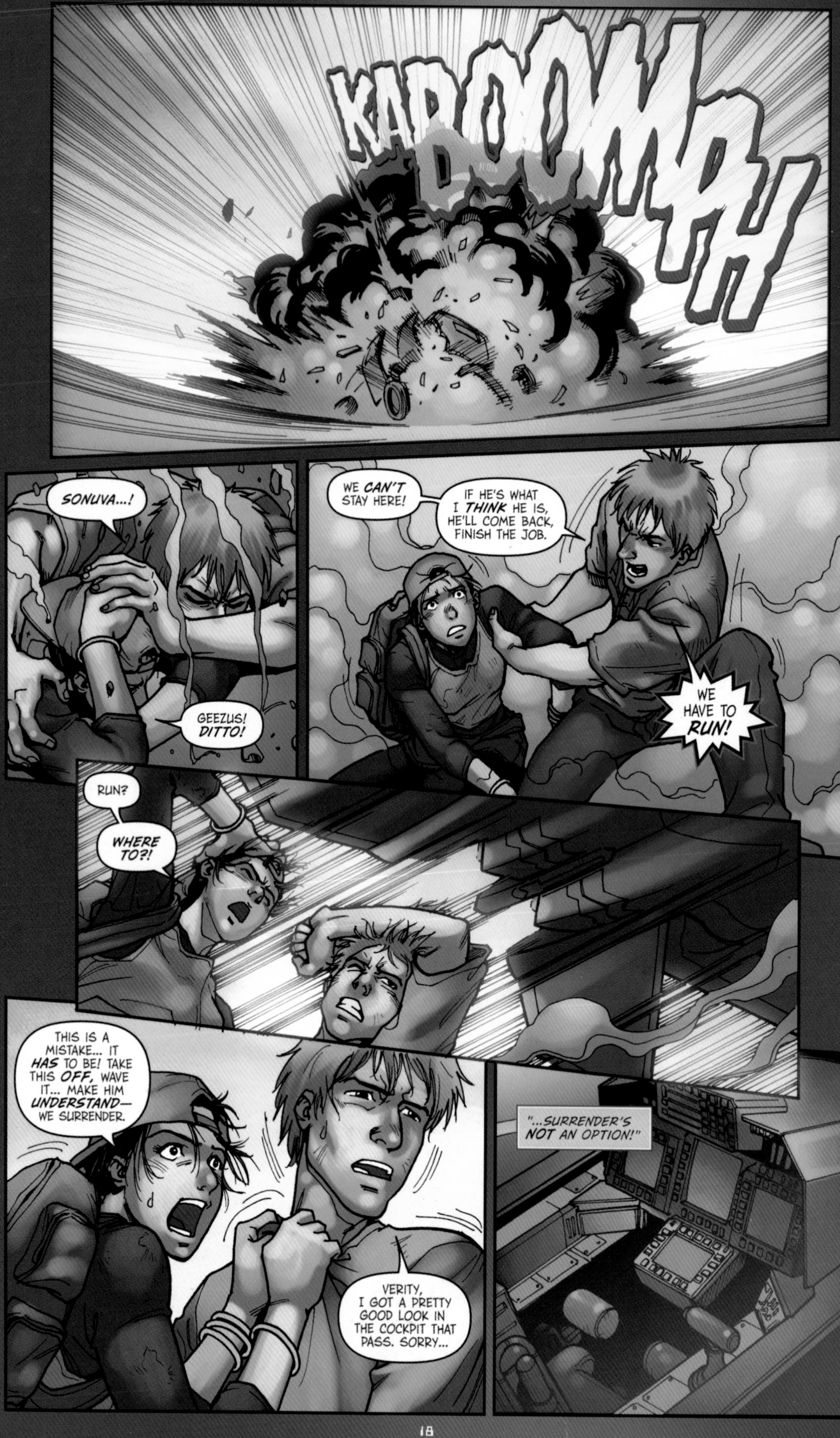
KADOOMPH
SONUVA...!
GEEZUS! DITTO!
WE CAN'T STAY HERE!
IF HE'S WHAT I THINK HE IS, HE'LL COME BACK, FINISH THE JOB.
WE HAVE TO RUN!
RUN?
WHERE TO?!
THIS IS A MISTAKE... IT HAS TO BE! TAKE THIS OFF, WAVE IT... MAKE HIM UNDERSTAND— WE SURRENDER.
VERITY, I GOT A PRETTY GOOD LOOK IN THE COCKPIT THAT PASS. SORRY...
"...SURRENDER'S NOT AN OPTION!"

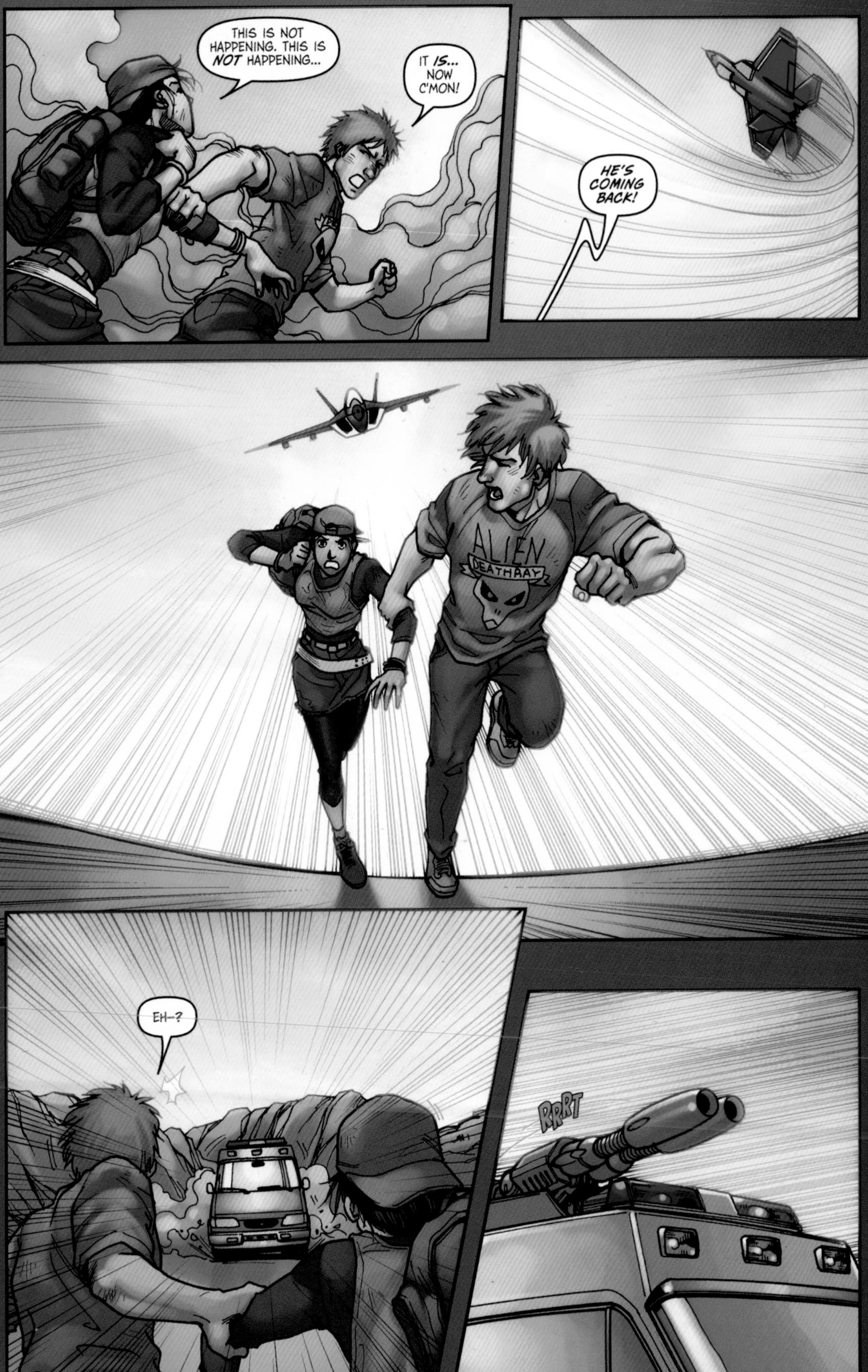

THIS IS NOT HAPPENING. THIS IS NOT HAPPENING...
IT IS... NOW C'MON!
HE'S COMING BACK!
ALIEN DEATHRAY
EH--?
RRRT

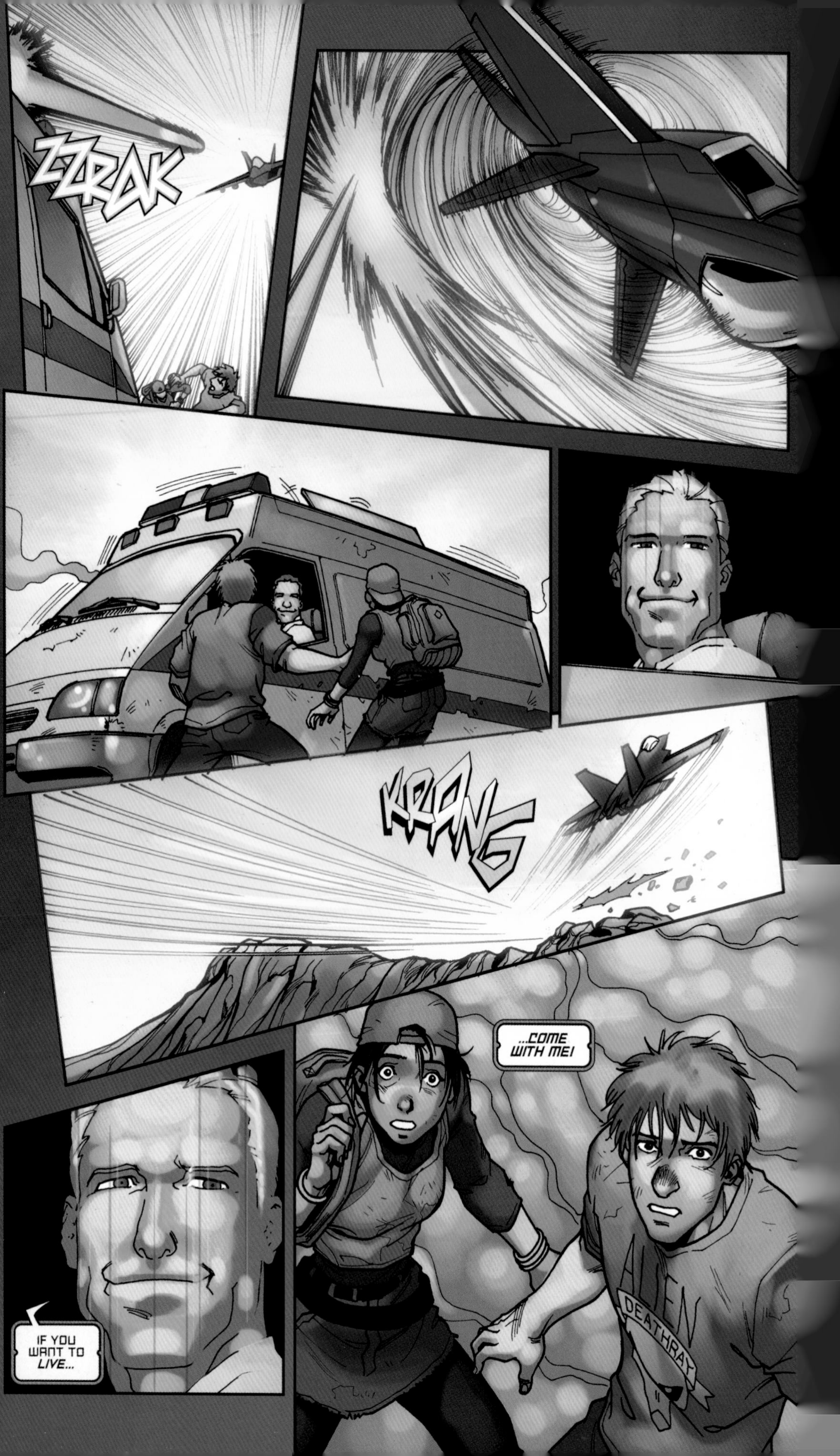
ZZRAK
KRANG
...COME WITH ME!
IF YOU WANT TO *LIVE*...
ALIEN DEATHRAY

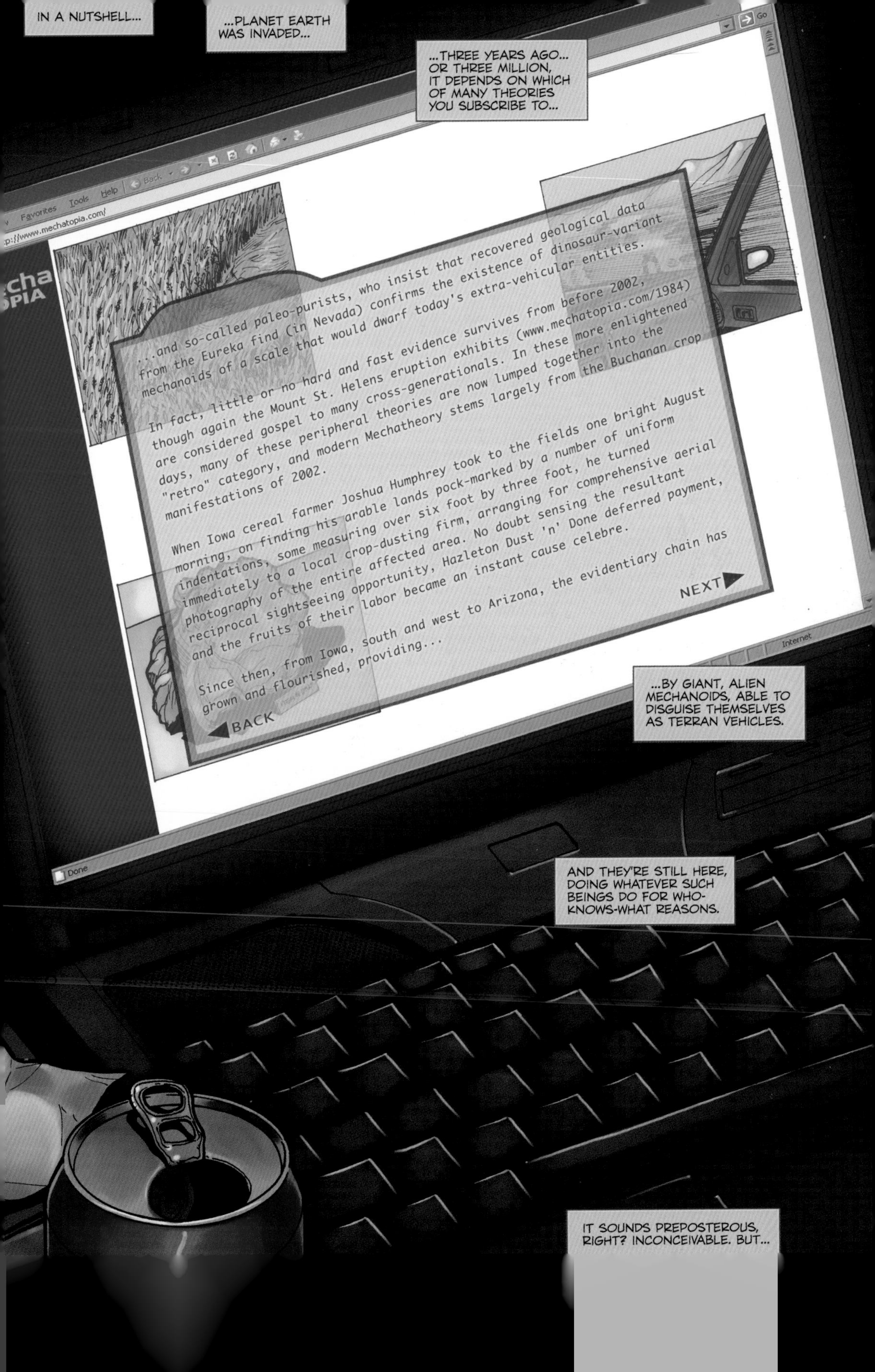
IN A NUTSHELL...
...PLANET EARTH WAS INVADED...
...THREE YEARS AGO... OR THREE MILLION, IT DEPENDS ON WHICH OF MANY THEORIES YOU SUBSCRIBE TO...
Favorites Tools Help
Back
Go
...and so-called paleo-purists, who insist that recovered geological data from the Eureka find (in Nevada) confirms the existence of dinosaur-variant mechanoids of a scale that would dwarf today's extra-vehicular entities.
In fact, little or no hard and fast evidence survives from before 2002, though again the Mount St. Helens eruption exhibits (www.mechatopia.com/1984) are considered gospel to many cross-generationals. In these more enlightened days, many of these peripheral theories are now lumped together into the "retro" category, and modern Mechatheory stems largely from the Buchanan crop manifestations of 2002.
When Iowa cereal farmer Joshua Humphrey took to the fields one bright August morning, on finding his arable lands pock-marked by a number of uniform indentations, some measuring over six foot by three foot, he turned immediately to a local crop-dusting firm, arranging for comprehensive aerial photography of the entire affected area. No doubt sensing the resultant reciprocal sightseeing opportunity, Hazleton Dust 'n' Done deferred payment, and the fruits of their labor became an instant cause celebre.
Since then, from Iowa, south and west to Arizona, the evidentiary chain has grown and flourished, providing...
NEXT
BACK
Internet
Done
...BY GIANT, ALIEN MECHANOIDS, ABLE TO DISGUISE THEMSELVES AS TERRAN VEHICLES.
AND THEY'RE STILL HERE, DOING WHATEVER SUCH BEINGS DO FOR WHO-KNOWS-WHAT REASONS.
IT SOUNDS PREPOSTEROUS, RIGHT? INCONCEIVABLE. BUT...

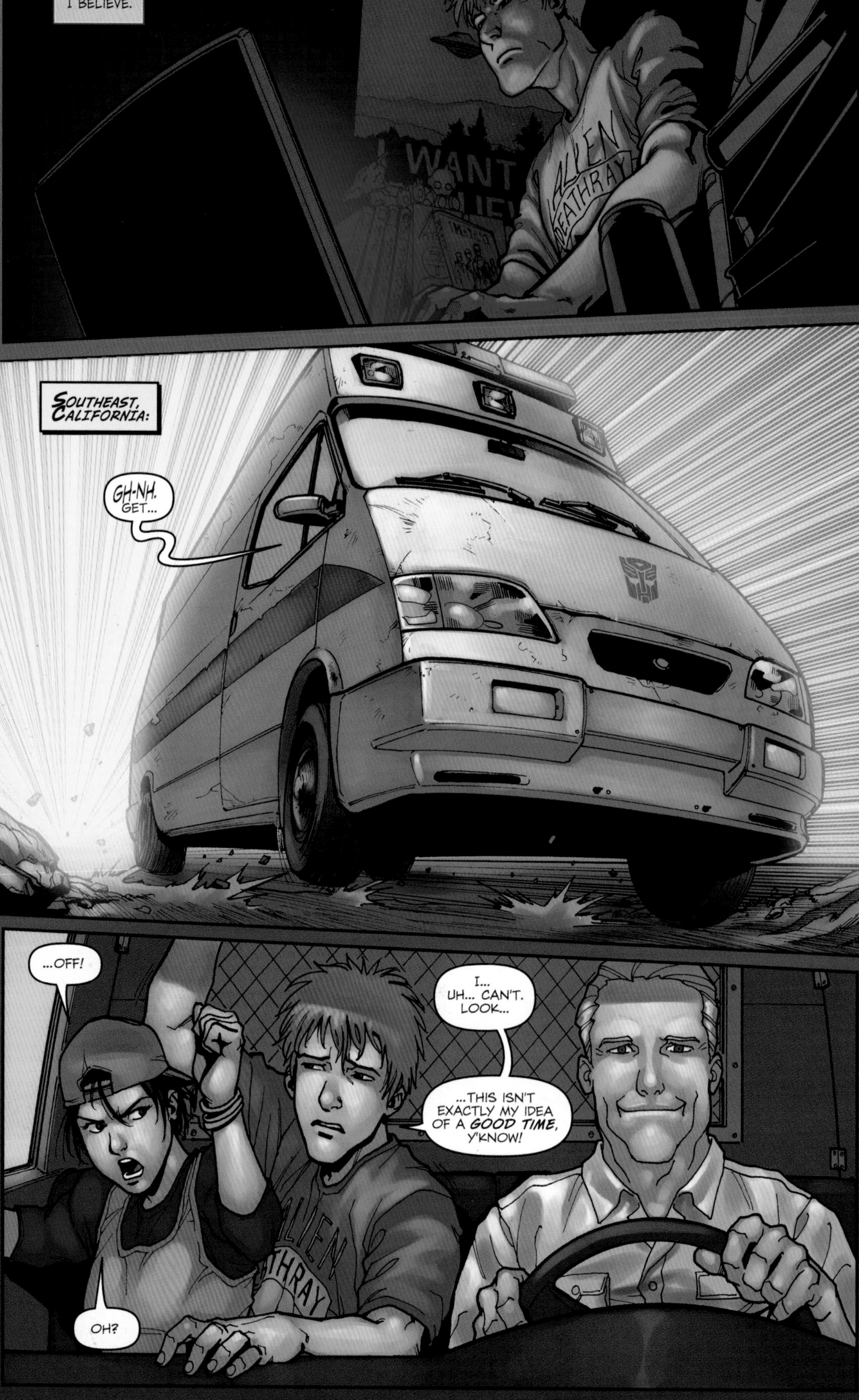
I BELIEVE.
SOUTHEAST, CALIFORNIA:
GH-NH. GET...
...OFF!
I... UH... CAN'T. LOOK...
...THIS ISN'T EXACTLY MY IDEA OF A GOOD TIME, Y'KNOW!
OH?

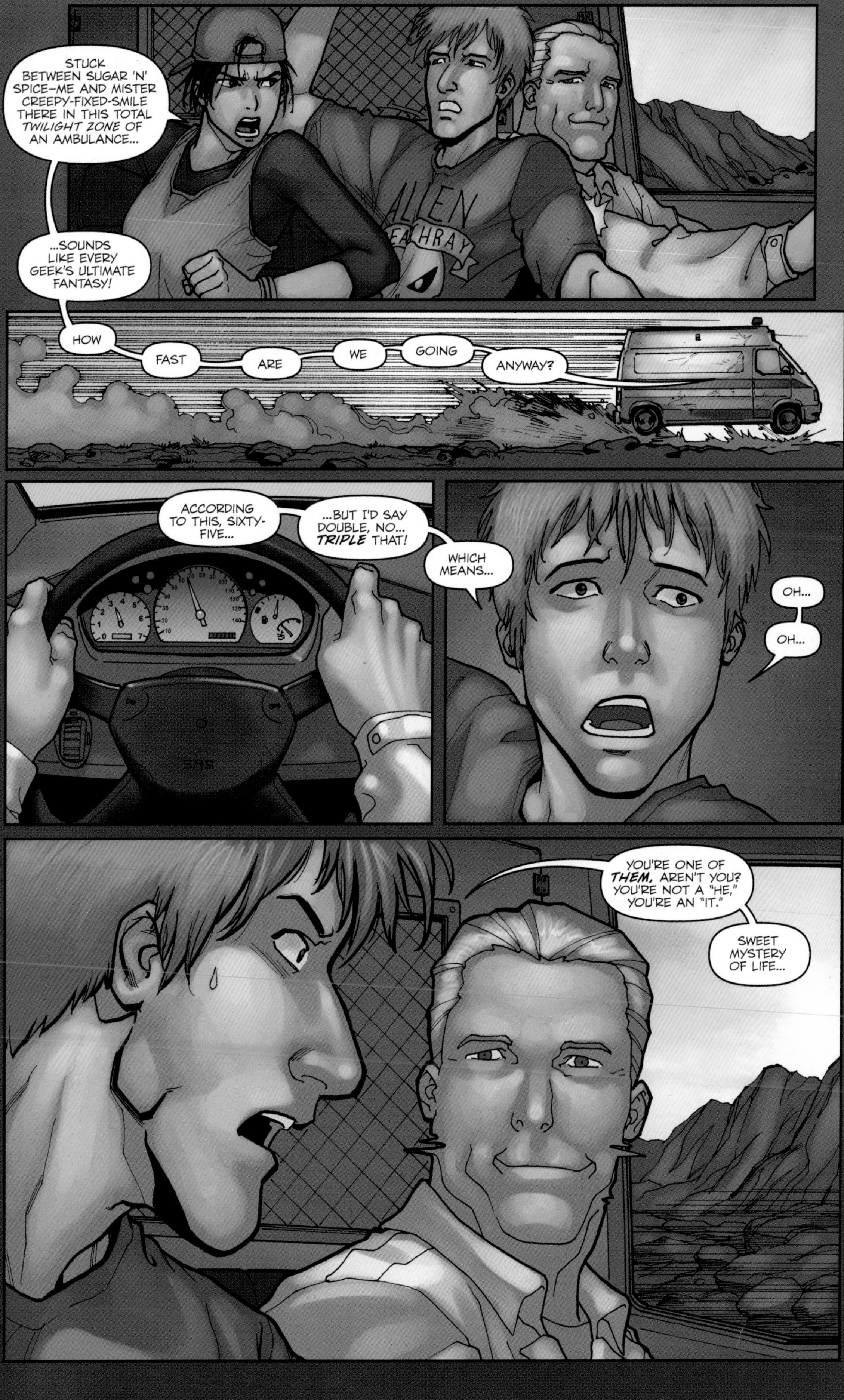
STUCK BETWEEN SUGAR 'N' SPICE—ME AND MISTER CREEPY-FIXED-SMILE THERE IN THIS TOTAL *TWILIGHT ZONE* OF AN AMBULANCE...
...SOUNDS LIKE EVERY GEEK'S ULTIMATE FANTASY!
ALIEN
HOW FAST ARE WE GOING ANYWAY?
ACCORDING TO THIS, SIXTY-FIVE...
...BUT I'D SAY DOUBLE, NO... ***TRIPLE*** THAT!
WHICH MEANS...
OH...
OH...
YOU'RE ONE OF ***THEM,*** AREN'T YOU? YOU'RE NOT A "HE," YOU'RE AN "IT."
SWEET MYSTERY OF LIFE...

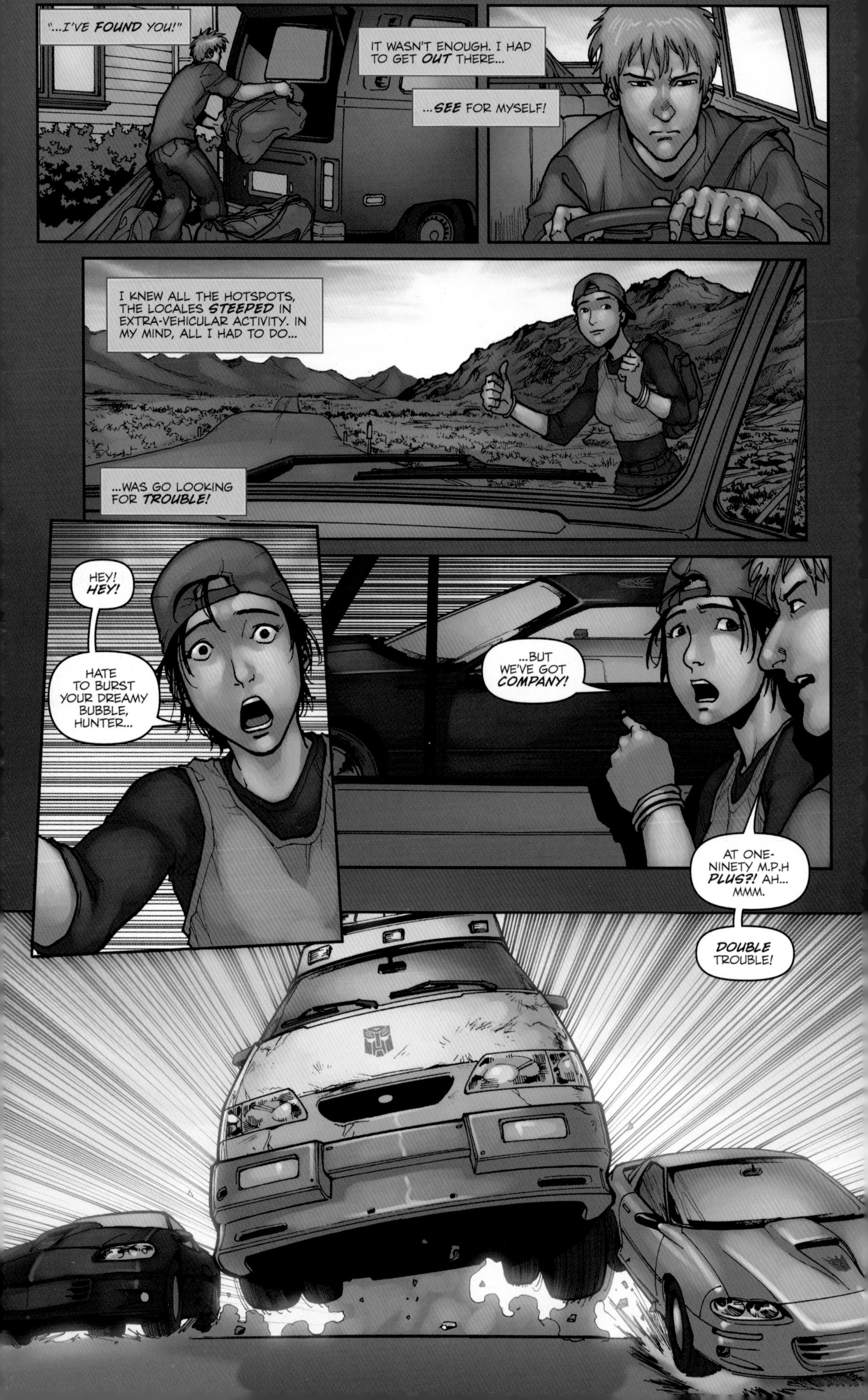
"...I'VE FOUND YOU!"
IT WASN'T ENOUGH. I HAD TO GET OUT THERE...
...SEE FOR MYSELF!
I KNEW ALL THE HOTSPOTS, THE LOCALES STEEPED IN EXTRA-VEHICULAR ACTIVITY. IN MY MIND, ALL I HAD TO DO...
...WAS GO LOOKING FOR TROUBLE!
HEY! HEY!
HATE TO BURST YOUR DREAMY BUBBLE, HUNTER...
...BUT WE'VE GOT COMPANY!
AT ONE-NINETY M.P.H PLUS?! AH... MMM.
DOUBLE TROUBLE!

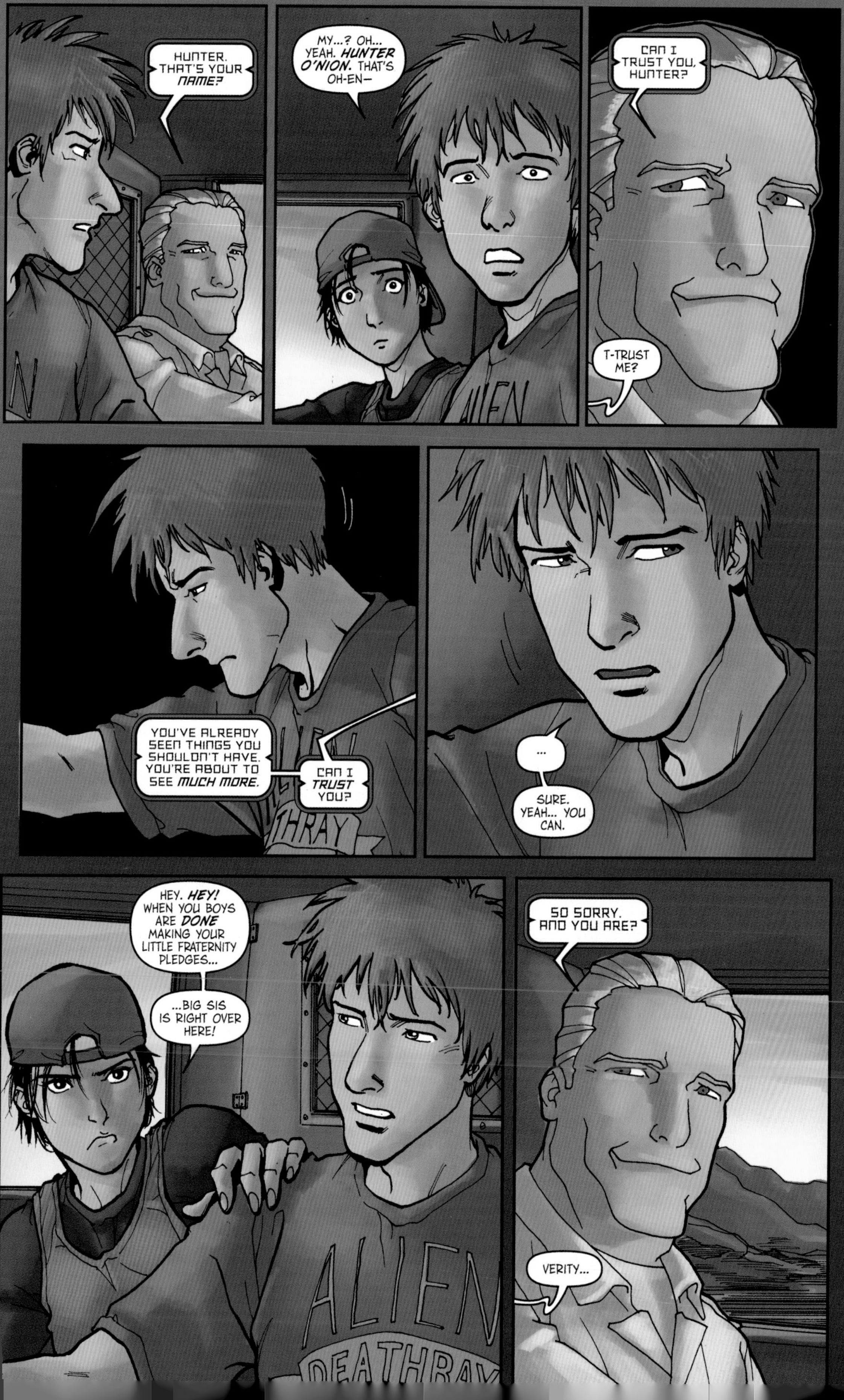
HUNTER. THAT'S YOUR *NAME?*
MY...? OH... YEAH. ***HUNTER O'NION.*** THAT'S OH-EN—
CAN I TRUST YOU, HUNTER?
T-TRUST ME?
YOU'VE ALREADY SEEN THINGS YOU SHOULDN'T HAVE. YOU'RE ABOUT TO SEE *MUCH MORE.*
CAN I *TRUST* YOU?
...
SURE. YEAH... YOU CAN.
HEY. ***HEY!*** WHEN YOU BOYS ARE ***DONE*** MAKING YOUR LITTLE FRATERNITY PLEDGES...
...BIG SIS IS RIGHT OVER HERE!
SO SORRY. AND YOU ARE?
VERITY...

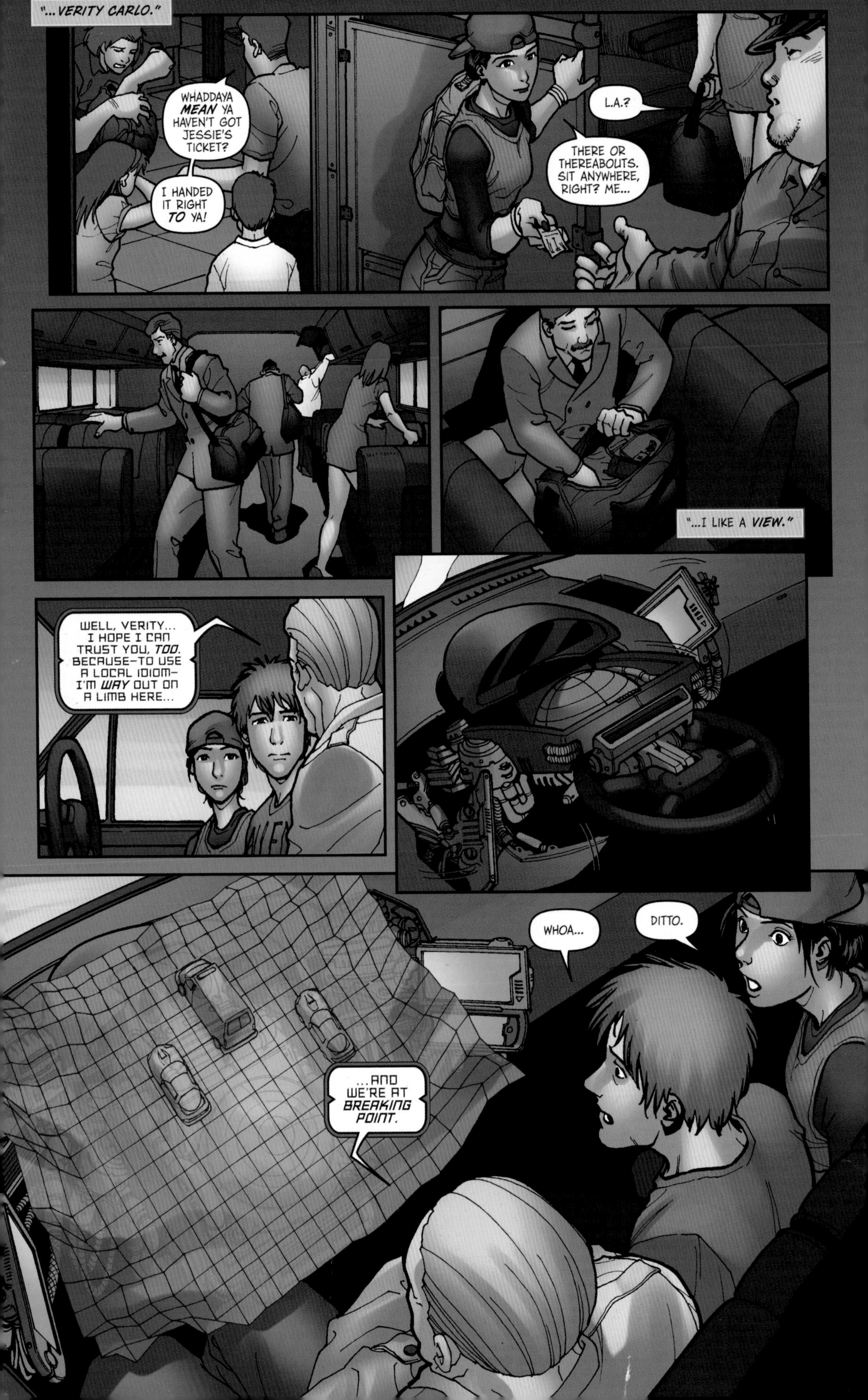
"...VERITY CARLO."
WHADDAYA MEAN YA HAVEN'T GOT JESSIE'S TICKET?
I HANDED IT RIGHT TO YA!
L.A.?
THERE OR THEREABOUTS. SIT ANYWHERE, RIGHT? ME...
"...I LIKE A VIEW."
WELL, VERITY... I HOPE I CAN TRUST YOU, TOO. BECAUSE–TO USE A LOCAL IDIOM– I'M WAY OUT ON A LIMB HERE...
WHOA...
DITTO.
...AND WE'RE AT BREAKING POINT.

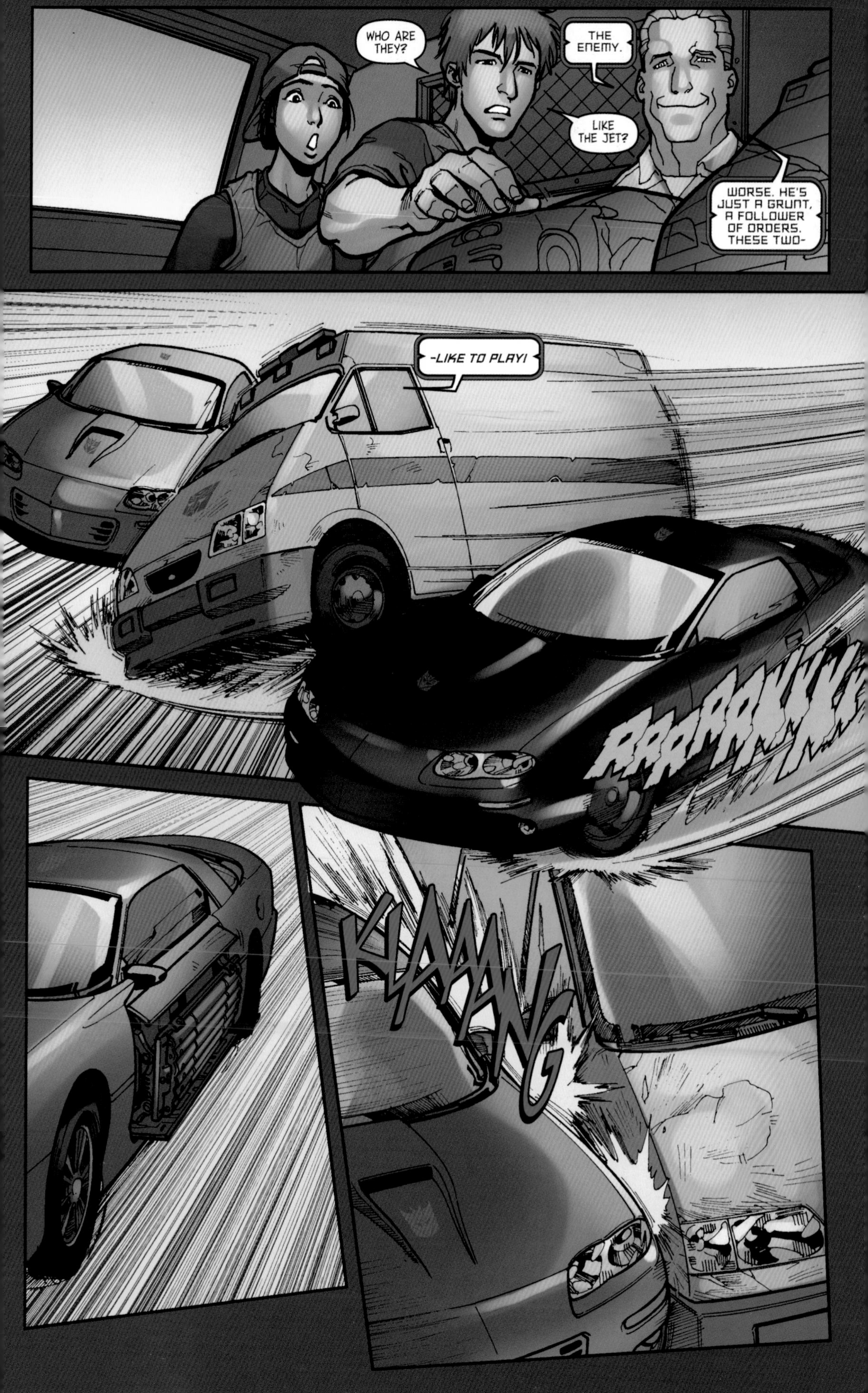
WHO ARE THEY?
THE ENEMY.
LIKE THE JET?
WORSE. HE'S JUST A GRUNT, A FOLLOWER OF ORDERS. THESE TWO-
-LIKE TO PLAY!
RRRRRKKK!
KLAAANG

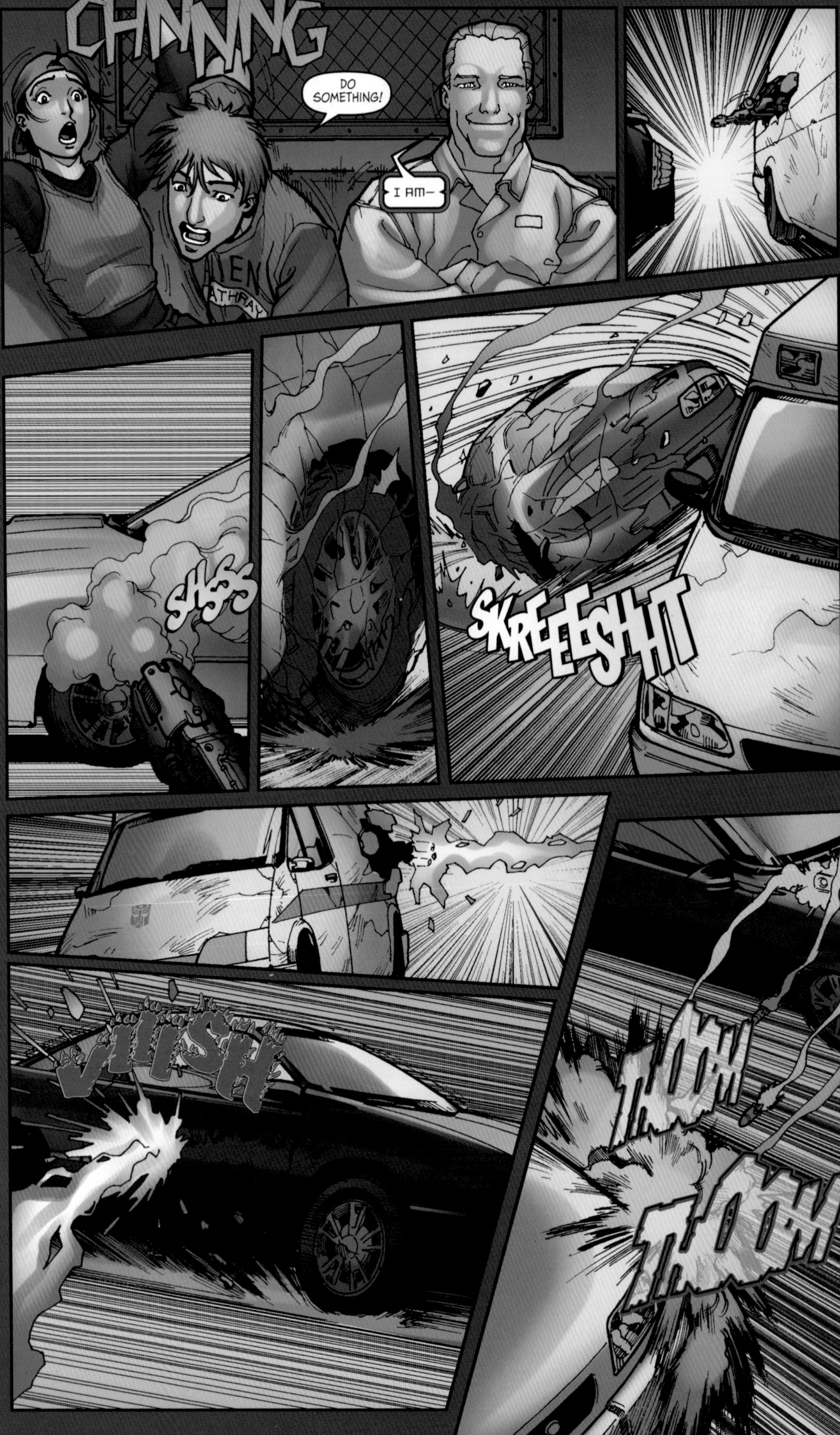
CHNNNG
DO SOMETHING!
I AM—
SHSSS
SKREEEESHHT
VIISH
THOOM
THOOM

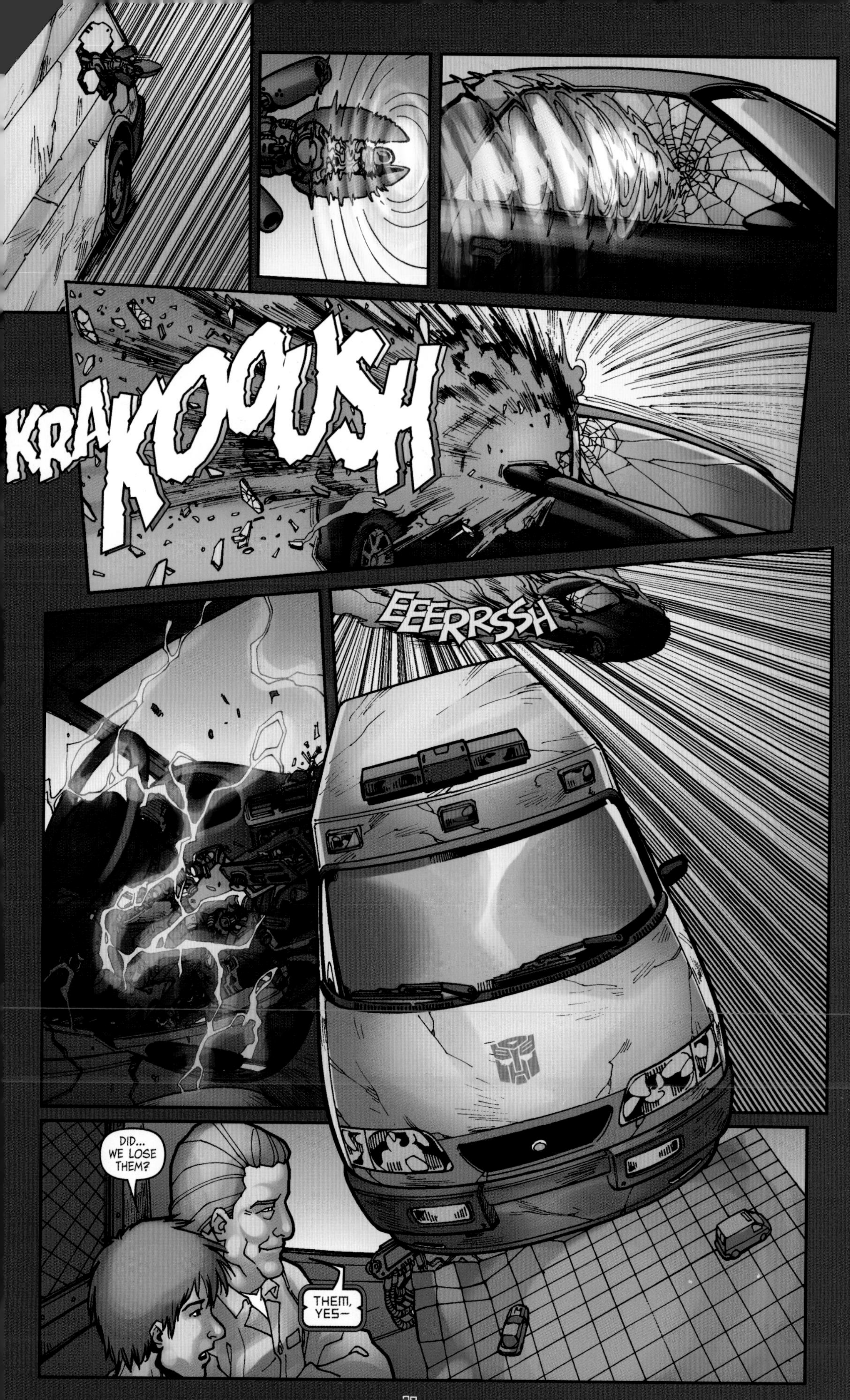
KRAKOOUSH
EEEERRSSH
DID... WE LOSE THEM?
THEM, YES—

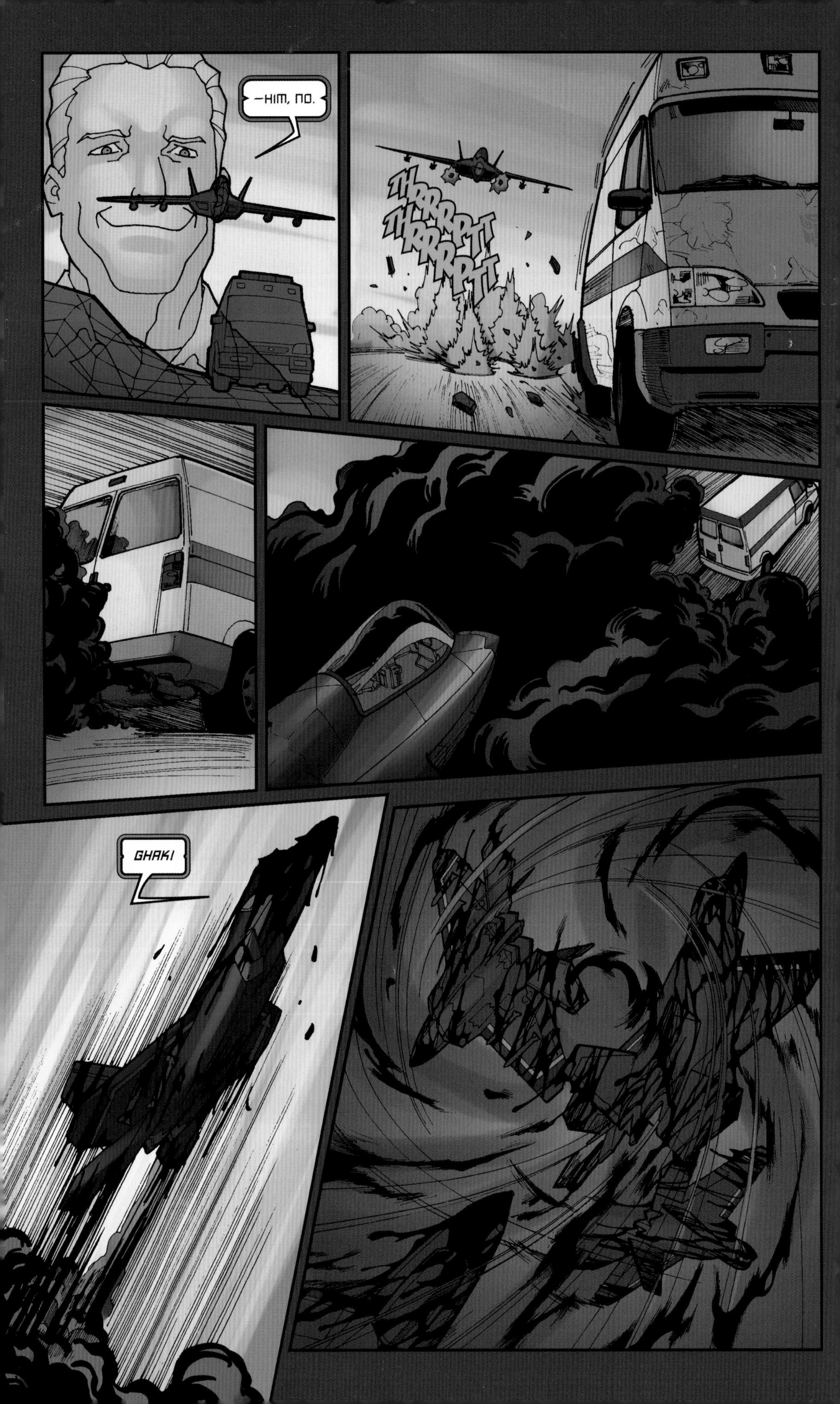
—HIM, NO.
THRRRPTT THRRRPTT
GHAK!

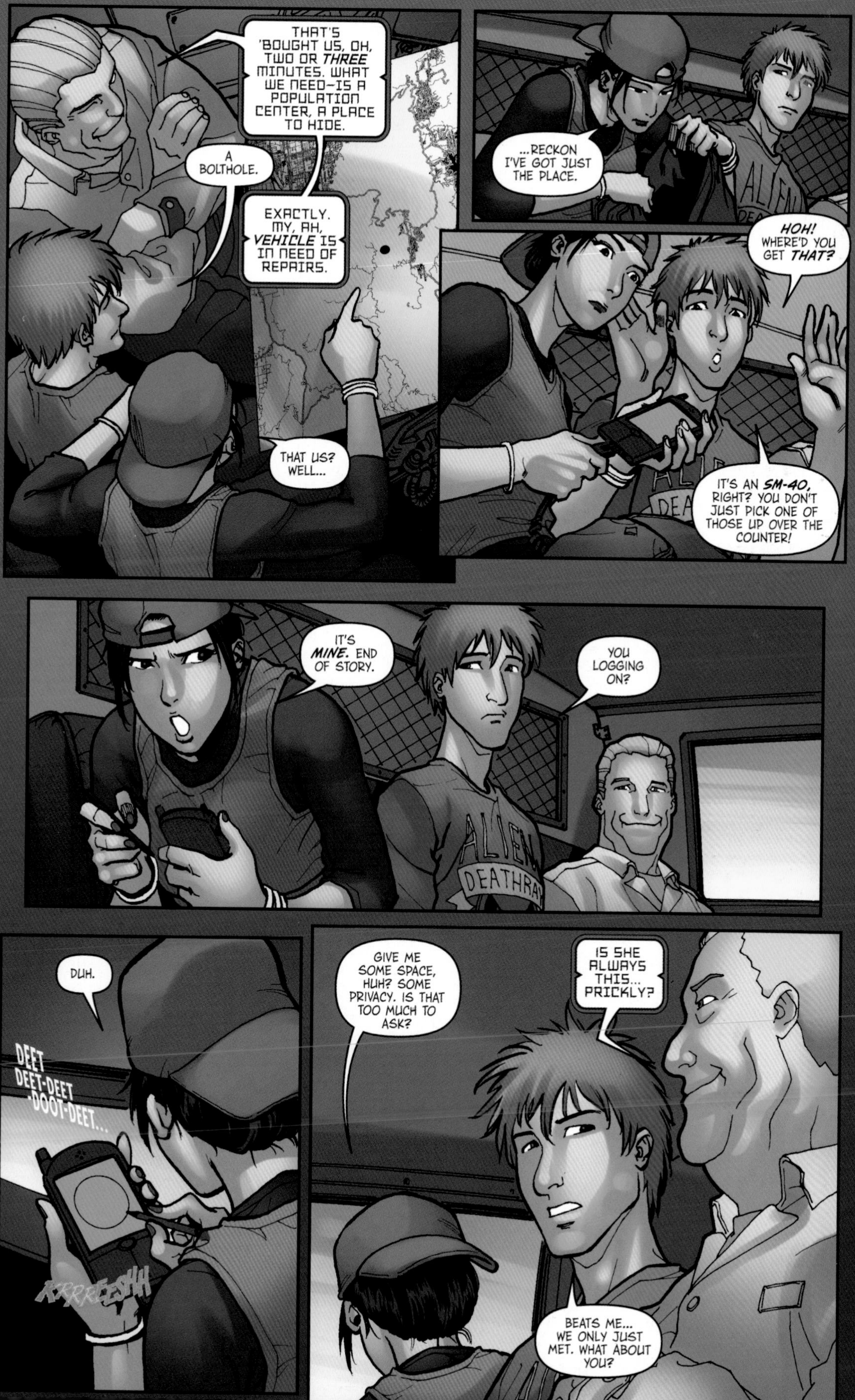
THAT'S 'BOUGHT US, OH, TWO OR *THREE* MINUTES. WHAT WE NEED--IS A POPULATION CENTER, A PLACE TO HIDE.
A BOLTHOLE.
EXACTLY. MY, AH, *VEHICLE* IS IN NEED OF REPAIRS.
THAT US? WELL...
...RECKON I'VE GOT JUST THE PLACE.
HOH! WHERE'D YOU GET *THAT?*
IT'S AN *SM-40,* RIGHT? YOU DON'T JUST PICK ONE OF THOSE UP OVER THE COUNTER!
IT'S *MINE.* END OF STORY.
YOU LOGGING ON?
DUH.
DEET DEET-DEET -DOOT-DEET...
KRRRCESHH
GIVE ME SOME SPACE, HUH? SOME PRIVACY. IS THAT TOO MUCH TO ASK?
IS SHE ALWAYS THIS... PRICKLY?
BEATS ME... WE ONLY JUST MET. WHAT ABOUT YOU?

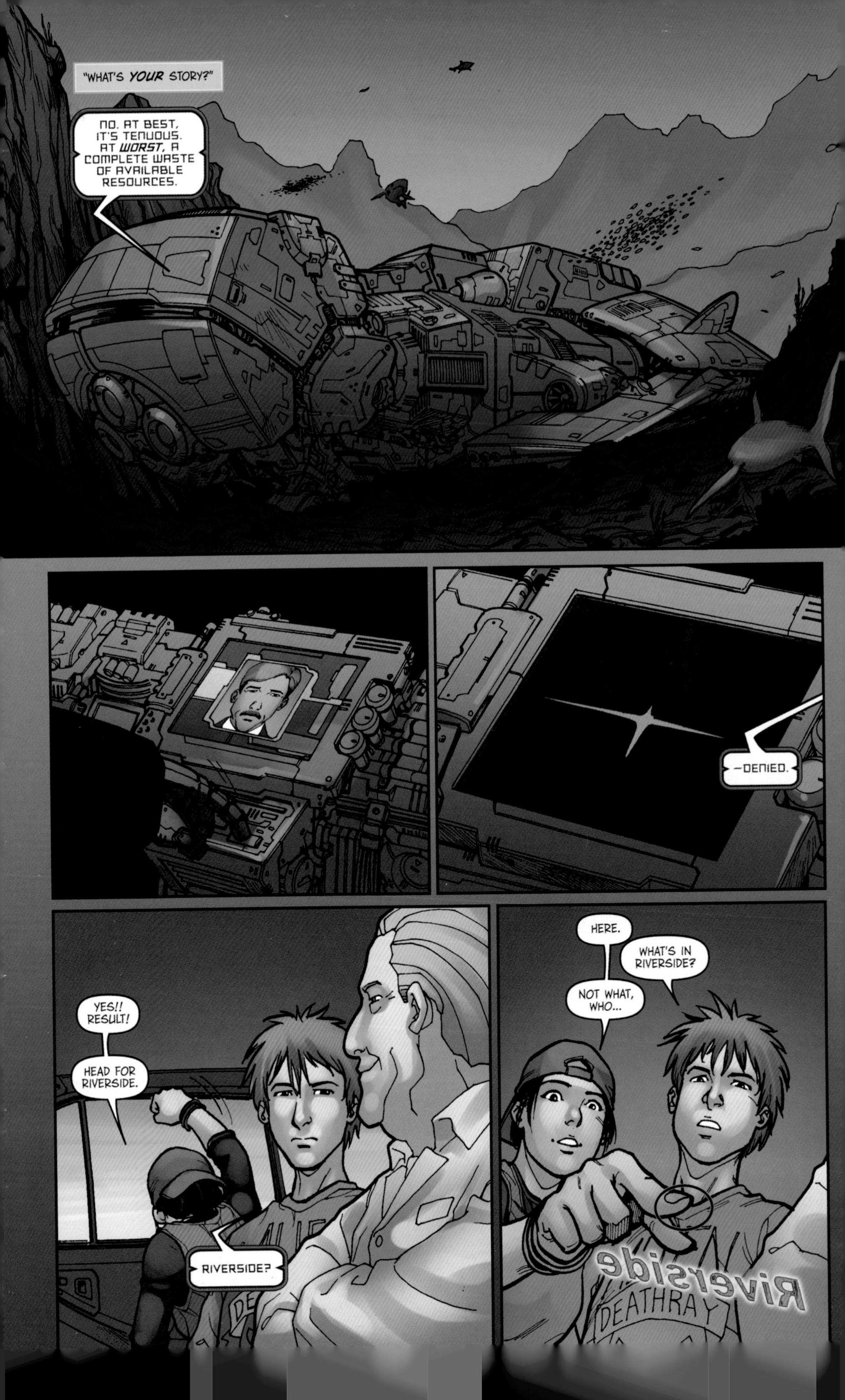
"WHAT'S YOUR STORY?"
NO. AT BEST, IT'S TENUOUS. AT WORST, A COMPLETE WASTE OF AVAILABLE RESOURCES.
—DENIED.
YES!! RESULT!
HEAD FOR RIVERSIDE.
RIVERSIDE?
HERE.
WHAT'S IN RIVERSIDE?
NOT WHAT, WHO...
DEATHRAY
Riverside

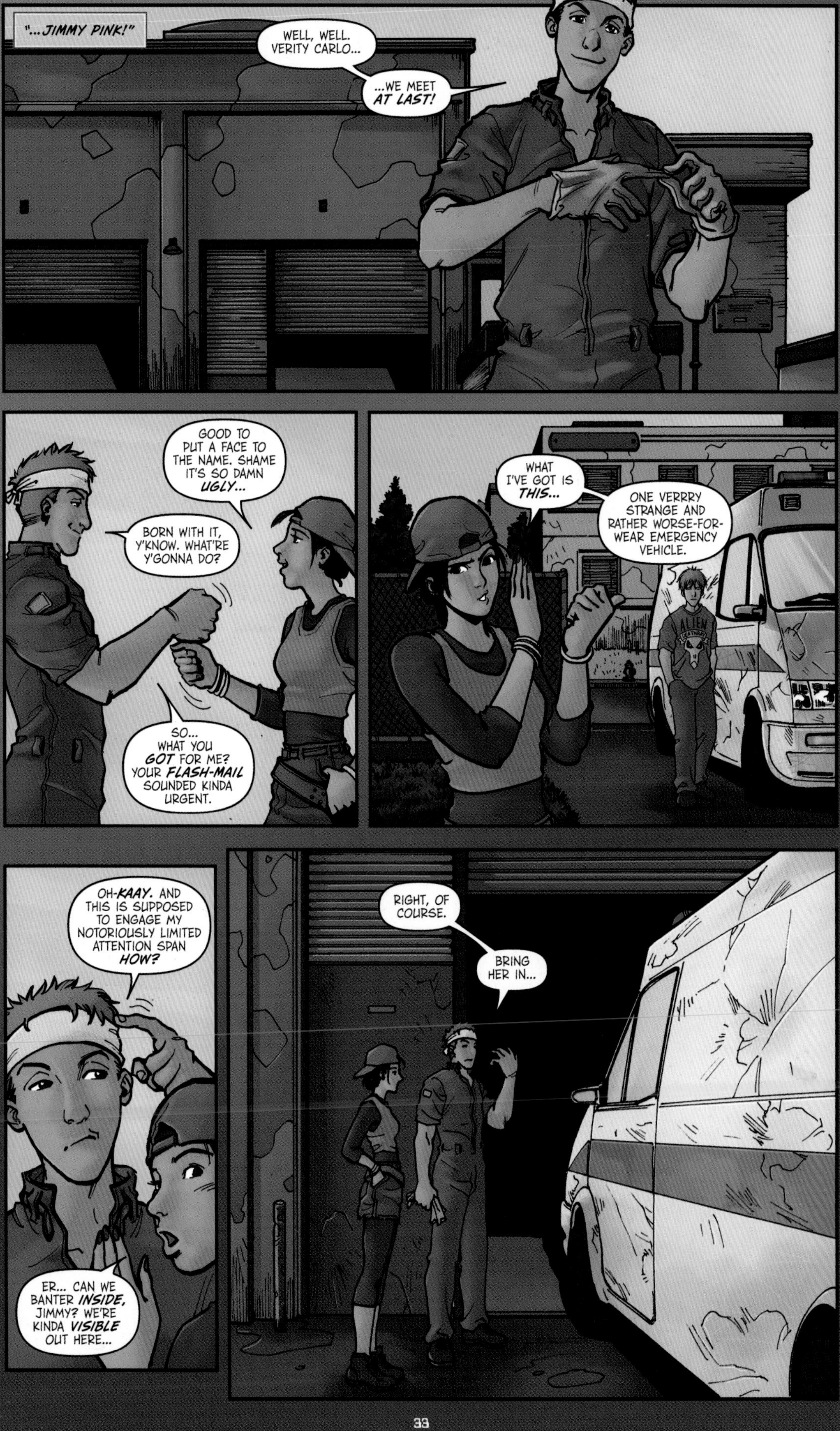
"...JIMMY PINK!"
WELL, WELL. VERITY CARLO...
...WE MEET AT LAST!
GOOD TO PUT A FACE TO THE NAME. SHAME IT'S SO DAMN UGLY...
BORN WITH IT, Y'KNOW. WHAT'RE Y'GONNA DO?
SO... WHAT YOU GOT FOR ME? YOUR FLASH-MAIL SOUNDED KINDA URGENT.
WHAT I'VE GOT IS THIS...
ONE VERRRY STRANGE AND RATHER WORSE-FOR-WEAR EMERGENCY VEHICLE.
ALIEN
OH-KAAY. AND THIS IS SUPPOSED TO ENGAGE MY NOTORIOUSLY LIMITED ATTENTION SPAN HOW?
ER... CAN WE BANTER INSIDE, JIMMY? WE'RE KINDA VISIBLE OUT HERE...
RIGHT, OF COURSE.
BRING HER IN...

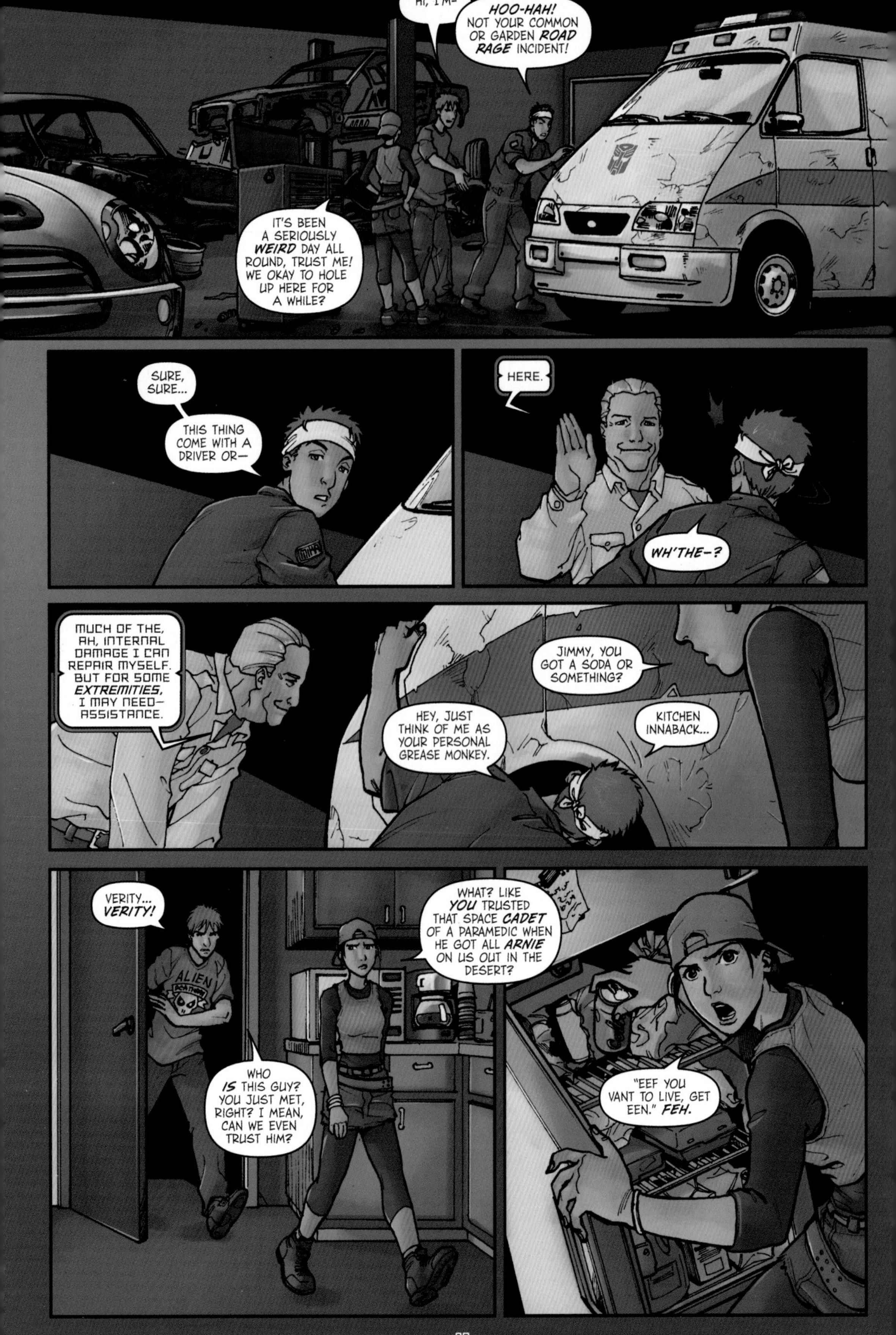
HI, I'M-
HOO-HAH! NOT YOUR COMMON OR GARDEN ROAD RAGE INCIDENT!
IT'S BEEN A SERIOUSLY WEIRD DAY ALL ROUND, TRUST ME! WE OKAY TO HOLE UP HERE FOR A WHILE?
SURE, SURE...
THIS THING COME WITH A DRIVER OR—
HERE.
WH'THE-?
MUCH OF THE, AH, INTERNAL DAMAGE I CAN REPAIR MYSELF. BUT FOR SOME EXTREMITIES, I MAY NEED-ASSISTANCE.
HEY, JUST THINK OF ME AS YOUR PERSONAL GREASE MONKEY.
JIMMY, YOU GOT A SODA OR SOMETHING?
KITCHEN INNABACK...
VERITY... VERITY!
WHO IS THIS GUY? YOU JUST MET, RIGHT? I MEAN, CAN WE EVEN TRUST HIM?
WHAT? LIKE YOU TRUSTED THAT SPACE CADET OF A PARAMEDIC WHEN HE GOT ALL ARNIE ON US OUT IN THE DESERT?
"EEF YOU VANT TO LIVE, GET EEN." FEH.

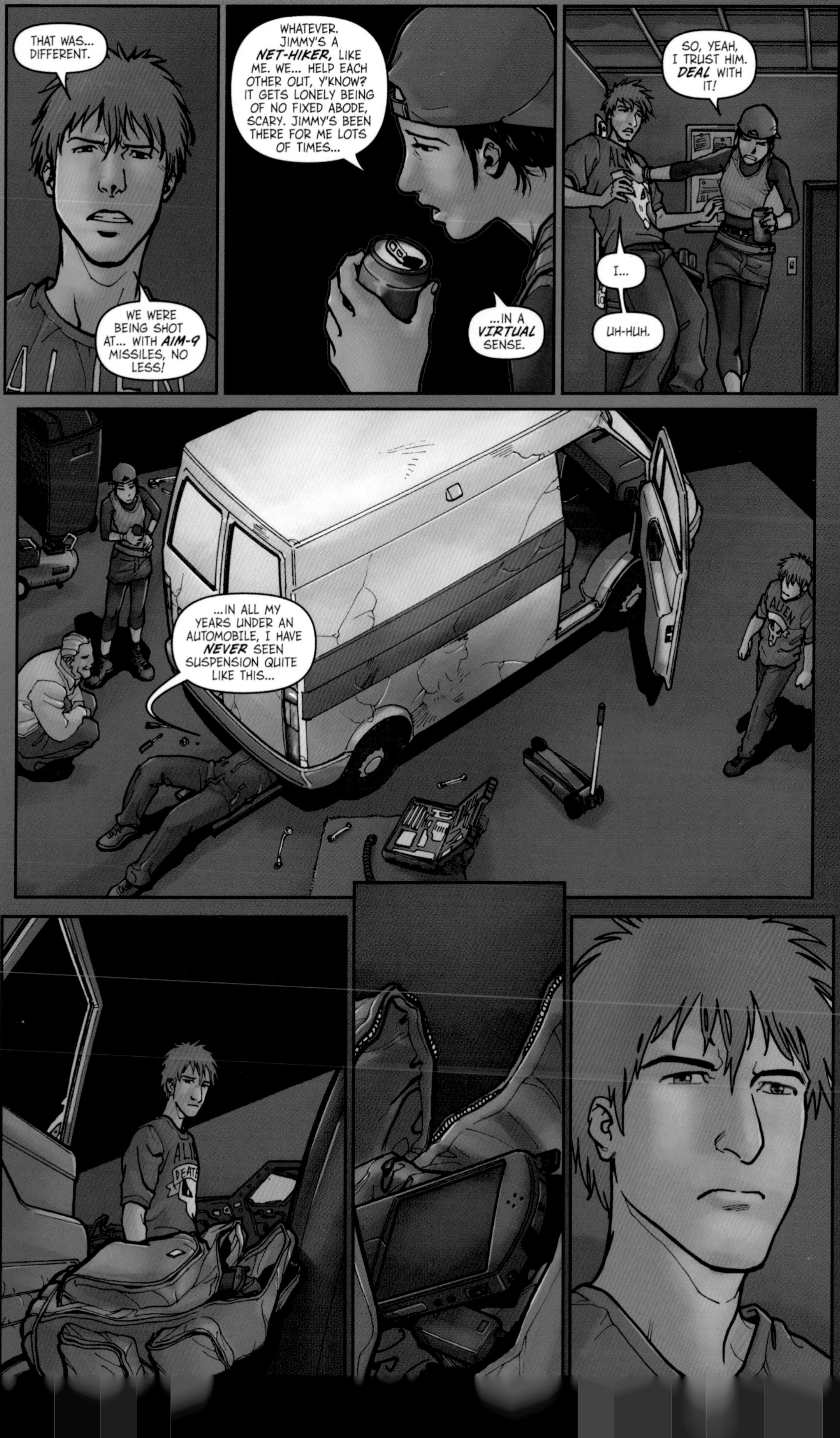

THAT WAS... DIFFERENT.
WE WERE BEING SHOT AT... WITH AIM-9 MISSILES, NO LESS!
WHATEVER. JIMMY'S A NET-HIKER, LIKE ME. WE... HELP EACH OTHER OUT, Y'KNOW? IT GETS LONELY BEING OF NO FIXED ABODE, SCARY. JIMMY'S BEEN THERE FOR ME LOTS OF TIMES...
...IN A VIRTUAL SENSE.
SO, YEAH, I TRUST HIM. DEAL WITH IT!
I...
UH-HUH.
...IN ALL MY YEARS UNDER AN AUTOMOBILE, I HAVE NEVER SEEN SUSPENSION QUITE LIKE THIS...

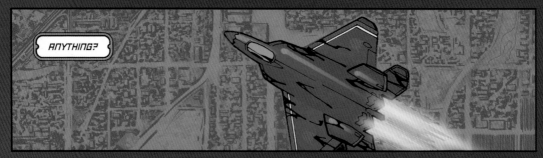

ANYTHING?

NEGATIVE. TARGETS HAVE GONE TO GROUND. CONTINUING RESONANT SIGNATURE SWEEP.

HE'LL BE SPITTING DIODE CLUSTERS RIGHT ABOUT NOW. THINK WE SHOULD DISCORPORATE THE *NULL BUBBLE* AND CHECK IN?

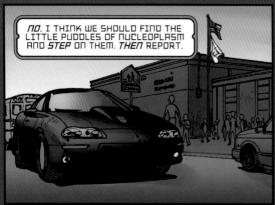

NO. I THINK WE SHOULD FIND THE LITTLE PUDDLES OF NUCLEOPLASM AND *STEP* ON THEM. *THEN* REPORT.

WE HAVE THE *ETHERGRID* PROFILE. SOONER OR LATER ONE OR OTHER BACTERIUM WILL BOOT UP, AND WHEN THEY *DO...*

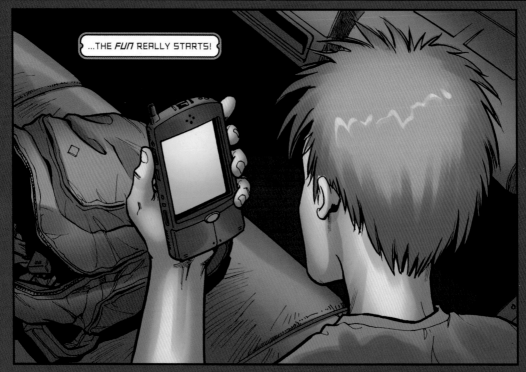

...THE *FUN* REALLY STARTS!

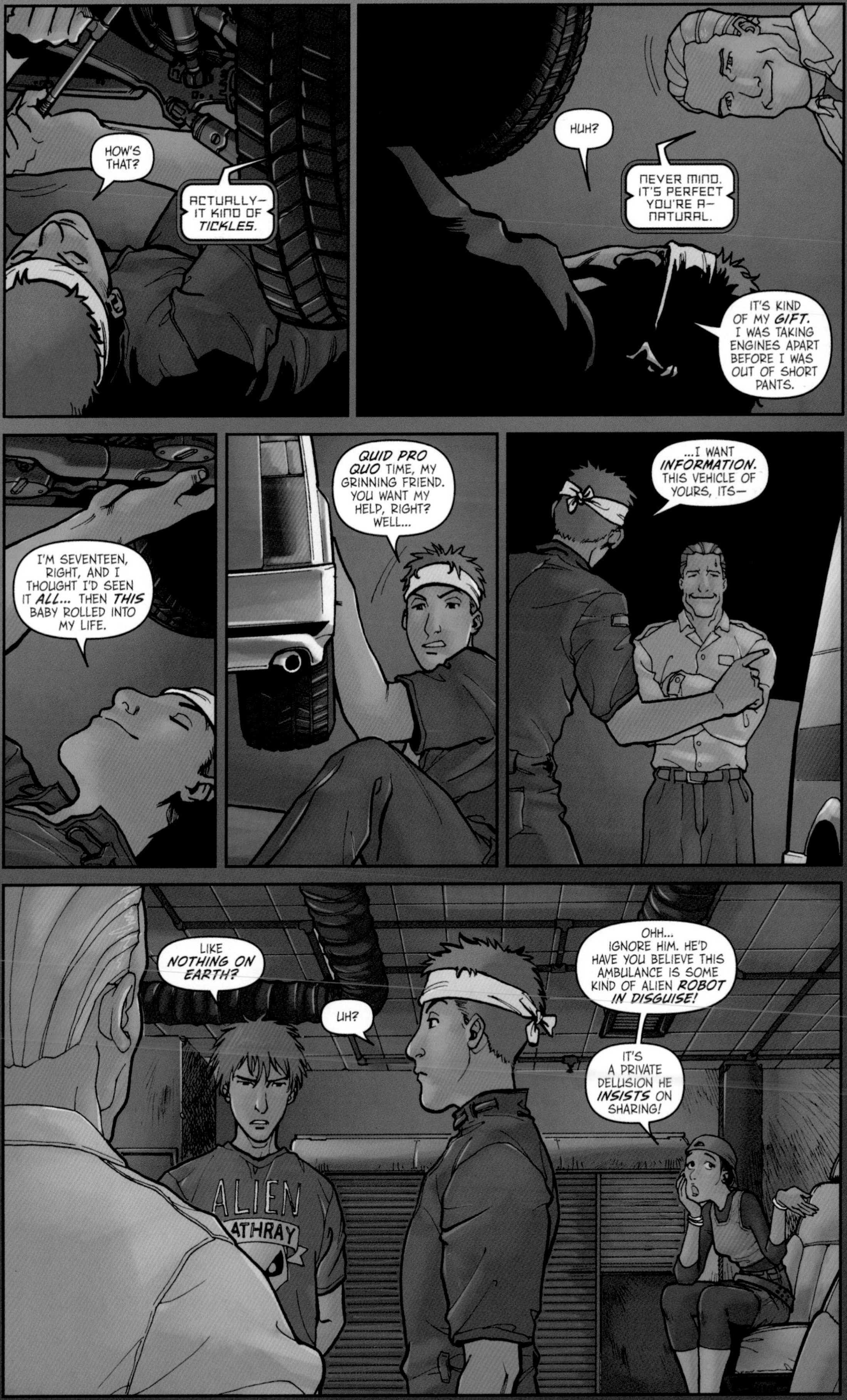
HOW'S THAT?
ACTUALLY— IT KIND OF TICKLES.
HUH?
NEVER MIND. IT'S PERFECT YOU'RE A— NATURAL.
IT'S KIND OF MY GIFT. I WAS TAKING ENGINES APART BEFORE I WAS OUT OF SHORT PANTS.
I'M SEVENTEEN, RIGHT, AND I THOUGHT I'D SEEN IT ALL... THEN THIS BABY ROLLED INTO MY LIFE.
QUID PRO QUO TIME, MY GRINNING FRIEND. YOU WANT MY HELP, RIGHT? WELL...
...I WANT INFORMATION. THIS VEHICLE OF YOURS, ITS—
LIKE NOTHING ON EARTH?
UH?
OHH... IGNORE HIM. HE'D HAVE YOU BELIEVE THIS AMBULANCE IS SOME KIND OF ALIEN ROBOT IN DISGUISE!
IT'S A PRIVATE DELUSION HE INSISTS ON SHARING!
ALIEN

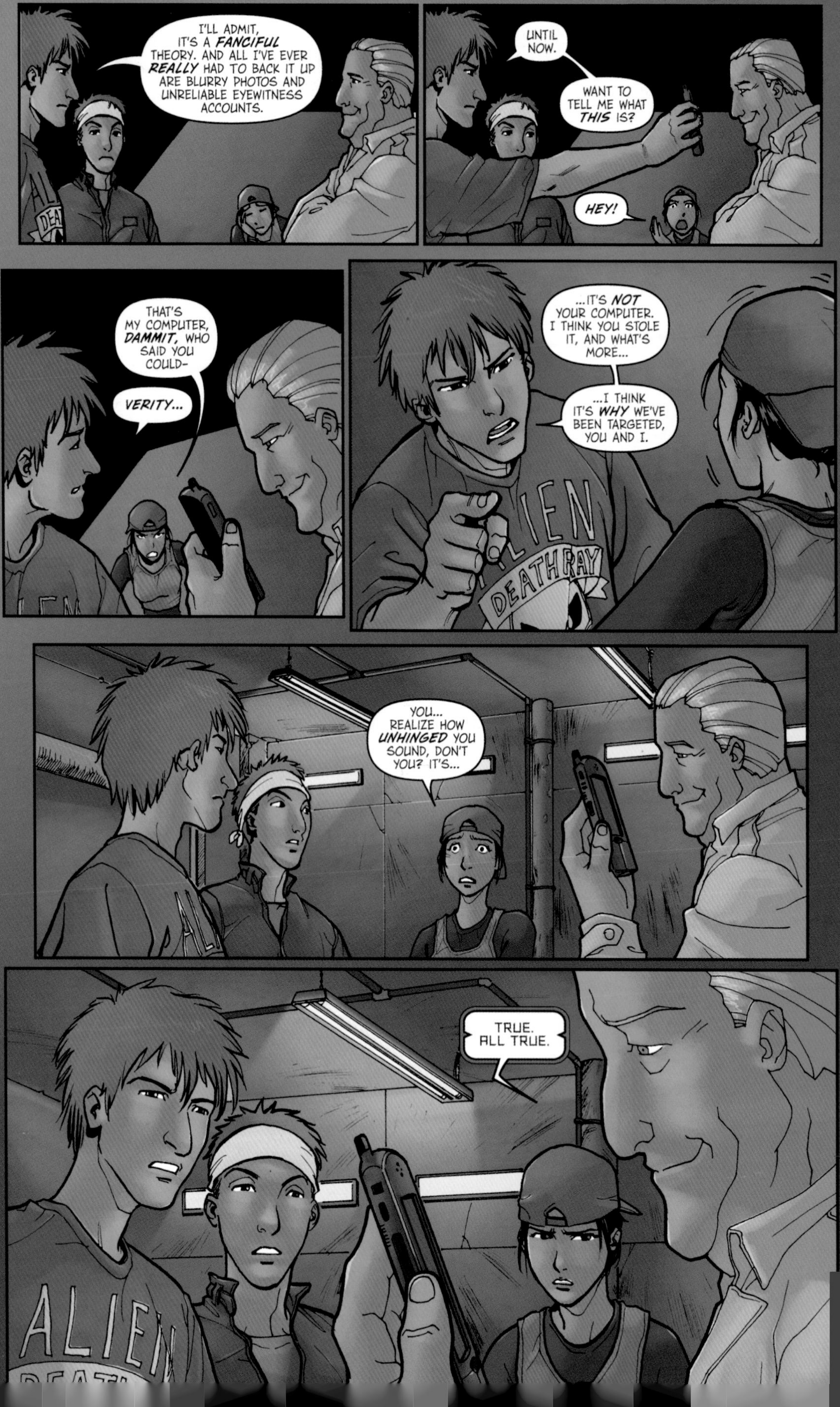

I'LL ADMIT, IT'S A FANCIFUL THEORY. AND ALL I'VE EVER REALLY HAD TO BACK IT UP ARE BLURRY PHOTOS AND UNRELIABLE EYEWITNESS ACCOUNTS.
UNTIL NOW.
WANT TO TELL ME WHAT THIS IS?
HEY!
THAT'S MY COMPUTER, DAMMIT, WHO SAID YOU COULD-
VERITY...
...IT'S NOT YOUR COMPUTER. I THINK YOU STOLE IT, AND WHAT'S MORE...
...I THINK IT'S WHY WE'VE BEEN TARGETED, YOU AND I.
YOU... REALIZE HOW UNHINGED YOU SOUND, DON'T YOU? IT'S...
TRUE. ALL TRUE.

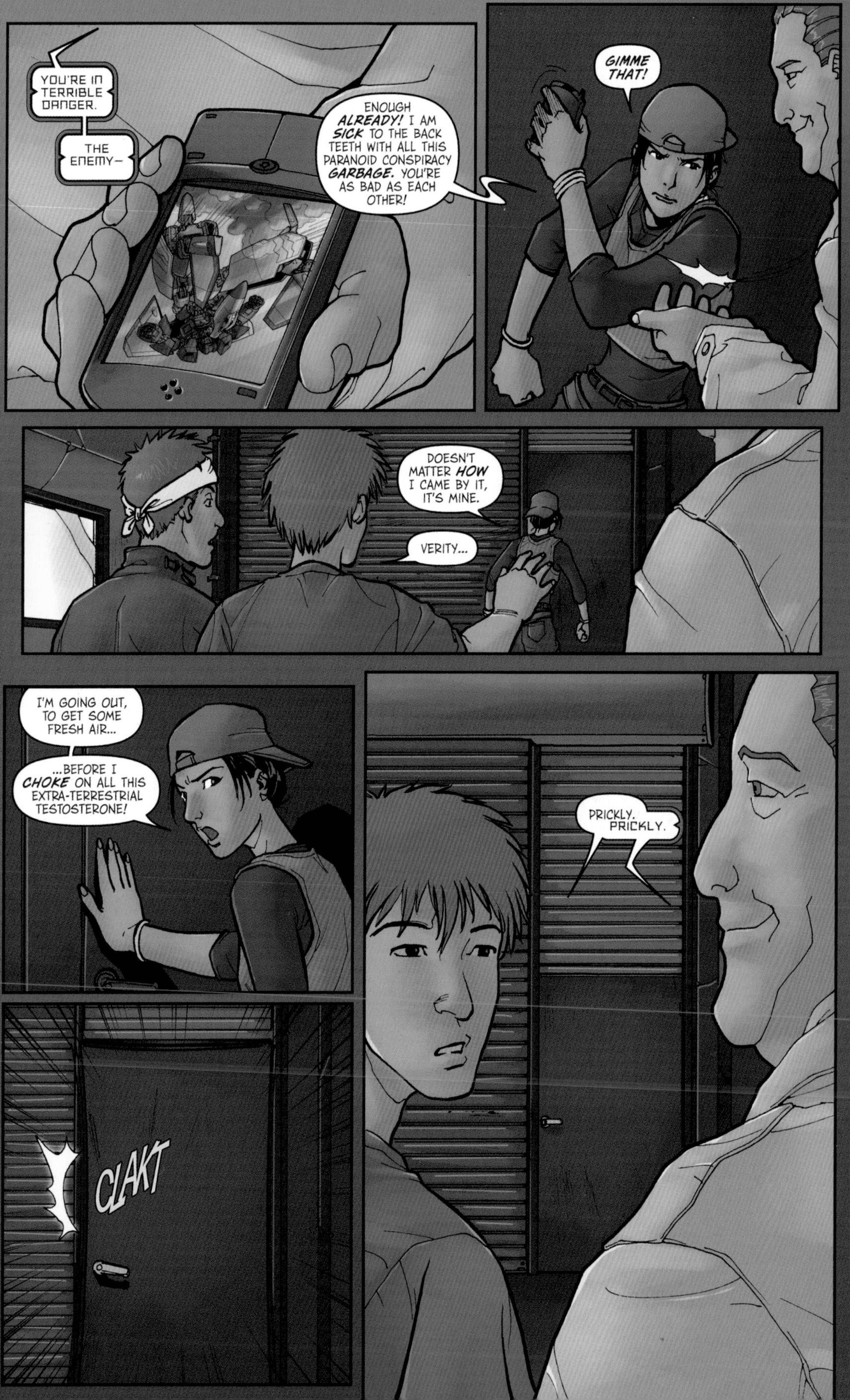

YOU'RE IN TERRIBLE DANGER.
THE ENEMY—
ENOUGH ALREADY! I AM SICK TO THE BACK TEETH WITH ALL THIS PARANOID CONSPIRACY GARBAGE. YOU'RE AS BAD AS EACH OTHER!
GIMME THAT!
DOESN'T MATTER HOW I CAME BY IT, IT'S MINE.
VERITY...
I'M GOING OUT, TO GET SOME FRESH AIR...
...BEFORE I CHOKE ON ALL THIS EXTRA-TERRESTRIAL TESTOSTERONE!
PRICKLY. PRICKLY.
CLAKT

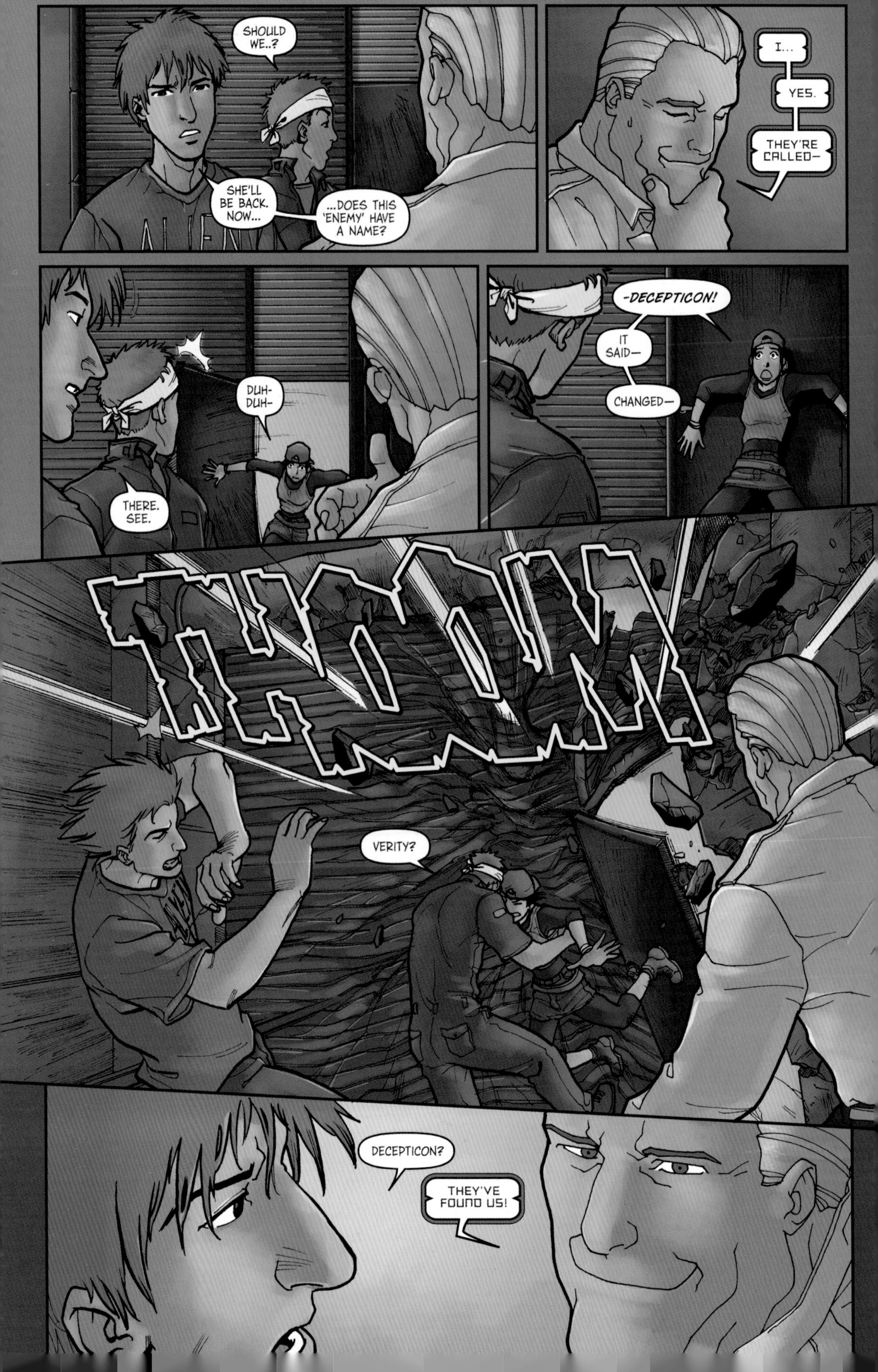

SHOULD WE..?
SHE'LL BE BACK. NOW...
...DOES THIS 'ENEMY' HAVE A NAME?
I...
YES.
THEY'RE CALLED—
DUH-DUH-
THERE. SEE.
-DECEPTICON!
IT SAID—
CHANGED—
THOOM
VERITY?
DECEPTICON?
THEY'VE FOUND US!

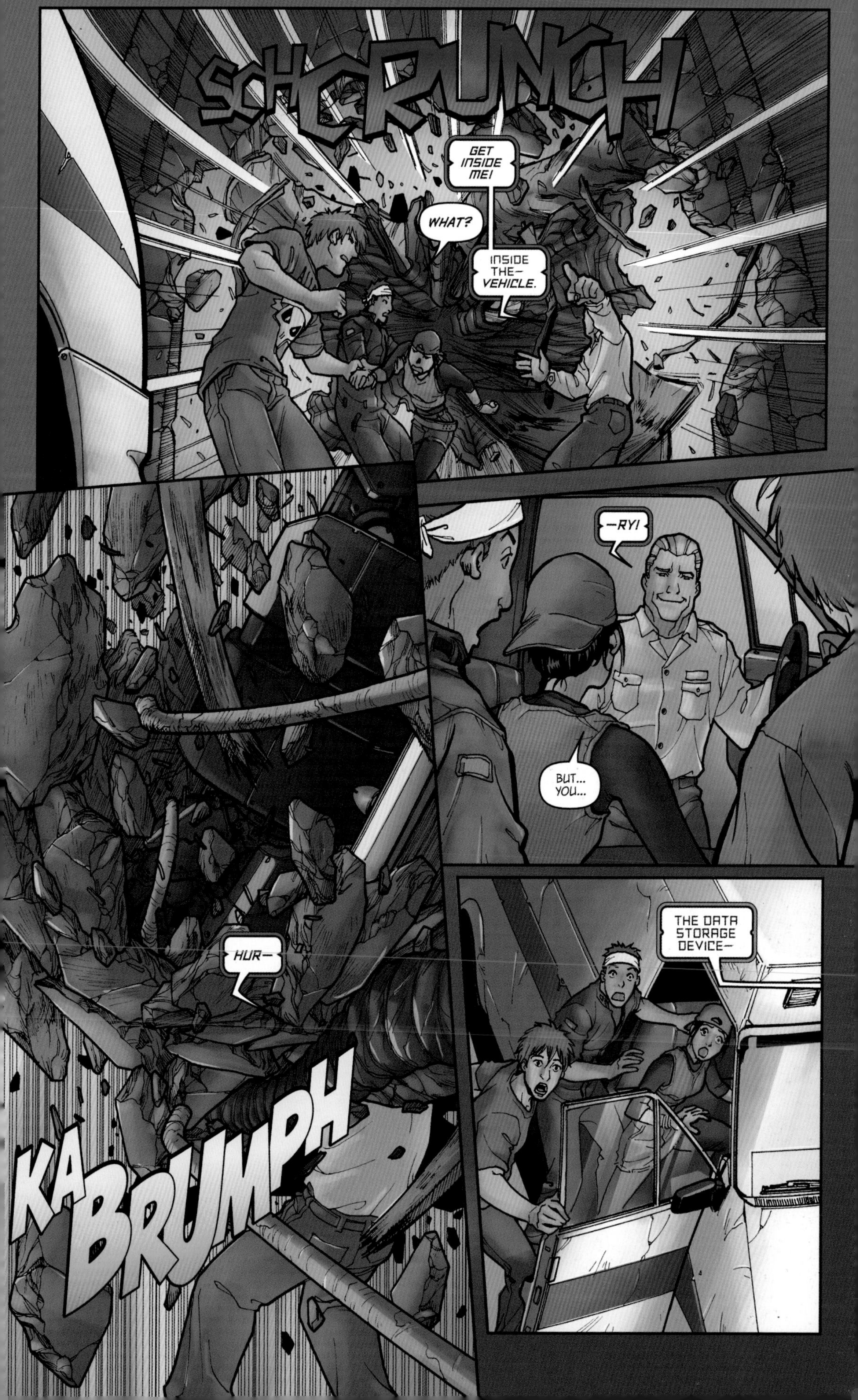
SCHCRUNCH
GET INSIDE ME!
WHAT?
INSIDE THE—VEHICLE.
HUR—
KA BRUMPH
—RY!
BUT... YOU...
THE DATA STORAGE DEVICE—

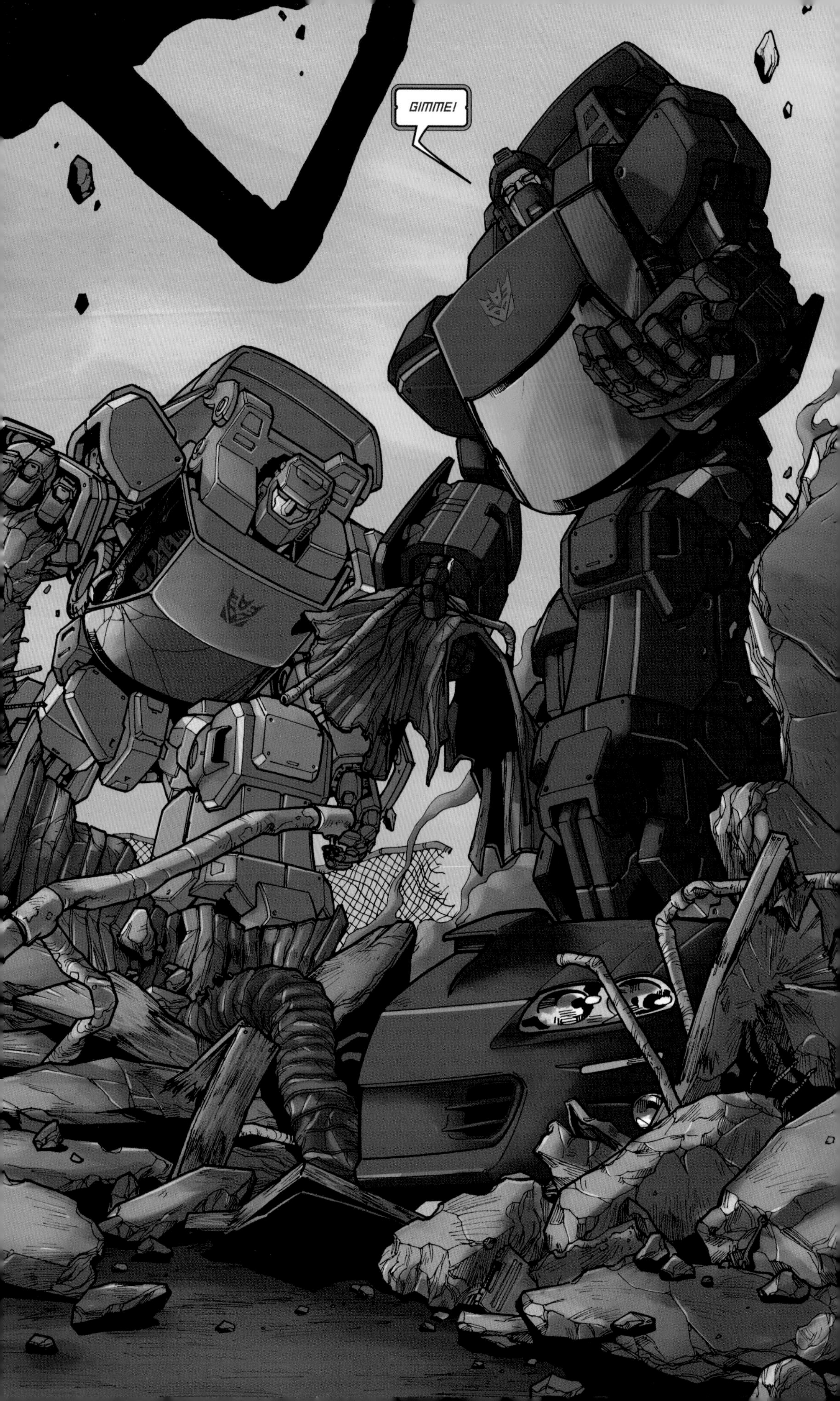
GIMME!

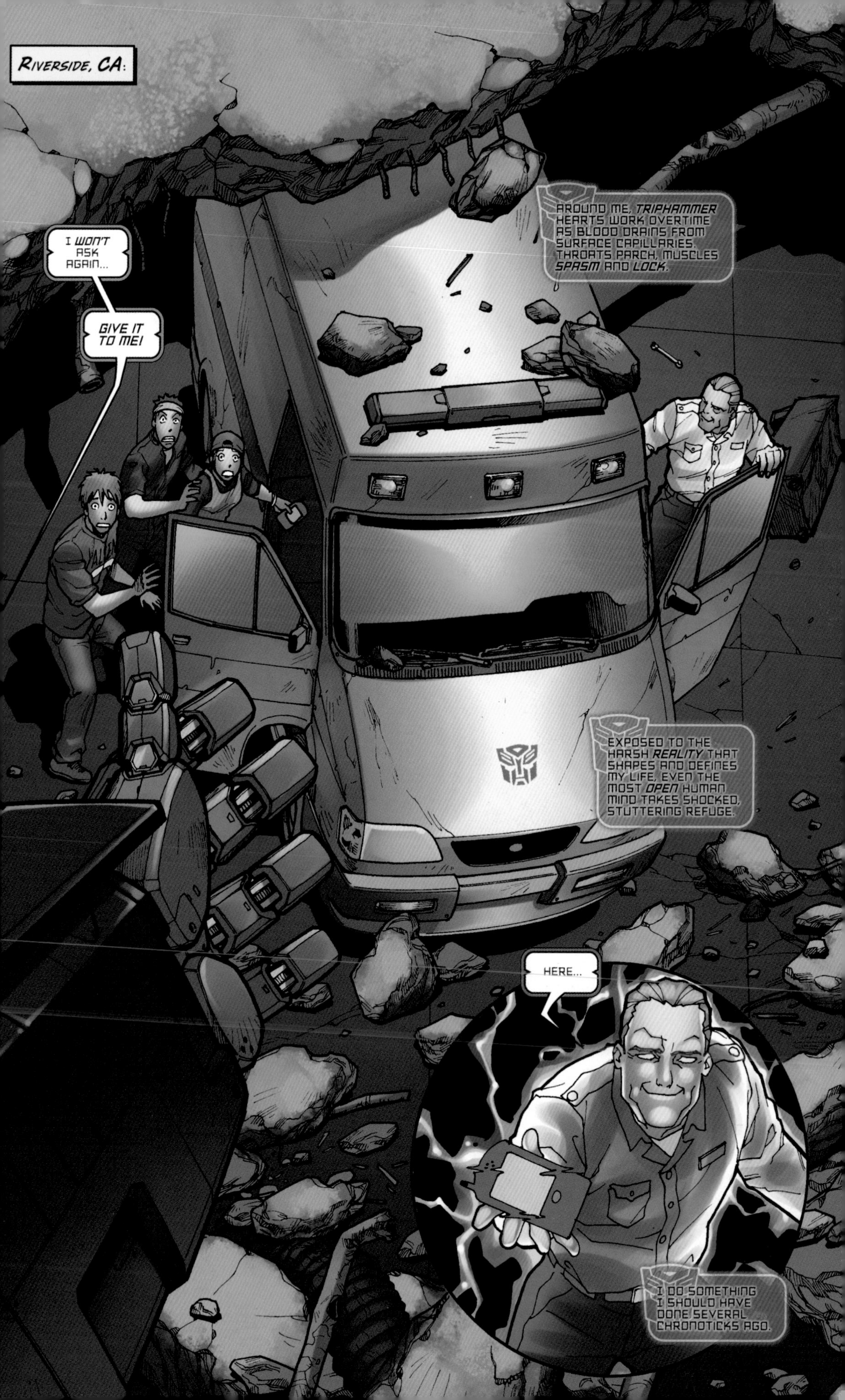

RIVERSIDE, CA:
I WON'T ASK AGAIN...
GIVE IT TO ME!
AROUND ME, TRIPHAMMER HEARTS WORK OVERTIME AS BLOOD DRAINS FROM SURFACE CAPILLARIES, THROATS PARCH, MUSCLES SPASM AND LOCK.
EXPOSED TO THE HARSH REALITY THAT SHAPES AND DEFINES MY LIFE, EVEN THE MOST OPEN HUMAN MIND TAKES SHOCKED, STUTTERING REFUGE.
HERE...
I DO SOMETHING I SHOULD HAVE DONE SEVERAL CHRONOTICKS AGO.

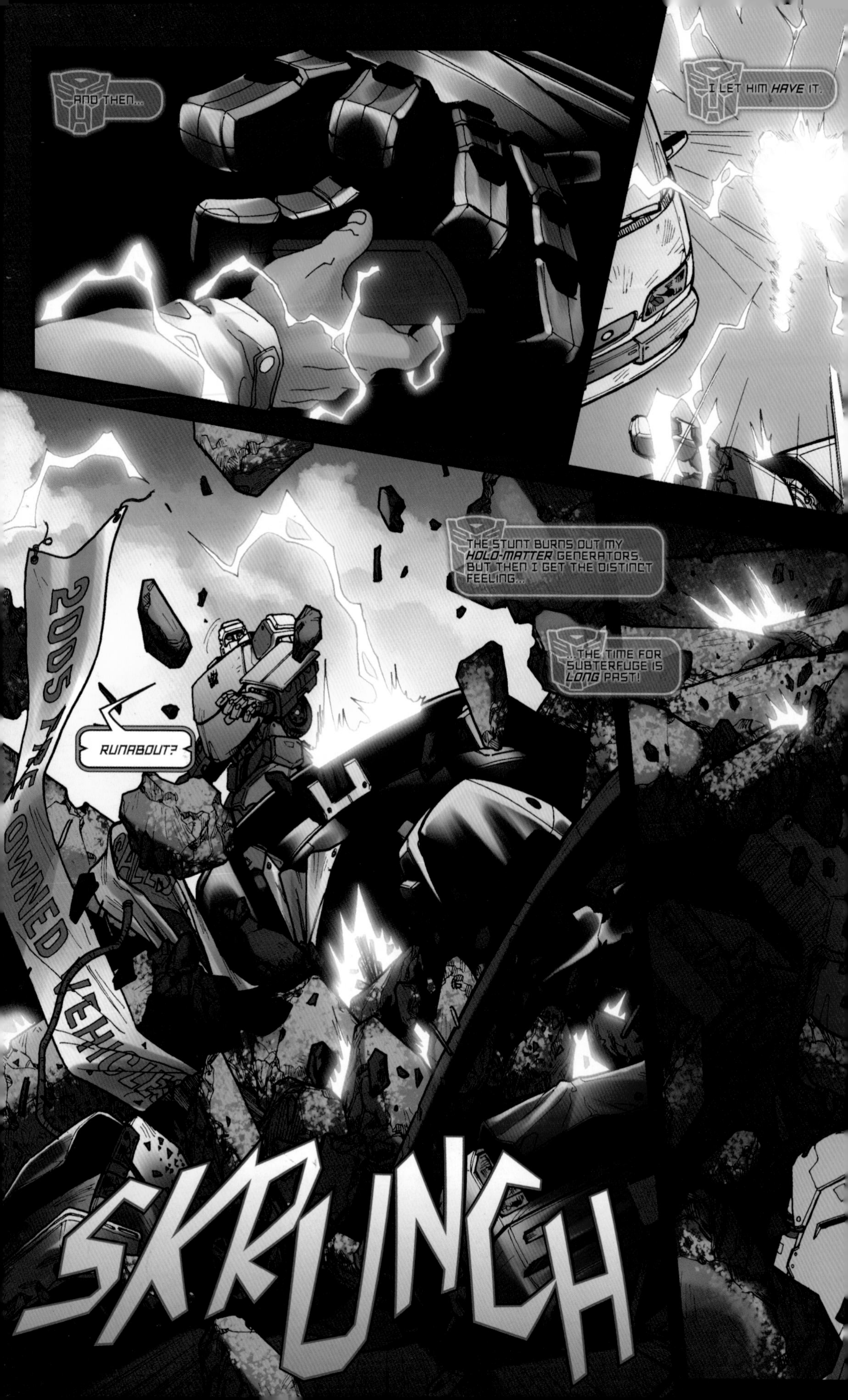
AND THEN...
I LET HIM HAVE IT.
THE STUNT BURNS OUT MY HOLO-MATTER GENERATORS. BUT THEN I GET THE DISTINCT FEELING...
...THE TIME FOR SUBTERFUGE IS LONG PAST!
RUNABOUT?
2005 PRE-OWNED VEHICLES
SKRUNCH

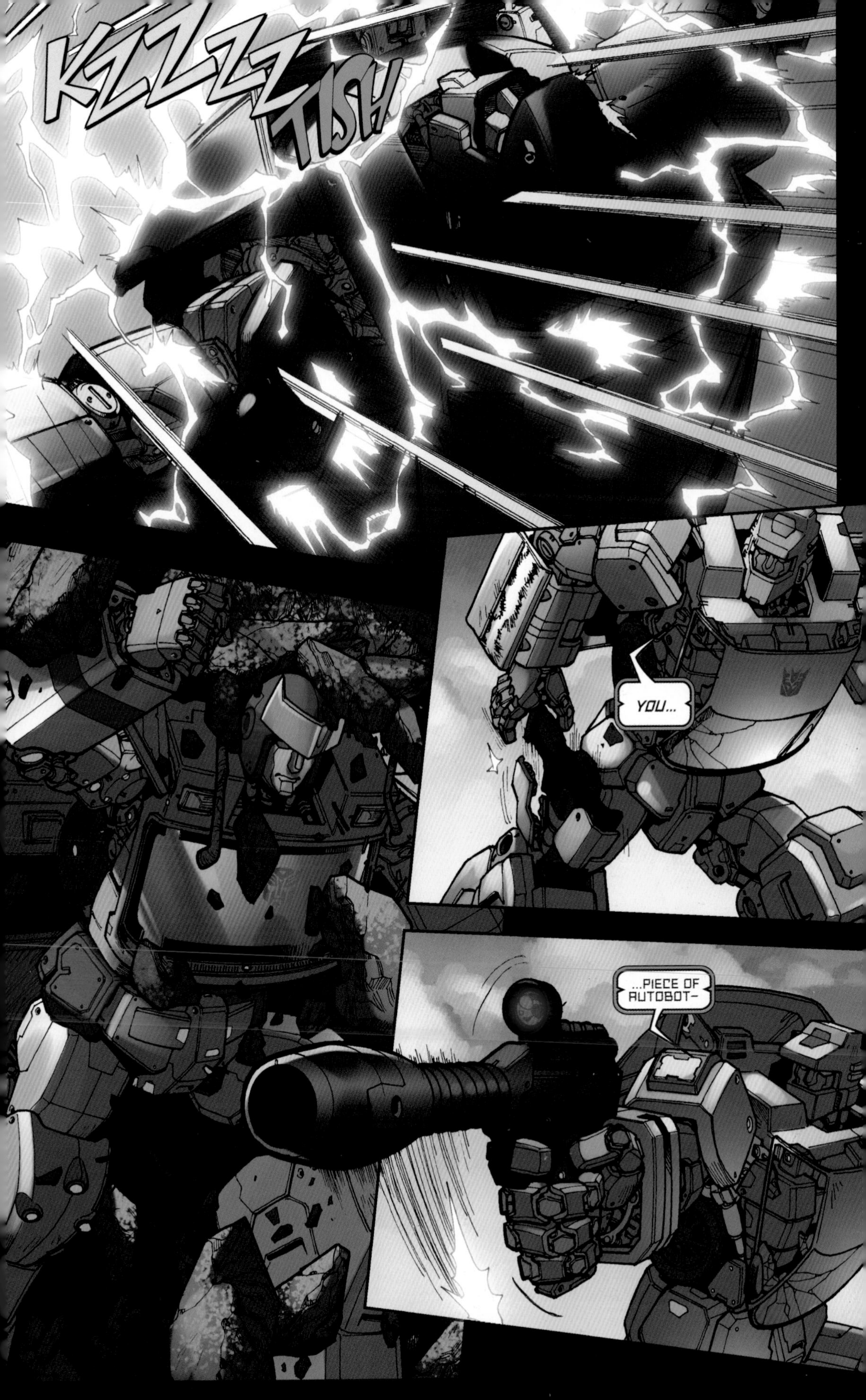
KZZZZZ TISH
YOU...
...PIECE OF AUTOBOT–

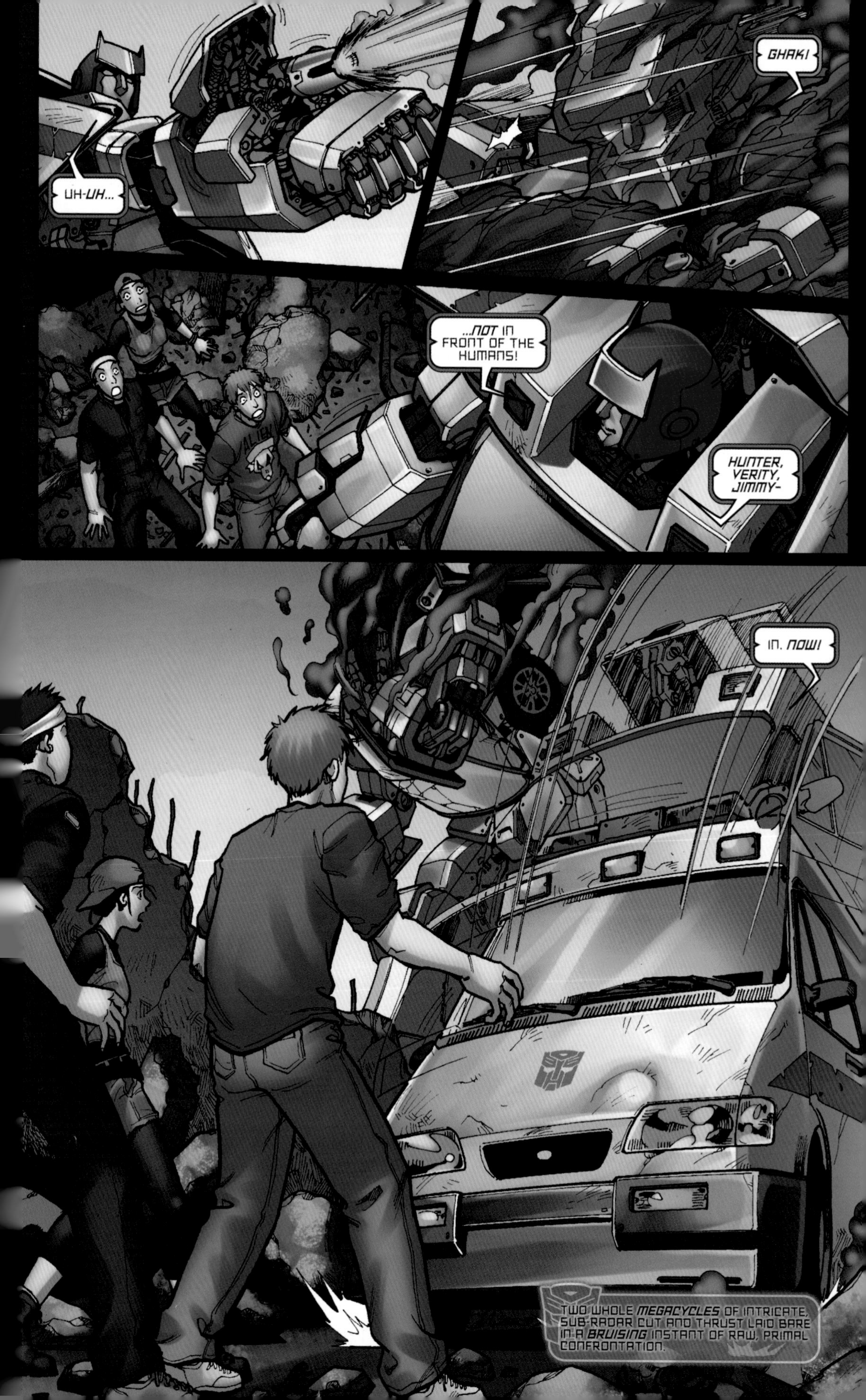
UH-UH...
GHAK!
...NOT IN FRONT OF THE HUMANS!
HUNTER, VERITY, JIMMY-
IN. NOW!
TWO WHOLE MEGACYCLES OF INTRICATE, SUB-RADAR CUT AND THRUST LAID BARE IN A BRUISING INSTANT OF RAW, PRIMAL CONFRONTATION.

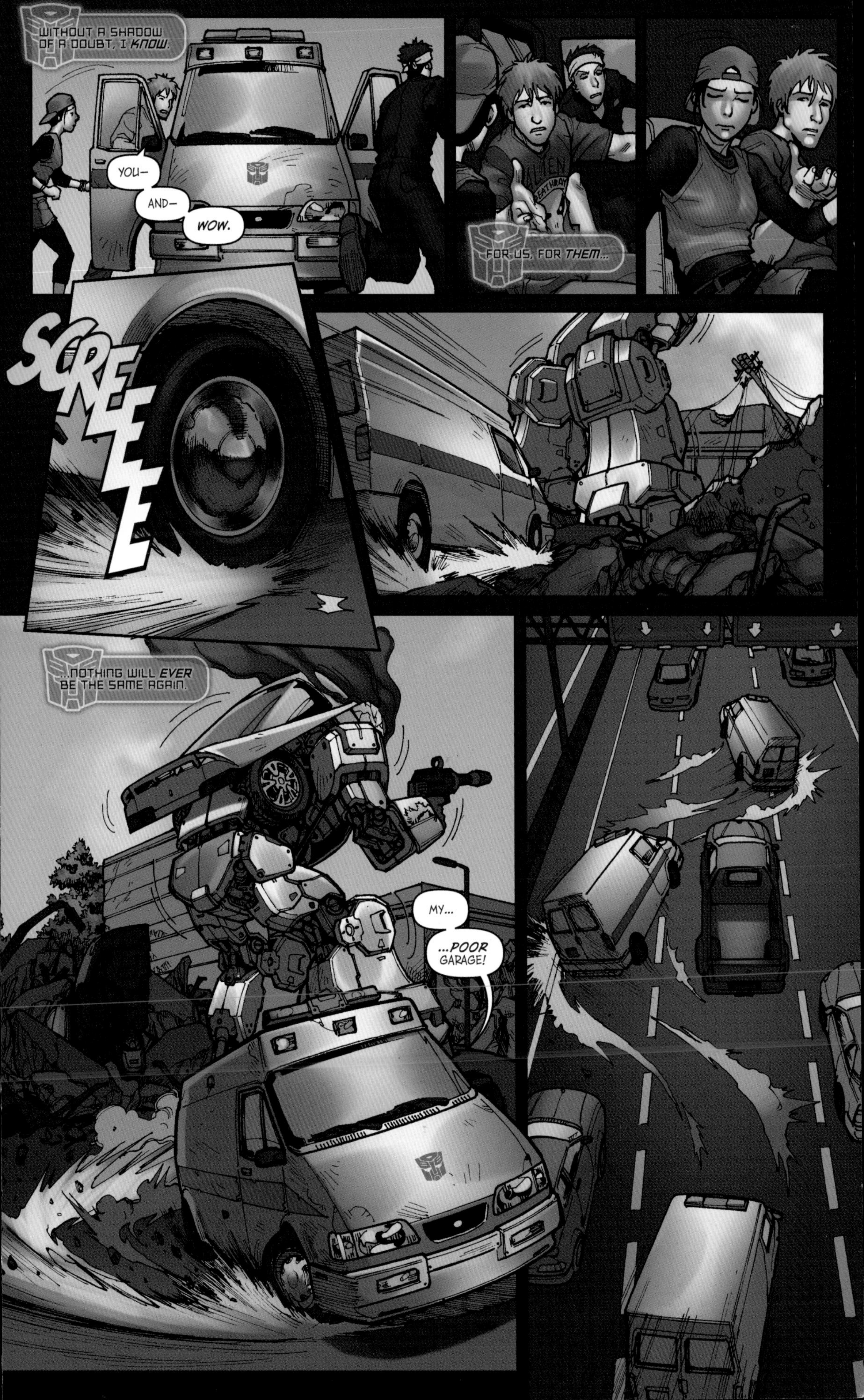
WITHOUT A SHADOW OF A DOUBT, I KNOW.
YOU—
AND—
WOW.
FOR US, FOR THEM...
SCREEEE
...NOTHING WILL EVER BE THE SAME AGAIN.
MY...
...POOR GARAGE!

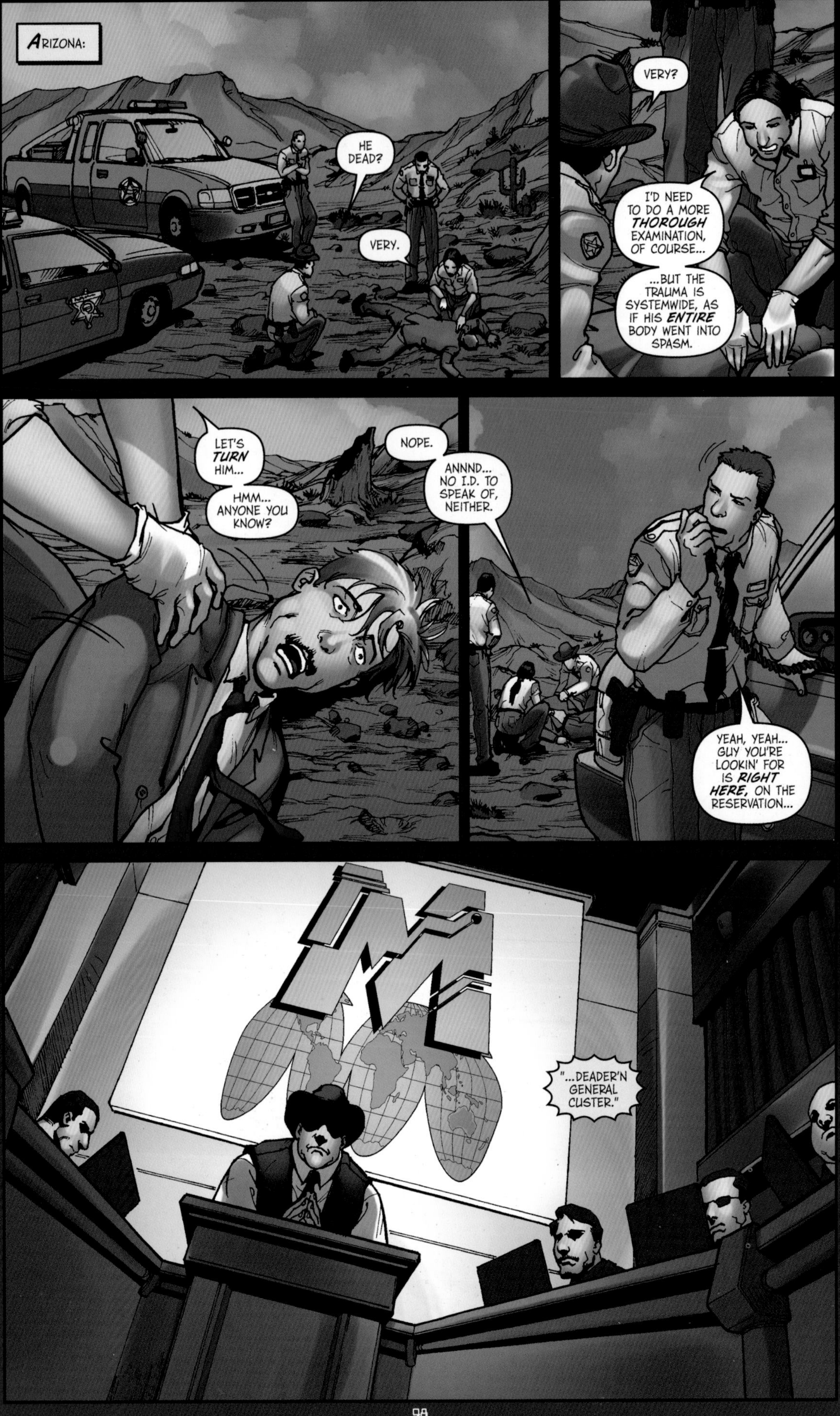
ARIZONA:
HE DEAD?
VERY.
VERY?
I'D NEED TO DO A MORE THOROUGH EXAMINATION, OF COURSE...
...BUT THE TRAUMA IS SYSTEMWIDE, AS IF HIS ENTIRE BODY WENT INTO SPASM.
LET'S TURN HIM...
HMM... ANYONE YOU KNOW?
NOPE.
ANNND... NO I.D. TO SPEAK OF, NEITHER.
YEAH, YEAH... GUY YOU'RE LOOKIN' FOR IS RIGHT HERE, ON THE RESERVATION...
"...DEADER'N GENERAL CUSTER."

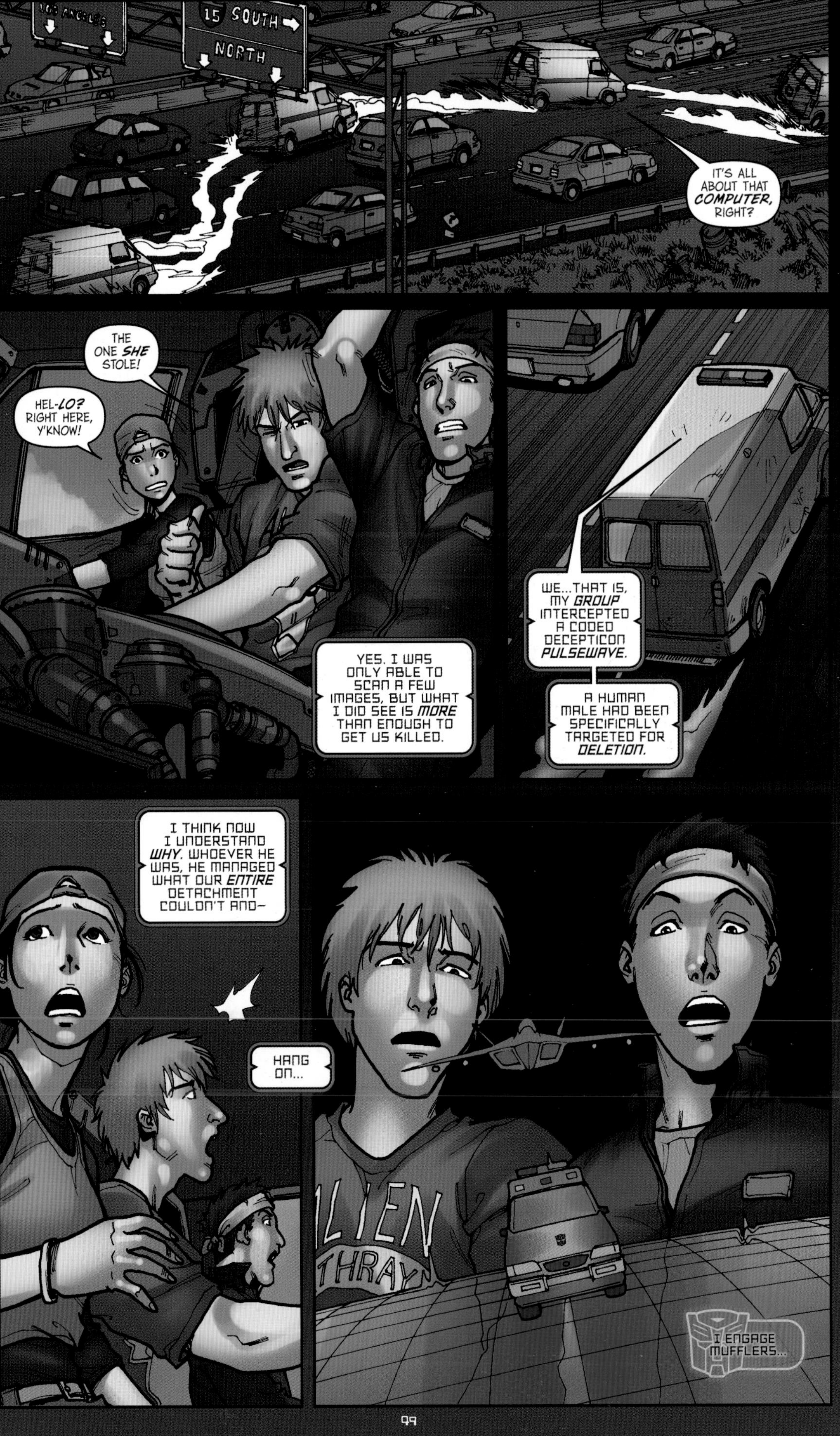

LOS ANGELES
15 SOUTH
NORTH
IT'S ALL ABOUT THAT *COMPUTER*, RIGHT?
THE ONE *SHE* STOLE!
HEL-*LO?* RIGHT HERE, Y'KNOW!
YES. I WAS ONLY ABLE TO SCAN A FEW IMAGES, BUT WHAT I DID SEE IS *MORE* THAN ENOUGH TO GET US KILLED.
WE...THAT IS, MY *GROUP* INTERCEPTED A CODED DECEPTICON *PULSEWAVE*.
A HUMAN MALE HAD BEEN SPECIFICALLY TARGETED FOR *DELETION*.
I THINK NOW I UNDERSTAND *WHY*. WHOEVER HE WAS, HE MANAGED WHAT OUR *ENTIRE* DETACHMENT COULDN'T AND–
HANG ON...
ALIEN THRAX
I ENGAGE MUFFLERS...

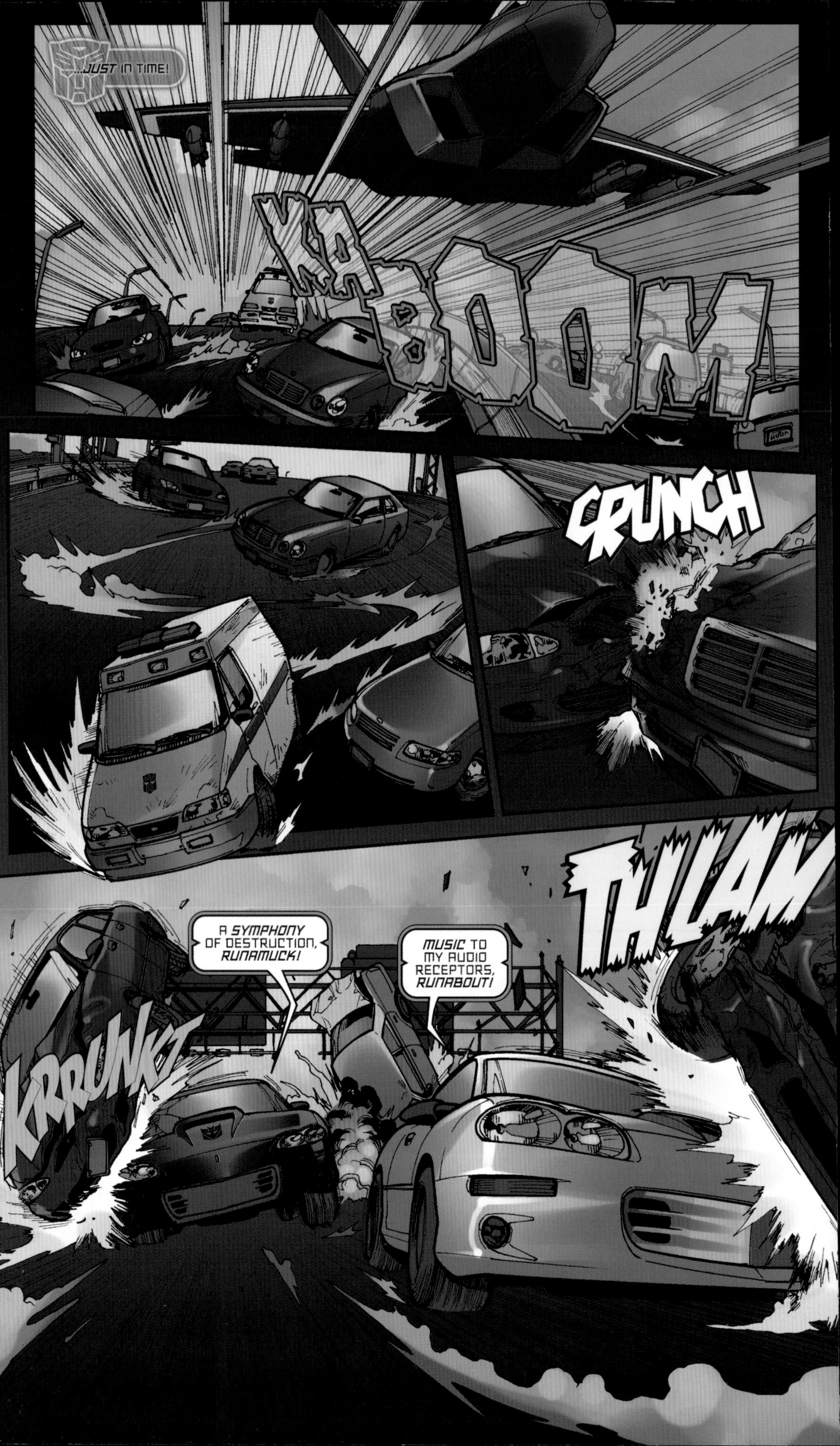
...JUST IN TIME!
KA-BOOM
CRUNCH
THLAM
A SYMPHONY OF DESTRUCTION, RUNAMUCK!
MUSIC TO MY AUDIO RECEPTORS, RUNABOUT!
KRRUNK!

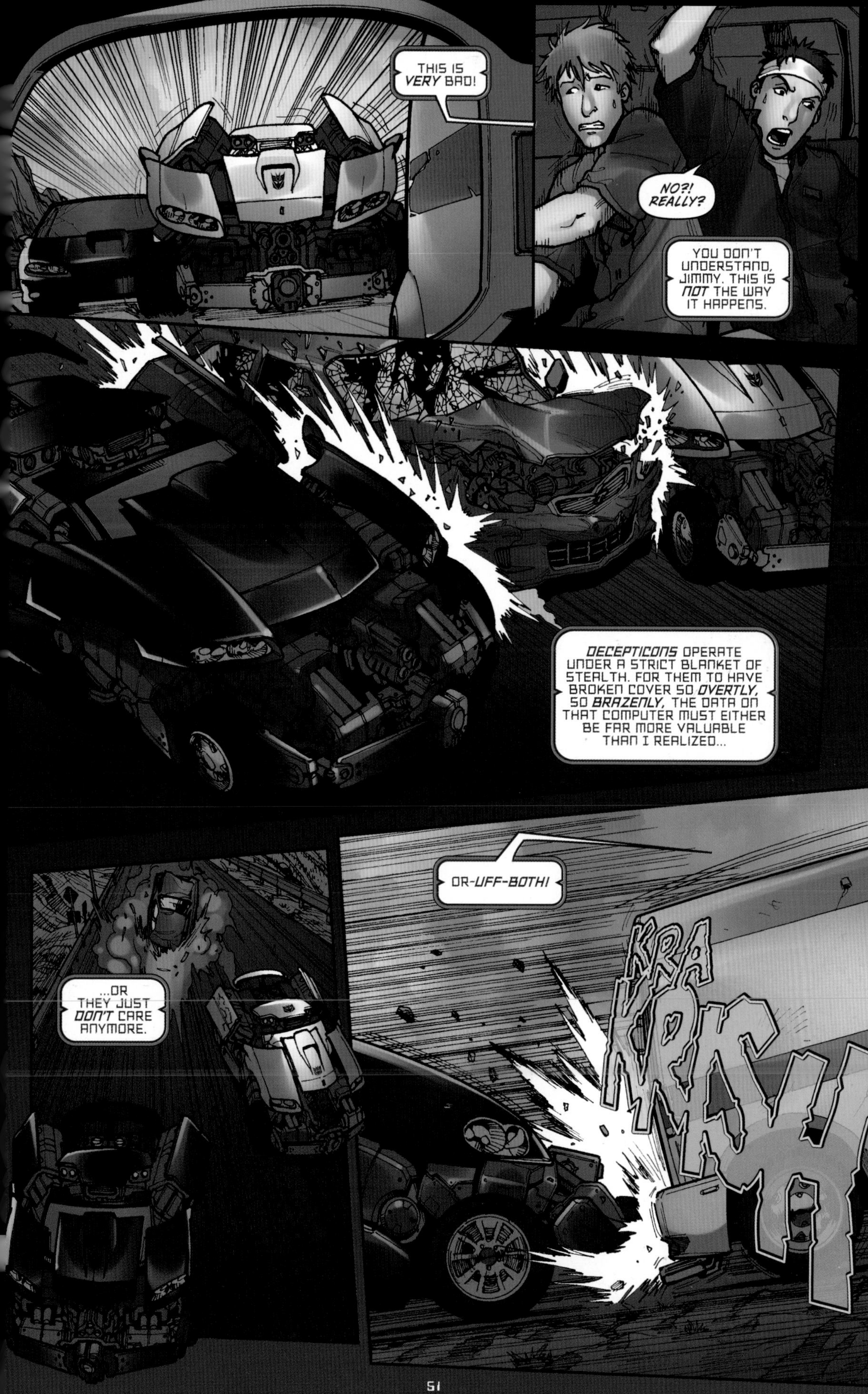
THIS IS VERY BAD!
NO?! REALLY?
YOU DON'T UNDERSTAND, JIMMY. THIS IS NOT THE WAY IT HAPPENS.
DECEPTICONS OPERATE UNDER A STRICT BLANKET OF STEALTH. FOR THEM TO HAVE BROKEN COVER SO OVERTLY, SO BRAZENLY, THE DATA ON THAT COMPUTER MUST EITHER BE FAR MORE VALUABLE THAN I REALIZED...
...OR THEY JUST DON'T CARE ANYMORE.
OR-UFF-BOTH!
KRA KRKKAY

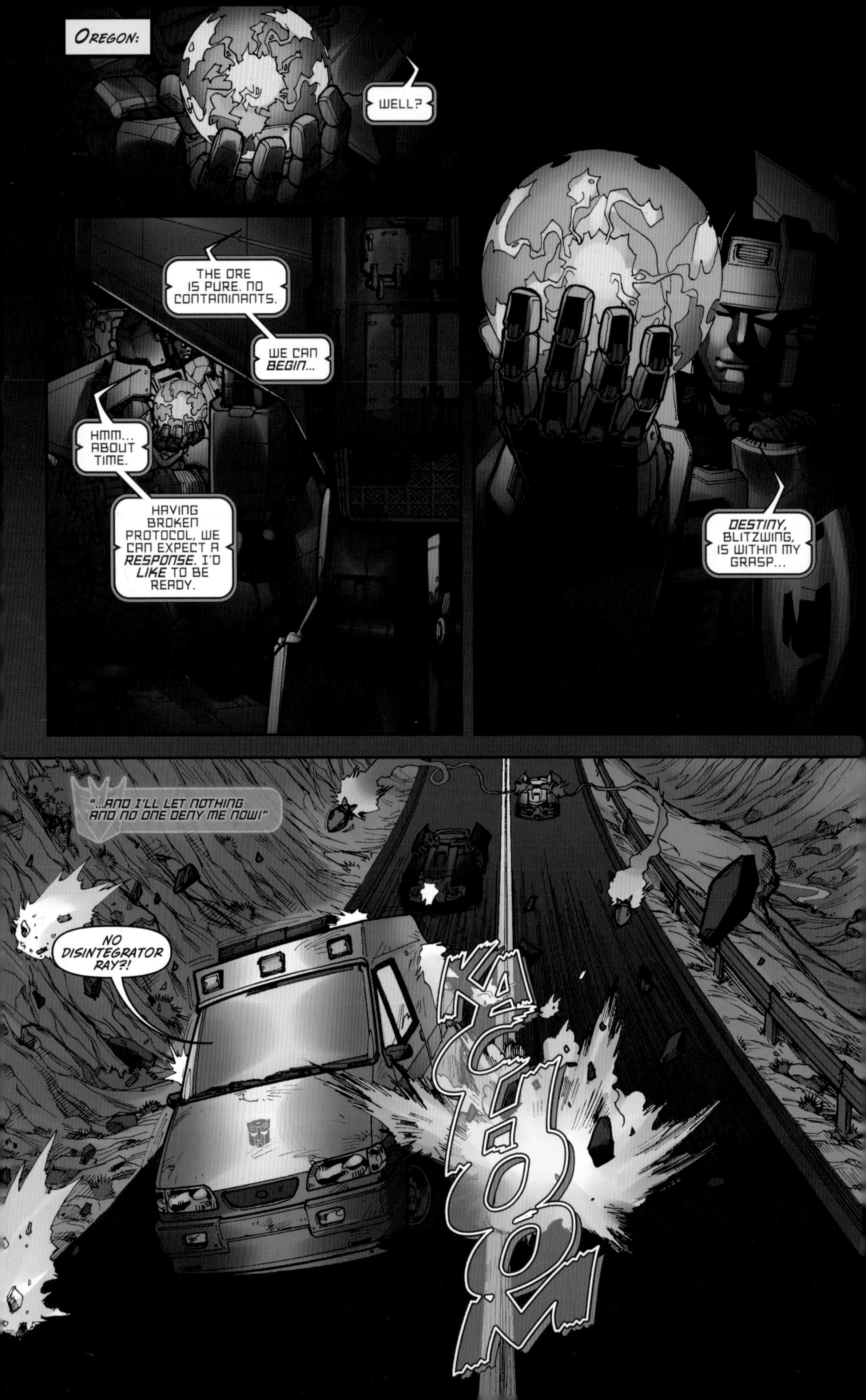
OREGON:
WELL?
THE ORE IS PURE. NO CONTAMINANTS.
WE CAN BEGIN...
HMM... ABOUT TIME.
HAVING BROKEN PROTOCOL, WE CAN EXPECT A RESPONSE. I'D LIKE TO BE READY.
DESTINY, BLITZWING, IS WITHIN MY GRASP...
"...AND I'LL LET NOTHING AND NO ONE DENY ME NOW!"
NO DISINTEGRATOR RAY?!
KA-BOOOM

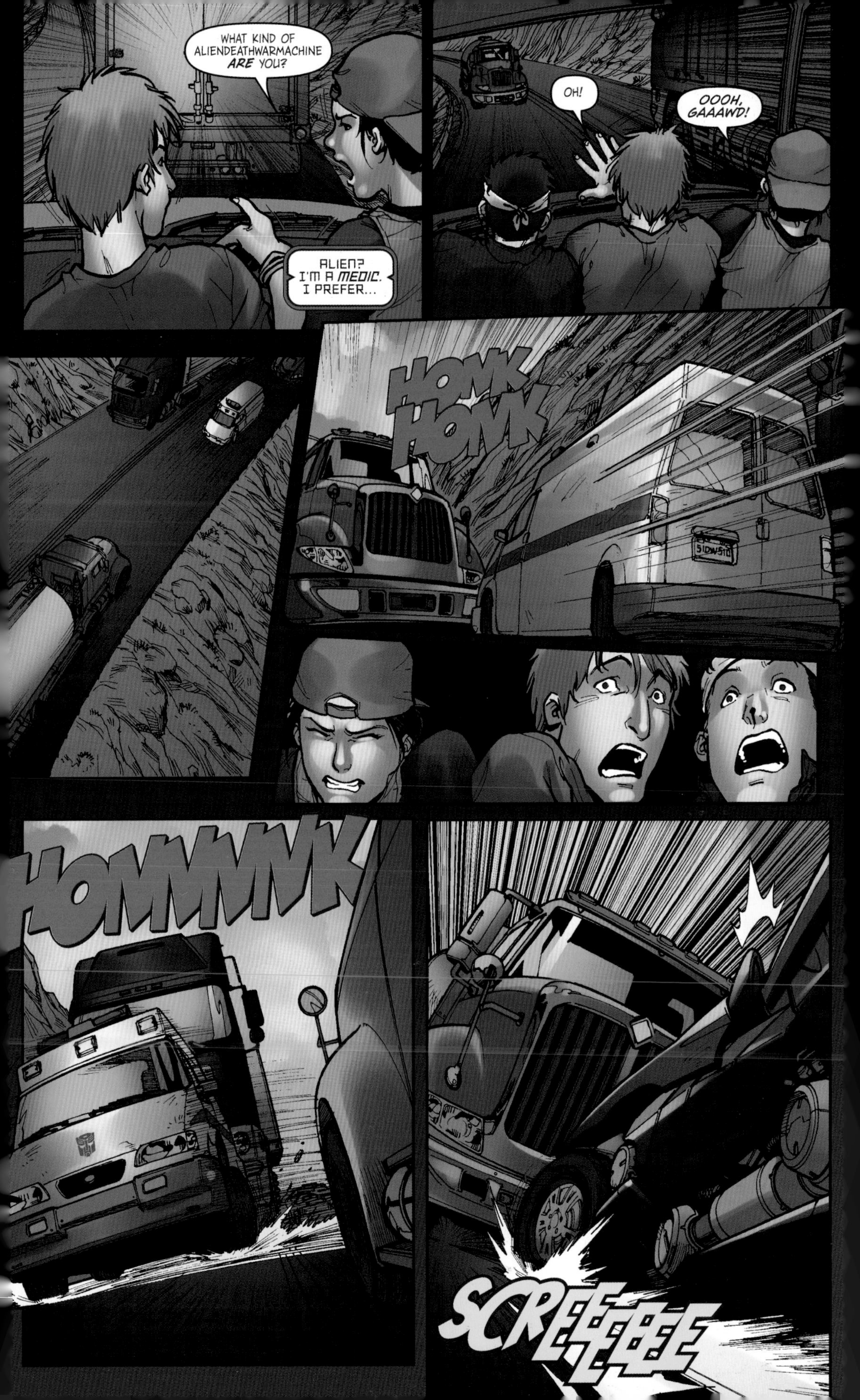
WHAT KIND OF ALIENDEATHWARMACHINE ARE YOU?
ALIEN? I'M A MEDIC. I PREFER...
OH!
OOOH, GAAAWD!
HONK HONK
HONNNNK
SCREEEEEE

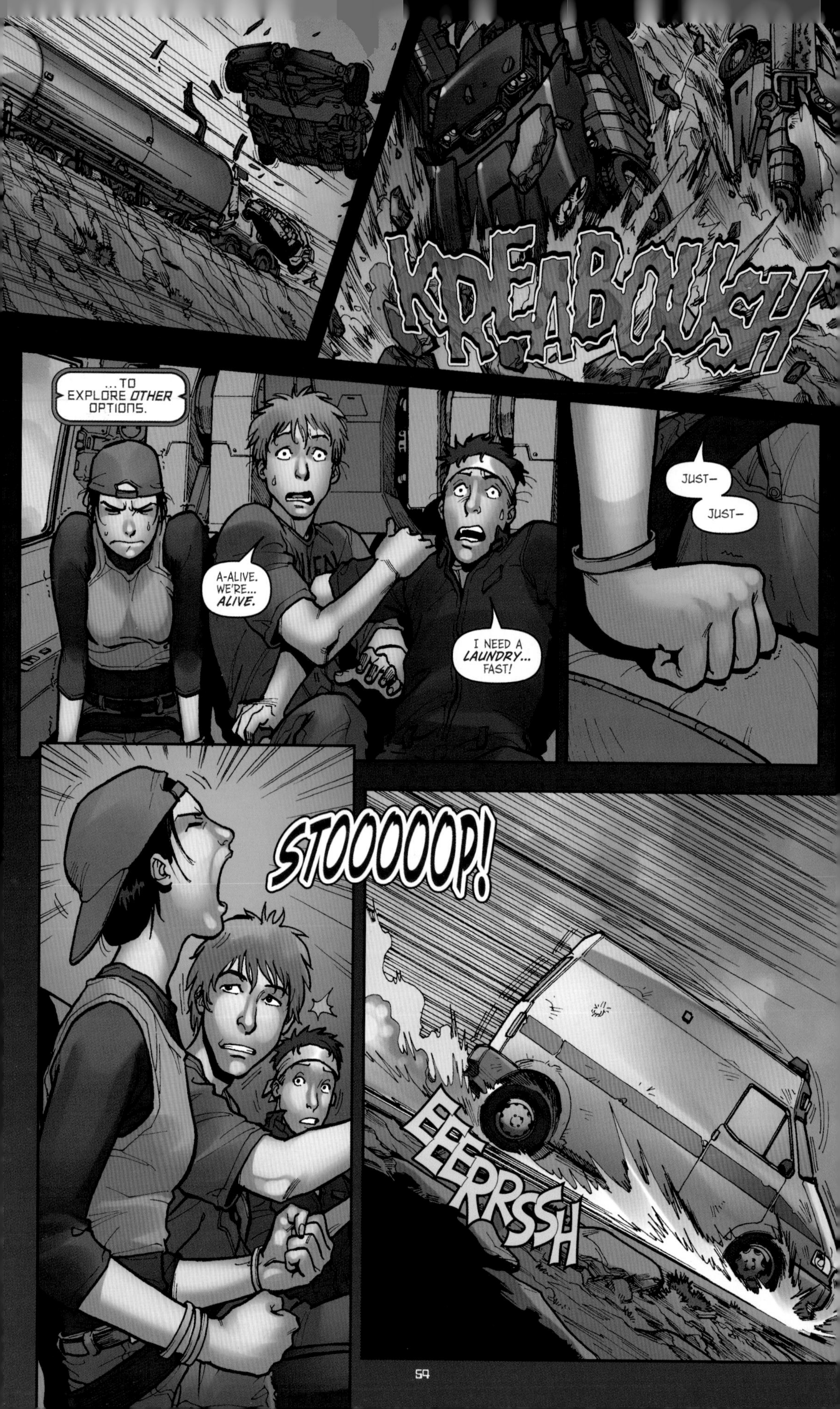
KREABOUSH
...TO EXPLORE OTHER OPTIONS.
A-ALIVE. WE'RE... ALIVE.
I NEED A LAUNDRY... FAST!
JUST—
JUST—
STOOOOOP!
EEERRSSH

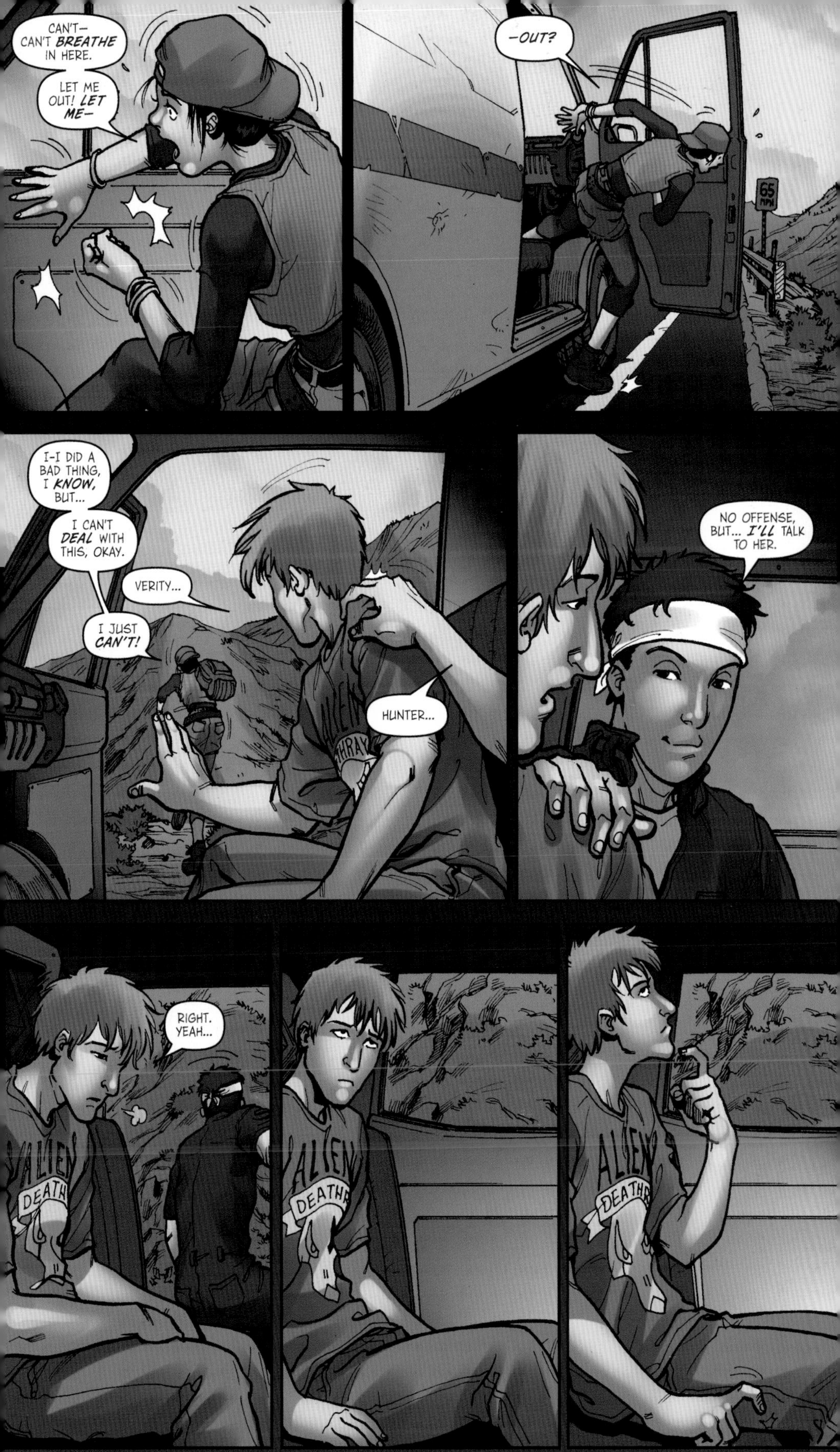
CAN'T—
CAN'T BREATHE IN HERE.
LET ME OUT! LET ME—
—OUT?
I-I DID A BAD THING, I KNOW, BUT...
I CAN'T DEAL WITH THIS, OKAY.
VERITY...
I JUST CAN'T!
HUNTER...
NO OFFENSE, BUT... I'LL TALK TO HER.
RIGHT. YEAH...

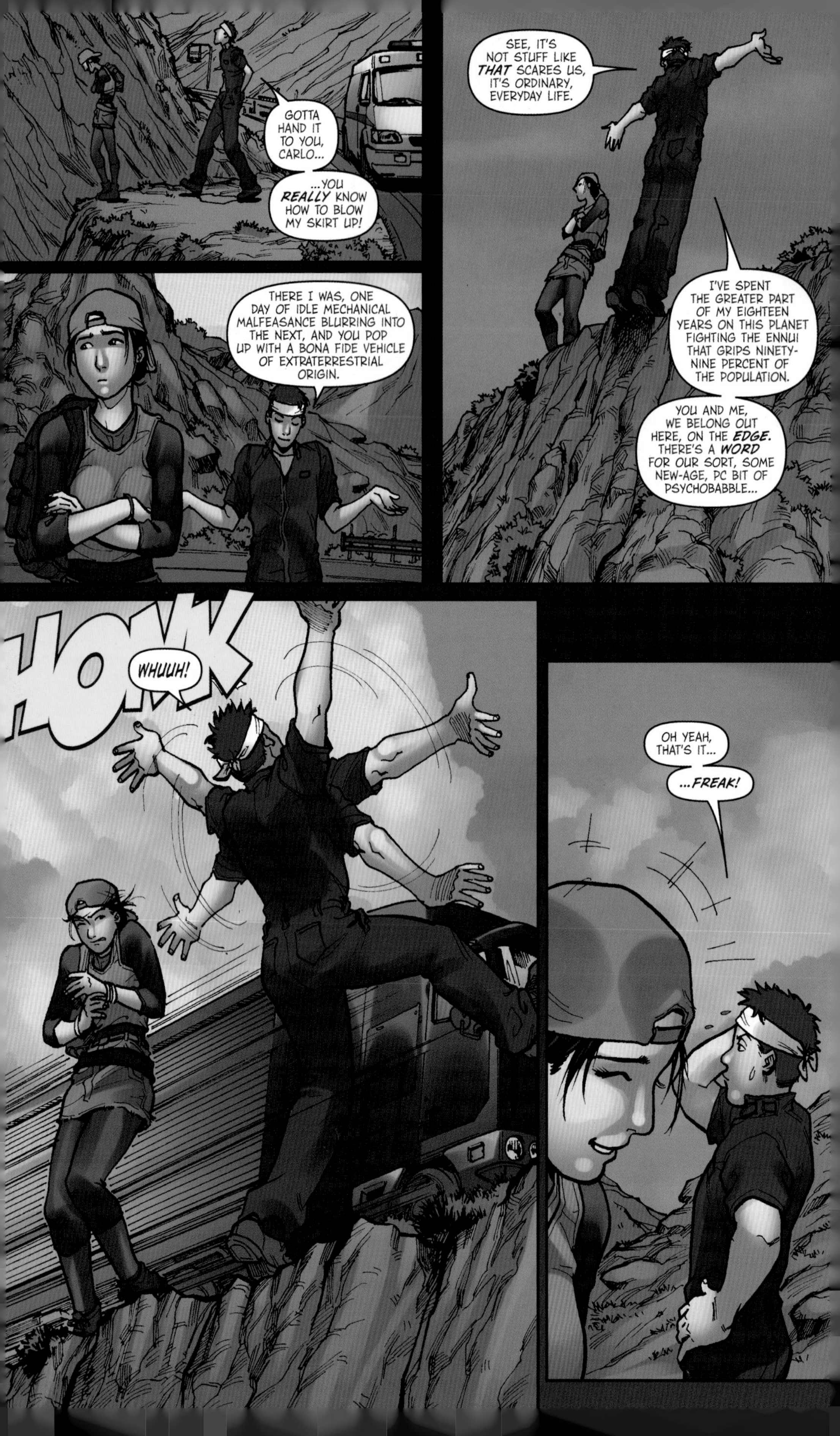
GOTTA HAND IT TO YOU, CARLO...
...YOU *REALLY* KNOW HOW TO BLOW MY SKIRT UP!
THERE I WAS, ONE DAY OF IDLE MECHANICAL MALFEASANCE BLURRING INTO THE NEXT, AND YOU POP UP WITH A BONA FIDE VEHICLE OF EXTRATERRESTRIAL ORIGIN.
SEE, IT'S NOT STUFF LIKE *THAT* SCARES US, IT'S ORDINARY, EVERYDAY LIFE.
I'VE SPENT THE GREATER PART OF MY EIGHTEEN YEARS ON THIS PLANET FIGHTING THE ENNUI THAT GRIPS NINETY-NINE PERCENT OF THE POPULATION.
YOU AND ME, WE BELONG OUT HERE, ON THE *EDGE.* THERE'S A *WORD* FOR OUR SORT, SOME NEW-AGE, PC BIT OF PSYCHOBABBLE...
HONK
WHUUH!
OH YEAH, THAT'S IT...
...FREAK!

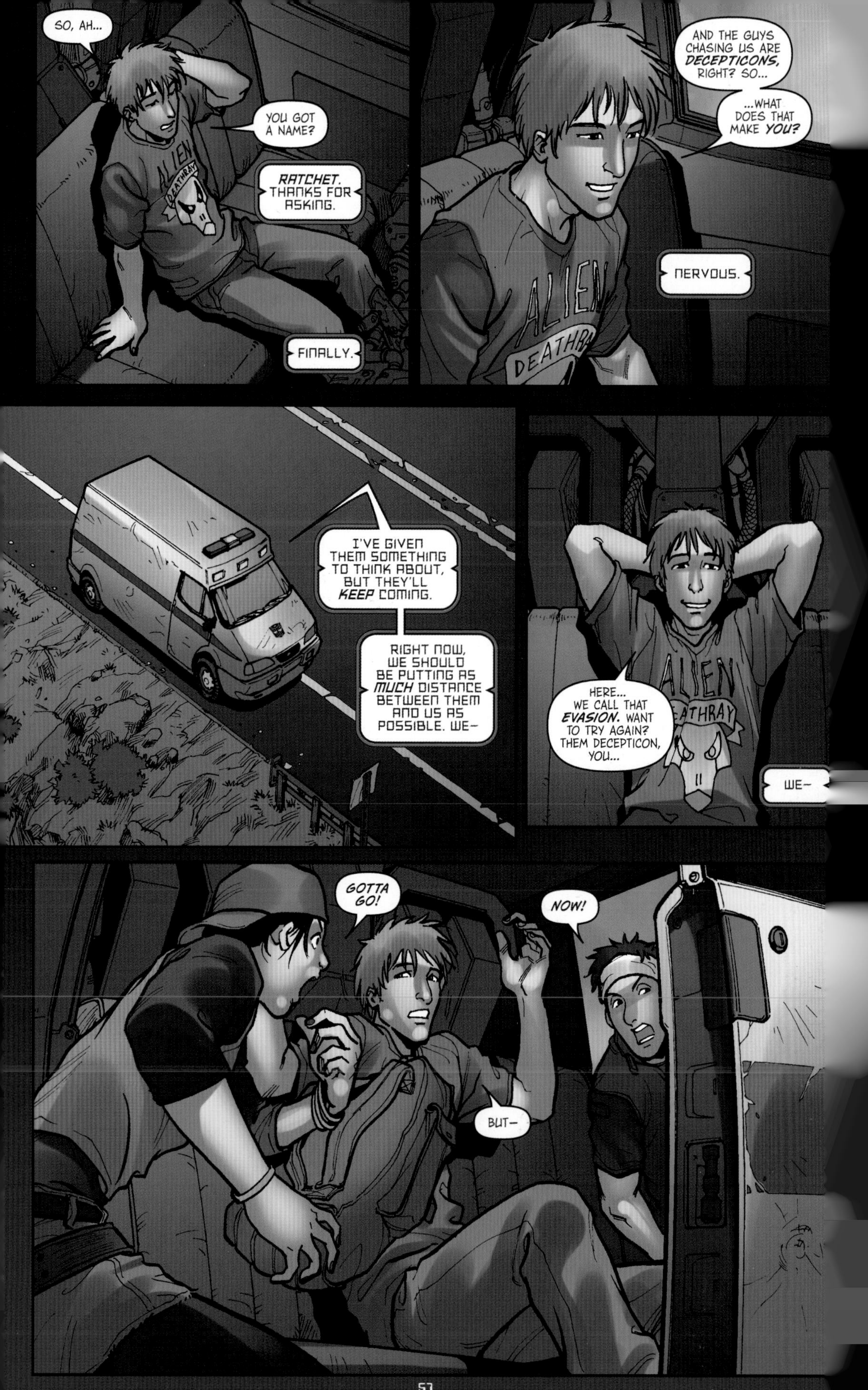
SO, AH...
YOU GOT A NAME?
RATCHET. THANKS FOR ASKING.
FINALLY.
AND THE GUYS CHASING US ARE DECEPTICONS, RIGHT? SO...
...WHAT DOES THAT MAKE YOU?
NERVOUS.
I'VE GIVEN THEM SOMETHING TO THINK ABOUT, BUT THEY'LL KEEP COMING.
RIGHT NOW, WE SHOULD BE PUTTING AS MUCH DISTANCE BETWEEN THEM AND US AS POSSIBLE. WE–
HERE... WE CALL THAT EVASION. WANT TO TRY AGAIN? THEM DECEPTICON, YOU...
WE–
GOTTA GO!
NOW!
BUT–

AH. OKAY.
IT'LL KEEP.
65 MPH
WHAT ARE YOU WAITING FOR?
GO!
NO.
GO-GO-GO!
...MARY, FULL OF GRACE...
NOT YET.

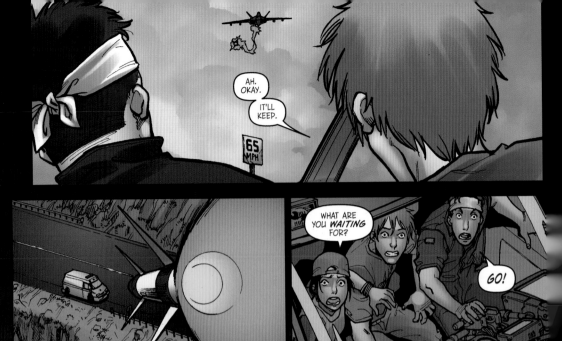

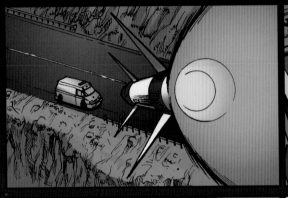

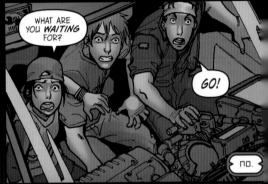

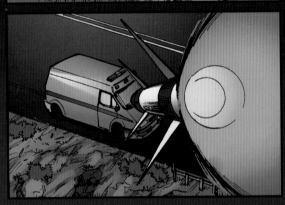

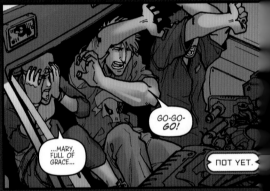

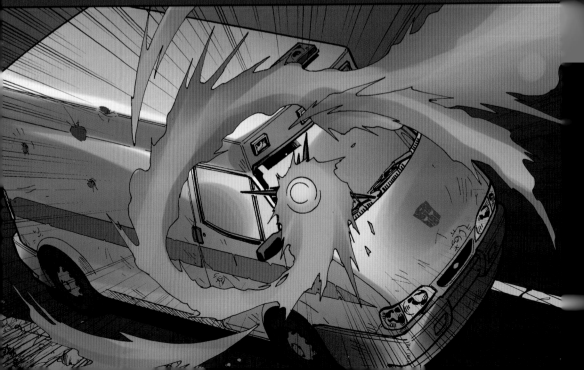

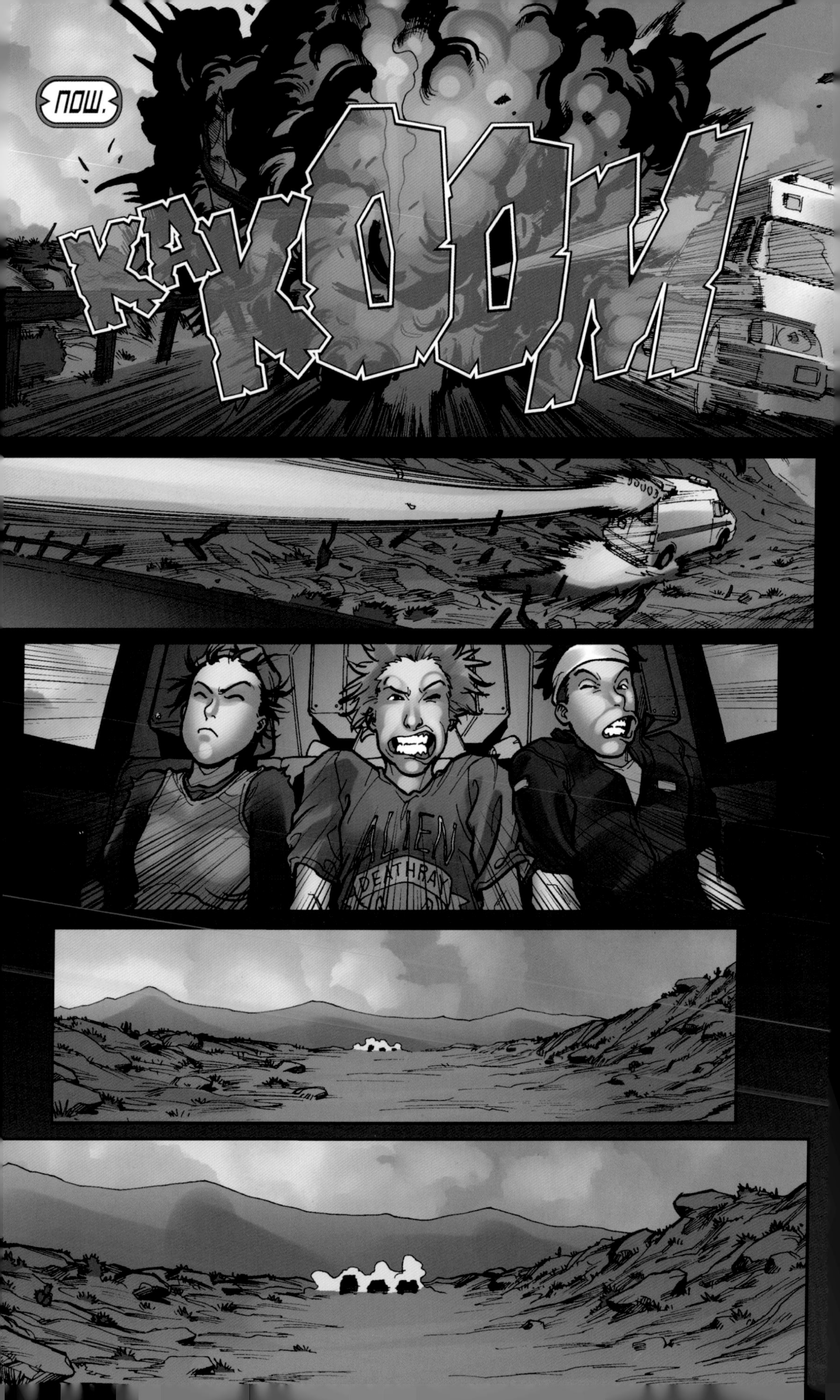
NOW.
KAKOOM
ALIEN
DEATHRAY

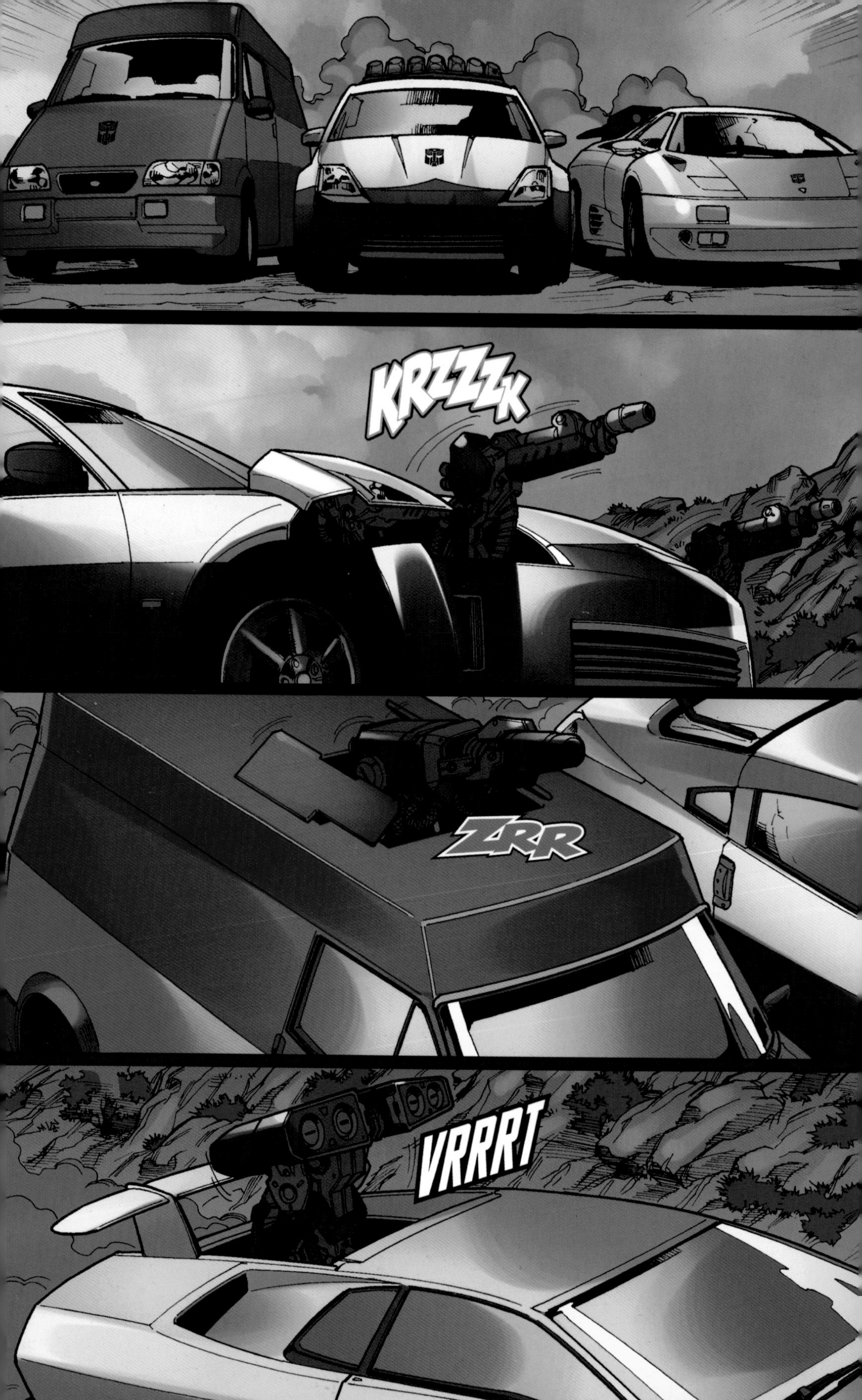
KRZZZK
ZRR
VRRRT

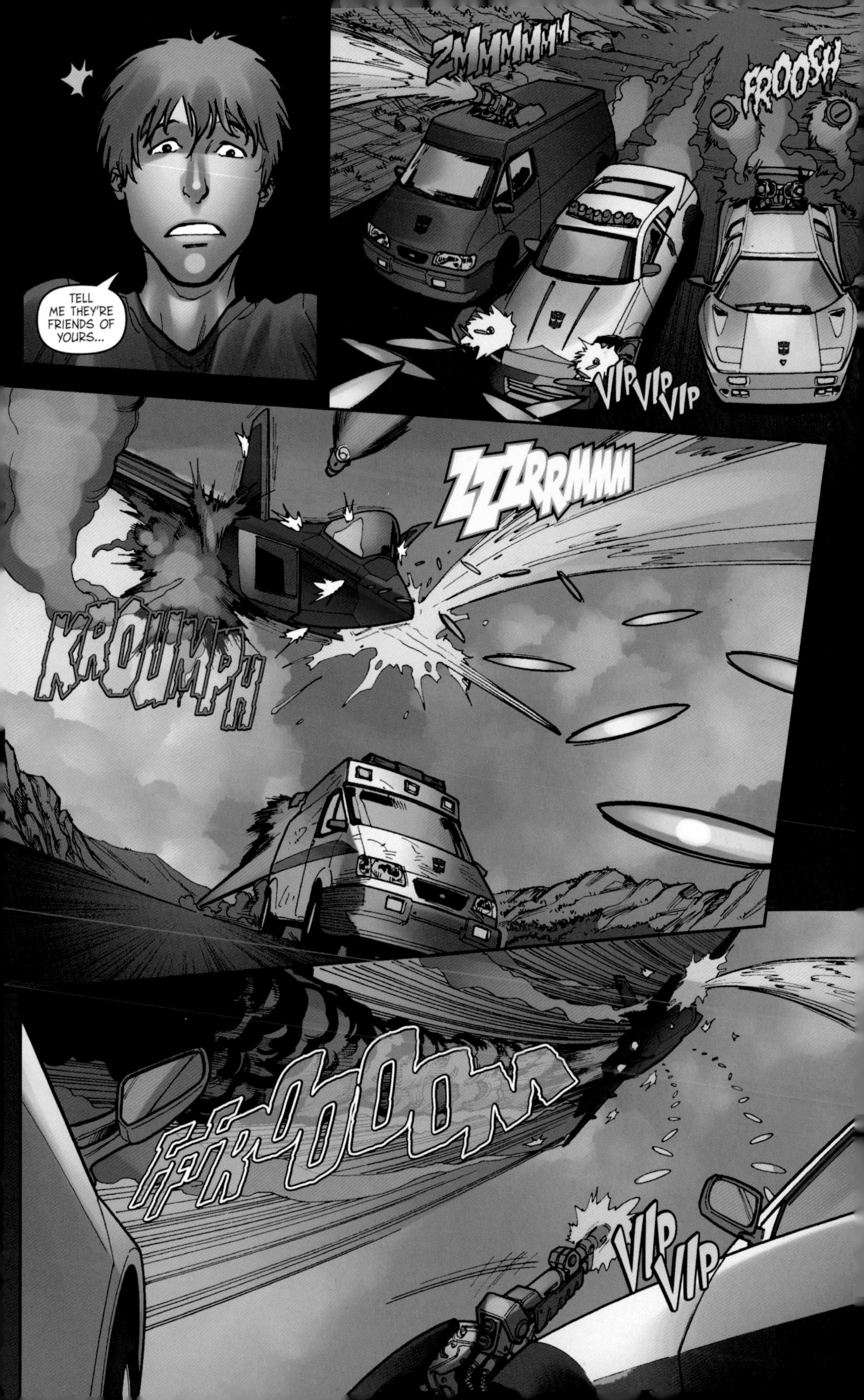
TELL ME THEY'RE FRIENDS OF YOURS...
ZMMMMMM
FROOSH
VIP VIP VIP
ZZZRRMMM
KROUMPH
FRROOOM
VIP VIP

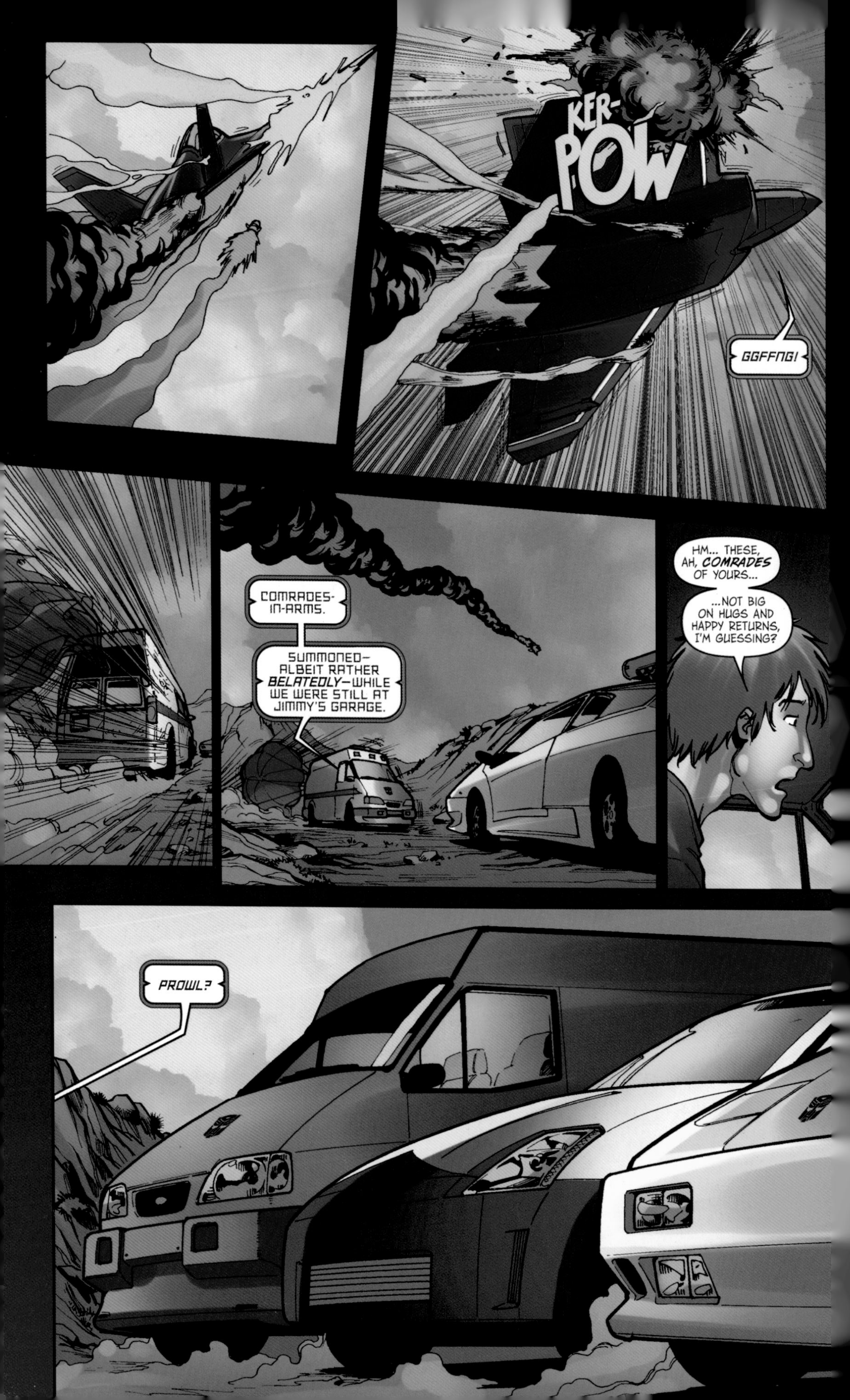
KER-POW
GGFFNG!
COMRADES-IN-ARMS.
SUMMONED—ALBEIT RATHER *BELATEDLY*—WHILE WE WERE STILL AT JIMMY'S GARAGE.
HM... THESE, AH, *COMRADES* OF YOURS...
...NOT BIG ON HUGS AND HAPPY RETURNS, I'M GUESSING?
PROWL?

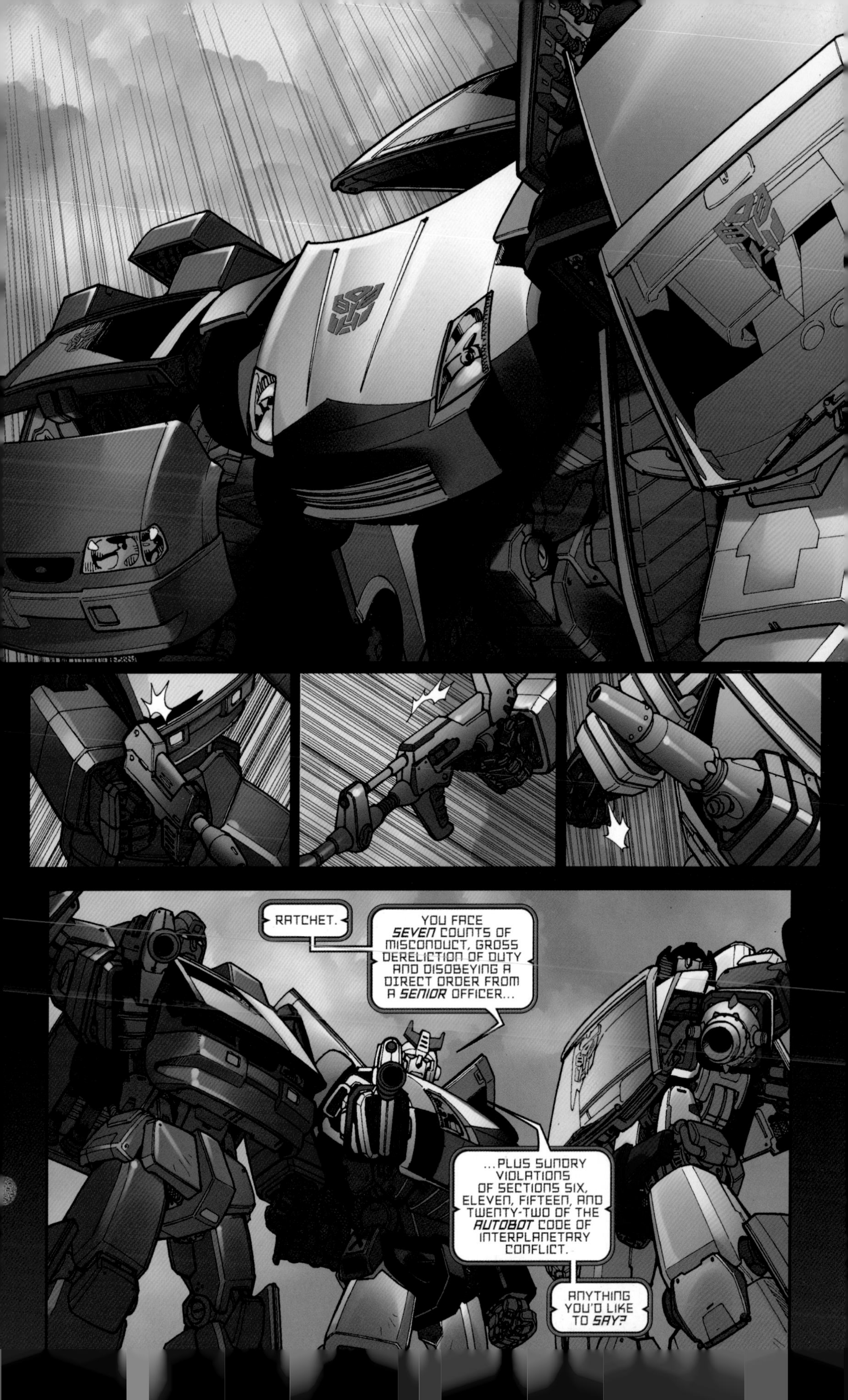
RATCHET.
YOU FACE SEVEN COUNTS OF MISCONDUCT, GROSS DERELICTION OF DUTY AND DISOBEYING A DIRECT ORDER FROM A SENIOR OFFICER...
...PLUS SUNDRY VIOLATIONS OF SECTIONS SIX, ELEVEN, FIFTEEN, AND TWENTY-TWO OF THE AUTOBOT CODE OF INTERPLANETARY CONFLICT.
ANYTHING YOU'D LIKE TO SAY?

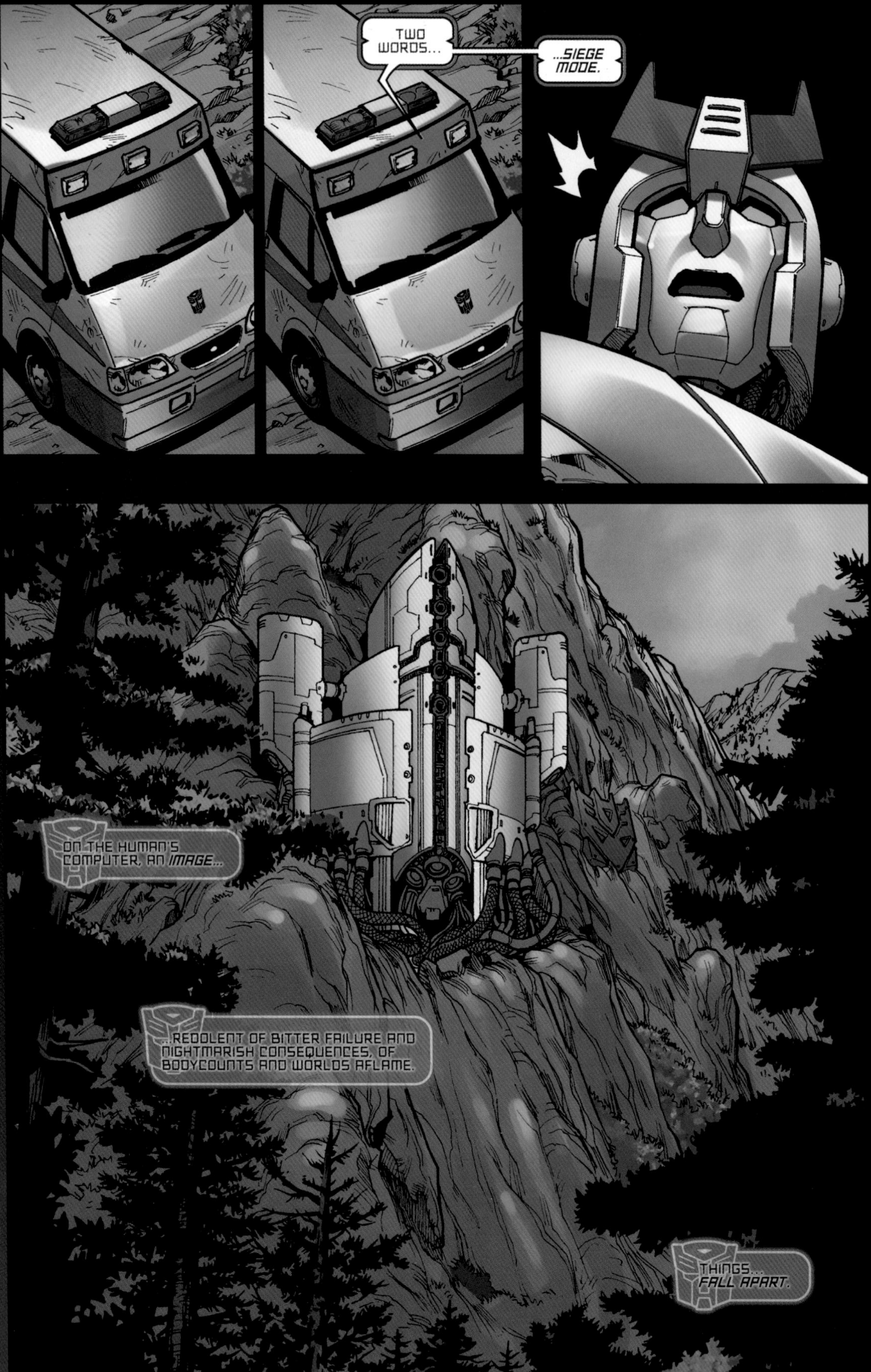
TWO WORDS...
...SIEGE MODE.
ON THE HUMAN'S COMPUTER, AN IMAGE...
...REDOLENT OF BITTER FAILURE AND NIGHTMARISH CONSEQUENCES, OF BODYCOUNTS AND WORLDS AFLAME.
THINGS... FALL APART.

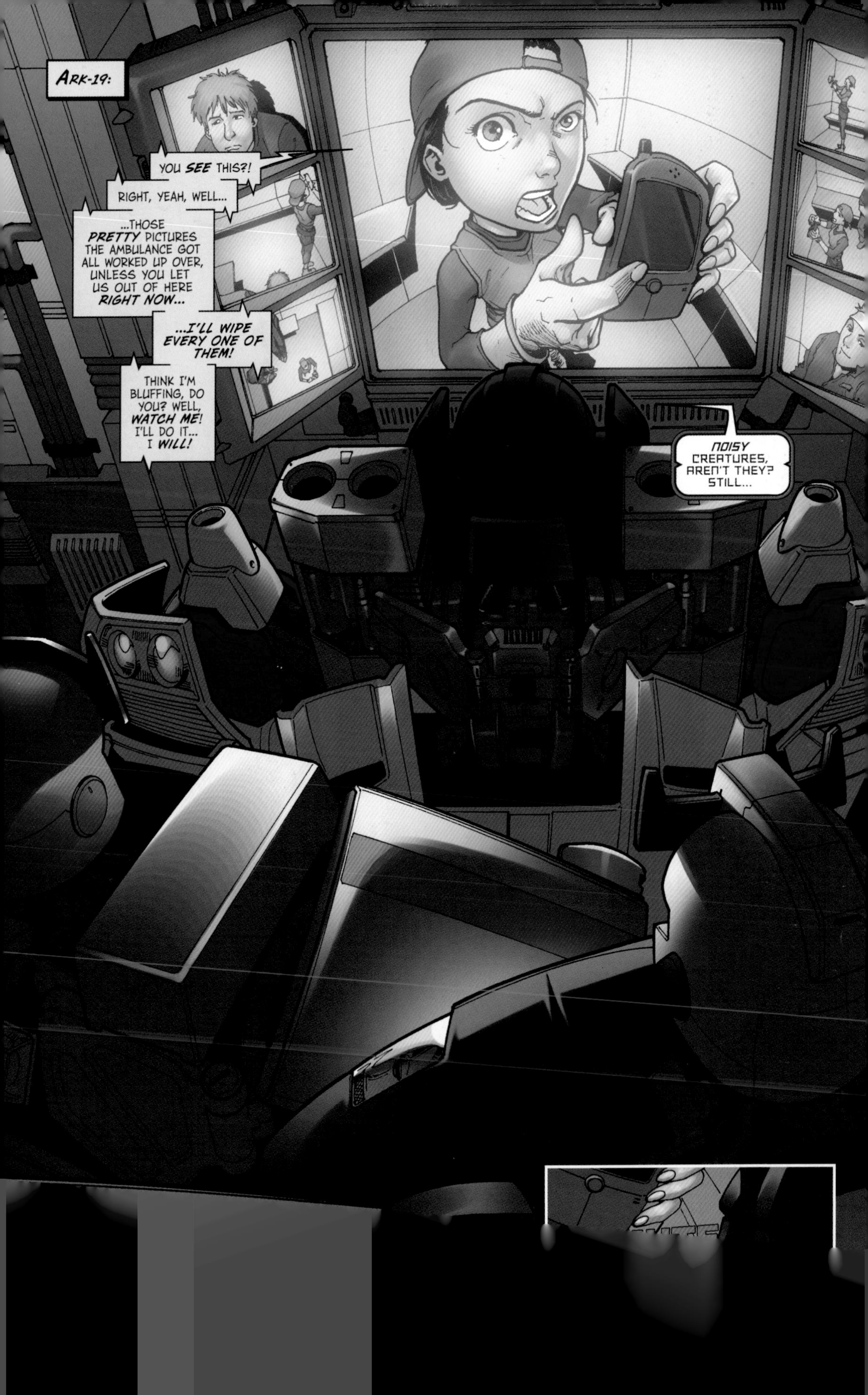

Ark-19:
YOU SEE THIS?!
RIGHT, YEAH, WELL...
...THOSE PRETTY PICTURES THE AMBULANCE GOT ALL WORKED UP OVER, UNLESS YOU LET US OUT OF HERE RIGHT NOW...
...I'LL WIPE EVERY ONE OF THEM!
THINK I'M BLUFFING, DO YOU? WELL, WATCH ME! I'LL DO IT... I WILL!
NOISY CREATURES, AREN'T THEY? STILL...

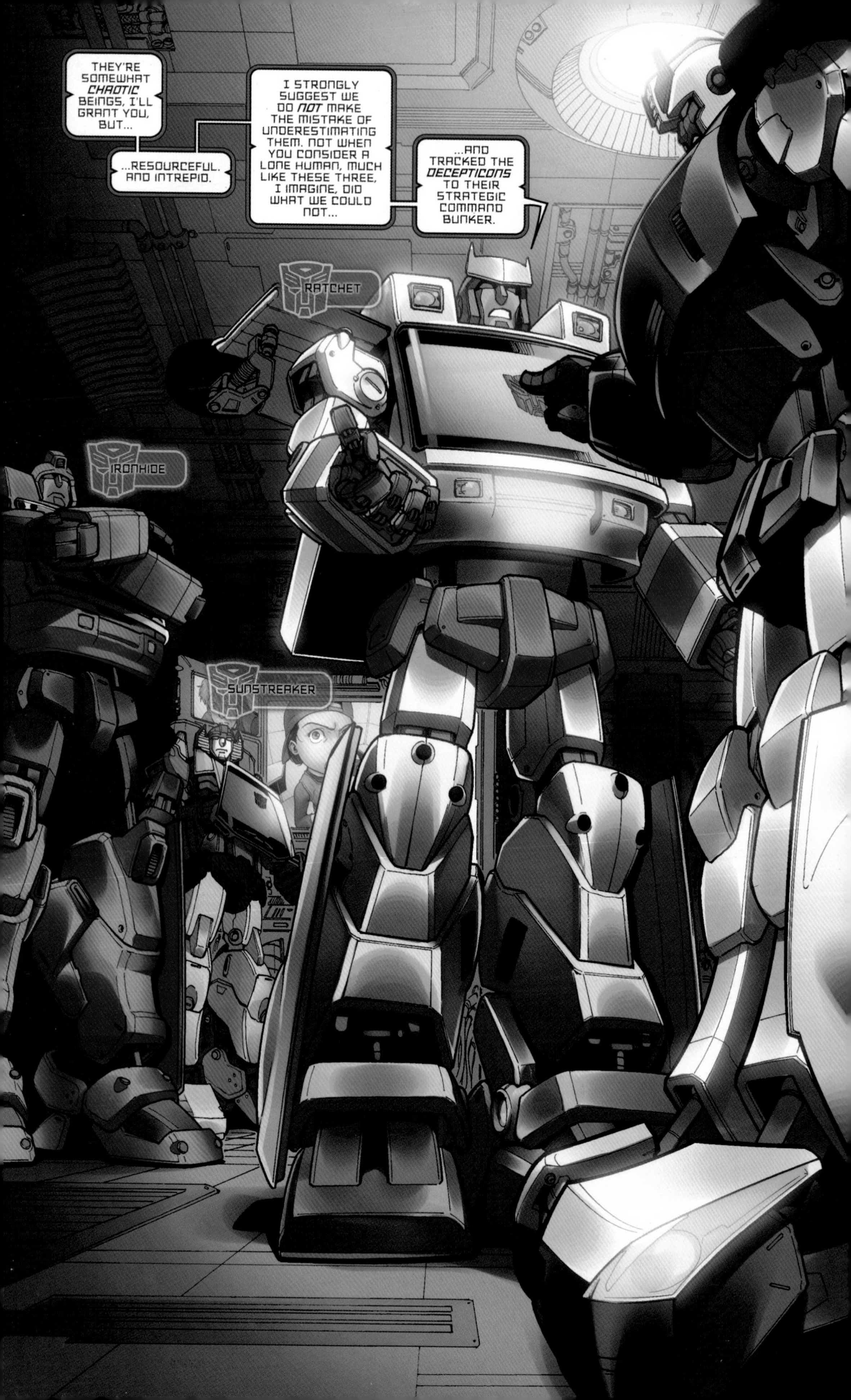
THEY'RE SOMEWHAT *CHAOTIC* BEINGS, I'LL GRANT YOU, BUT...
...RESOURCEFUL. AND INTREPID.
I STRONGLY SUGGEST WE DO *NOT* MAKE THE MISTAKE OF UNDERESTIMATING THEM. NOT WHEN YOU CONSIDER A LONE HUMAN, MUCH LIKE THESE THREE, I IMAGINE, DID WHAT WE COULD NOT...
...AND TRACKED THE *DECEPTICONS* TO THEIR STRATEGIC COMMAND BUNKER.
RATCHET
IRONHIDE
SUNSTREAKER

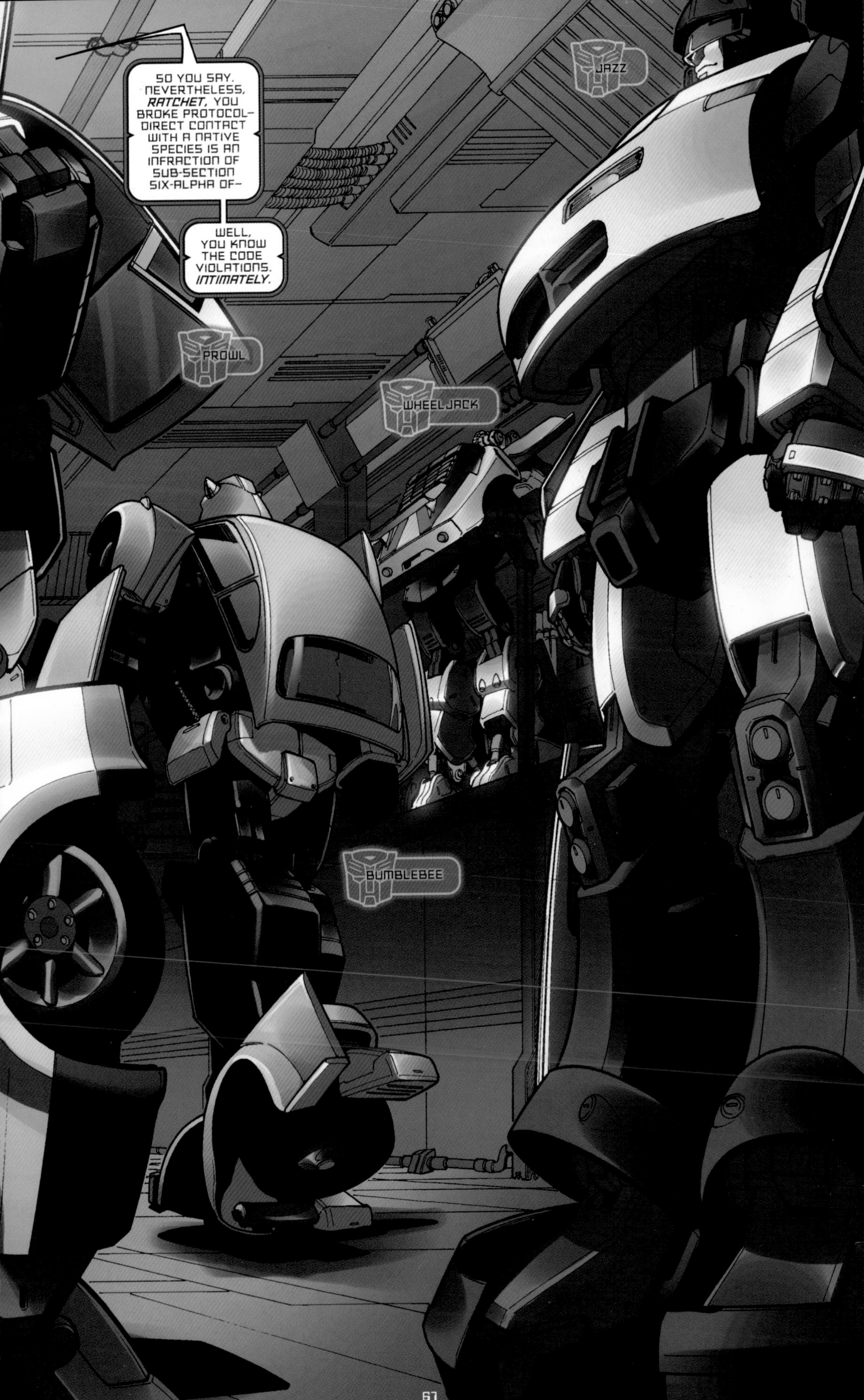

SO YOU SAY. NEVERTHELESS, *RATCHET*, YOU BROKE PROTOCOL–DIRECT CONTACT WITH A NATIVE SPECIES IS AN INFRACTION OF SUB-SECTION SIX-ALPHA OF–
WELL, YOU KNOW THE CODE VIOLATIONS. *INTIMATELY*.
JAZZ
PROWL
WHEELJACK
BUMBLEBEE

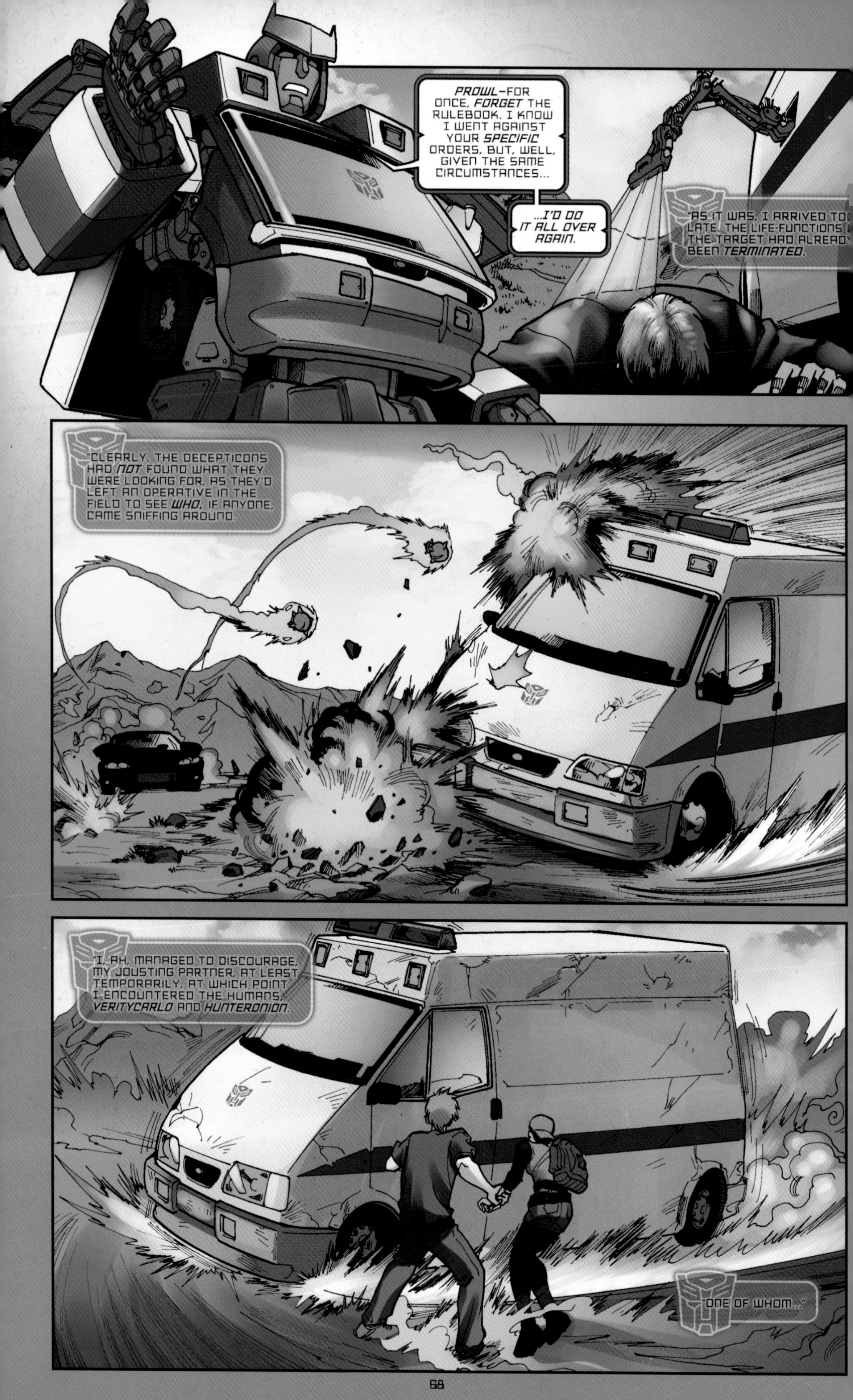
PROWL—FOR ONCE, FORGET THE RULEBOOK. I KNOW I WENT AGAINST YOUR SPECIFIC ORDERS, BUT, WELL, GIVEN THE SAME CIRCUMSTANCES...
...I'D DO IT ALL OVER AGAIN.
"AS IT WAS, I ARRIVED TOO LATE. THE LIFE-FUNCTIONS OF THE TARGET HAD ALREADY BEEN TERMINATED.
"CLEARLY, THE DECEPTICONS HAD NOT FOUND WHAT THEY WERE LOOKING FOR, AS THEY'D LEFT AN OPERATIVE IN THE FIELD TO SEE WHO, IF ANYONE, CAME SNIFFING AROUND.
"I, AH, MANAGED TO DISCOURAGE MY JOUSTING PARTNER, AT LEAST TEMPORARILY, AT WHICH POINT I ENCOUNTERED THE HUMANS VERITYCARLO AND HUNTERONION.
"ONE OF WHOM..."

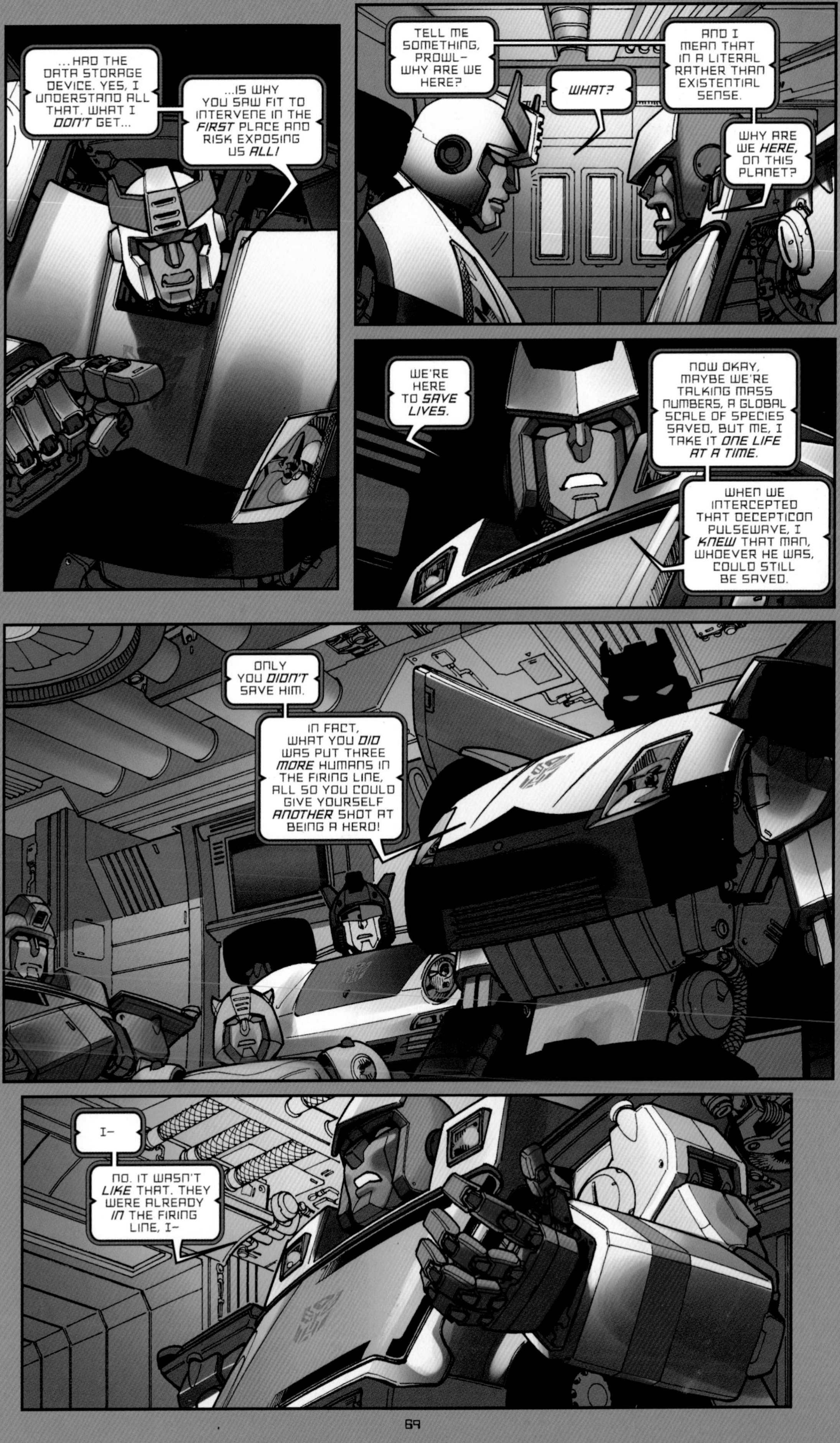
...HAD THE DATA STORAGE DEVICE. YES, I UNDERSTAND ALL THAT. WHAT I DON'T GET...
...IS WHY YOU SAW FIT TO INTERVENE IN THE FIRST PLACE AND RISK EXPOSING US ALL!
TELL ME SOMETHING, PROWL– WHY ARE WE HERE?
WHAT?
AND I MEAN THAT IN A LITERAL RATHER THAN EXISTENTIAL SENSE.
WHY ARE WE HERE, ON THIS PLANET?
WE'RE HERE TO SAVE LIVES.
NOW OKAY, MAYBE WE'RE TALKING MASS NUMBERS, A GLOBAL SCALE OF SPECIES SAVED, BUT ME, I TAKE IT ONE LIFE AT A TIME.
WHEN WE INTERCEPTED THAT DECEPTICON PULSEWAVE, I KNEW THAT MAN, WHOEVER HE WAS, COULD STILL BE SAVED.
ONLY YOU DIDN'T SAVE HIM.
IN FACT, WHAT YOU DID WAS PUT THREE MORE HUMANS IN THE FIRING LINE, ALL SO YOU COULD GIVE YOURSELF ANOTHER SHOT AT BEING A HERO!
I–
NO. IT WASN'T LIKE THAT. THEY WERE ALREADY IN THE FIRING LINE, I–

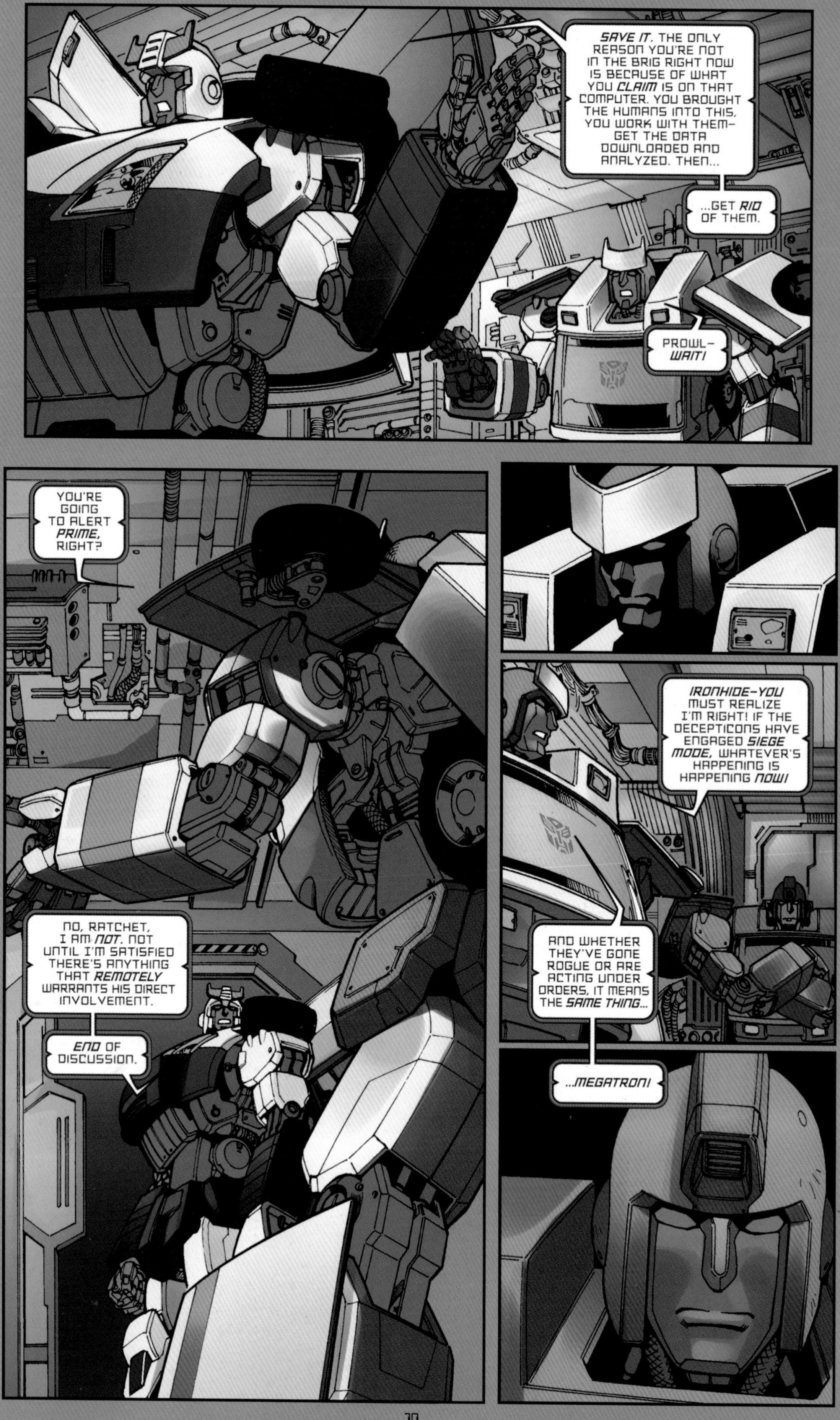
SAVE IT. THE ONLY REASON YOU'RE NOT IN THE BRIG RIGHT NOW IS BECAUSE OF WHAT YOU CLAIM IS ON THAT COMPUTER. YOU BROUGHT THE HUMANS INTO THIS, YOU WORK WITH THEM-- GET THE DATA DOWNLOADED AND ANALYZED. THEN...
...GET RID OF THEM.
PROWL-- WAIT!
YOU'RE GOING TO ALERT PRIME, RIGHT?
NO, RATCHET, I AM NOT. NOT UNTIL I'M SATISFIED THERE'S ANYTHING THAT REMOTELY WARRANTS HIS DIRECT INVOLVEMENT.
END OF DISCUSSION.
IRONHIDE--YOU MUST REALIZE I'M RIGHT! IF THE DECEPTICONS HAVE ENGAGED SIEGE MODE, WHATEVER'S HAPPENING IS HAPPENING NOW!
AND WHETHER THEY'VE GONE ROGUE OR ARE ACTING UNDER ORDERS, IT MEANS THE SAME THING...
...MEGATRON!

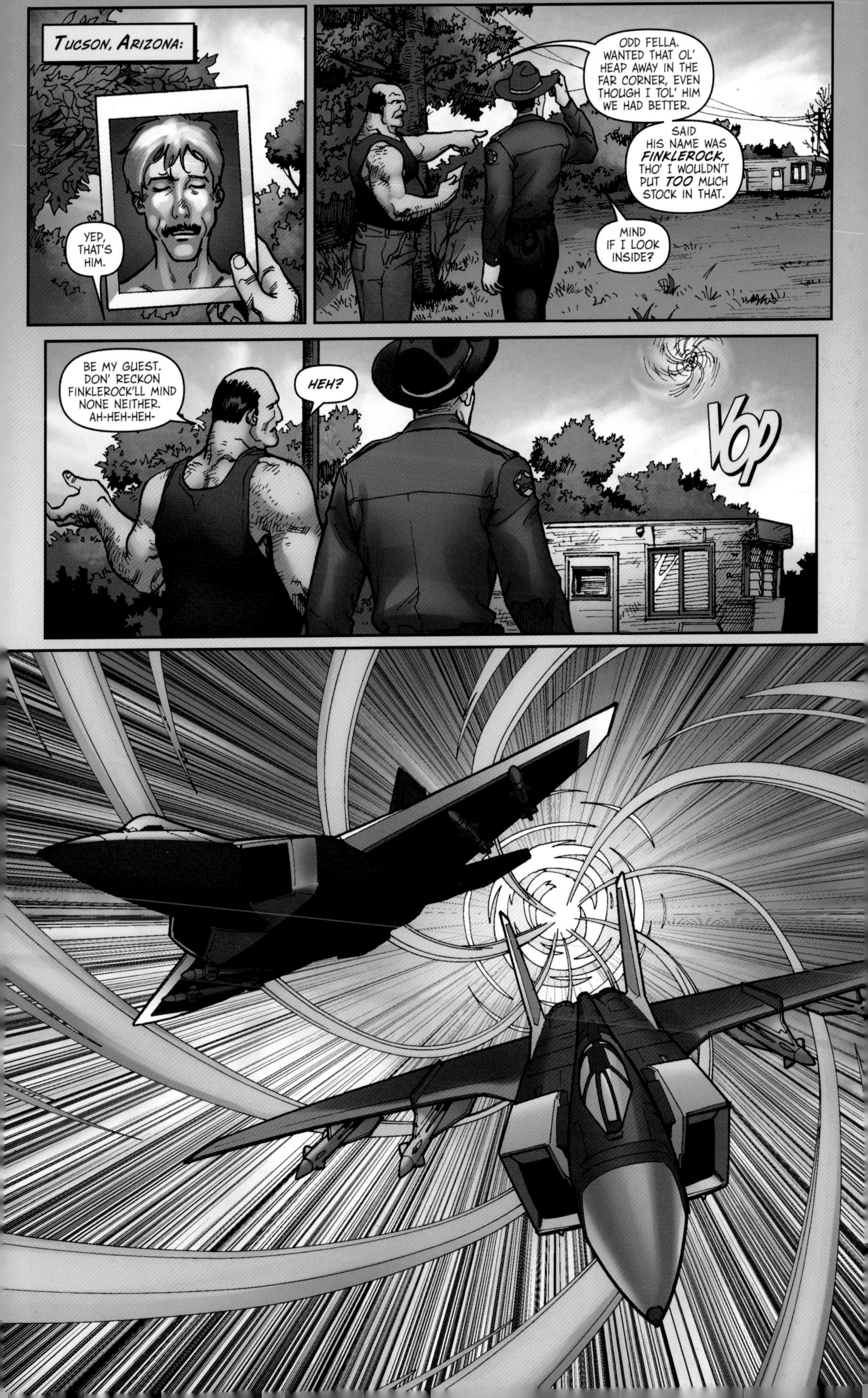

TUCSON, ARIZONA:
YEP, THAT'S HIM.
ODD FELLA. WANTED THAT OL' HEAP AWAY IN THE FAR CORNER, EVEN THOUGH I TOL' HIM WE HAD BETTER.
SAID HIS NAME WAS FINKLEROCK, THO' I WOULDN'T PUT TOO MUCH STOCK IN THAT.
MIND IF I LOOK INSIDE?
BE MY GUEST. DON' RECKON FINKLEROCK'LL MIND NONE NEITHER. AH-HEH-HEH-
HEH?
VOP

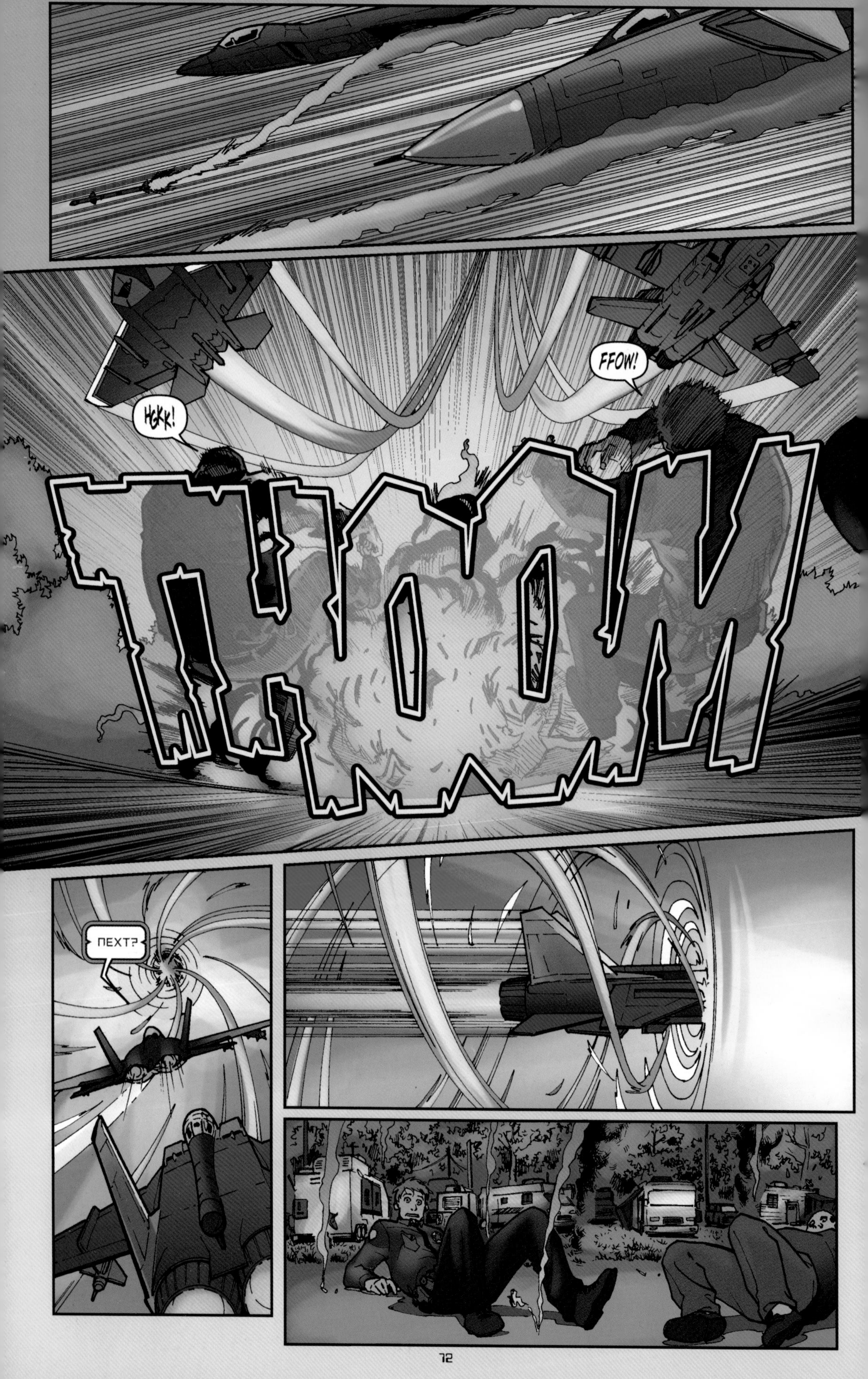
HGKK!
FFOW!
THOOM
NEXT?

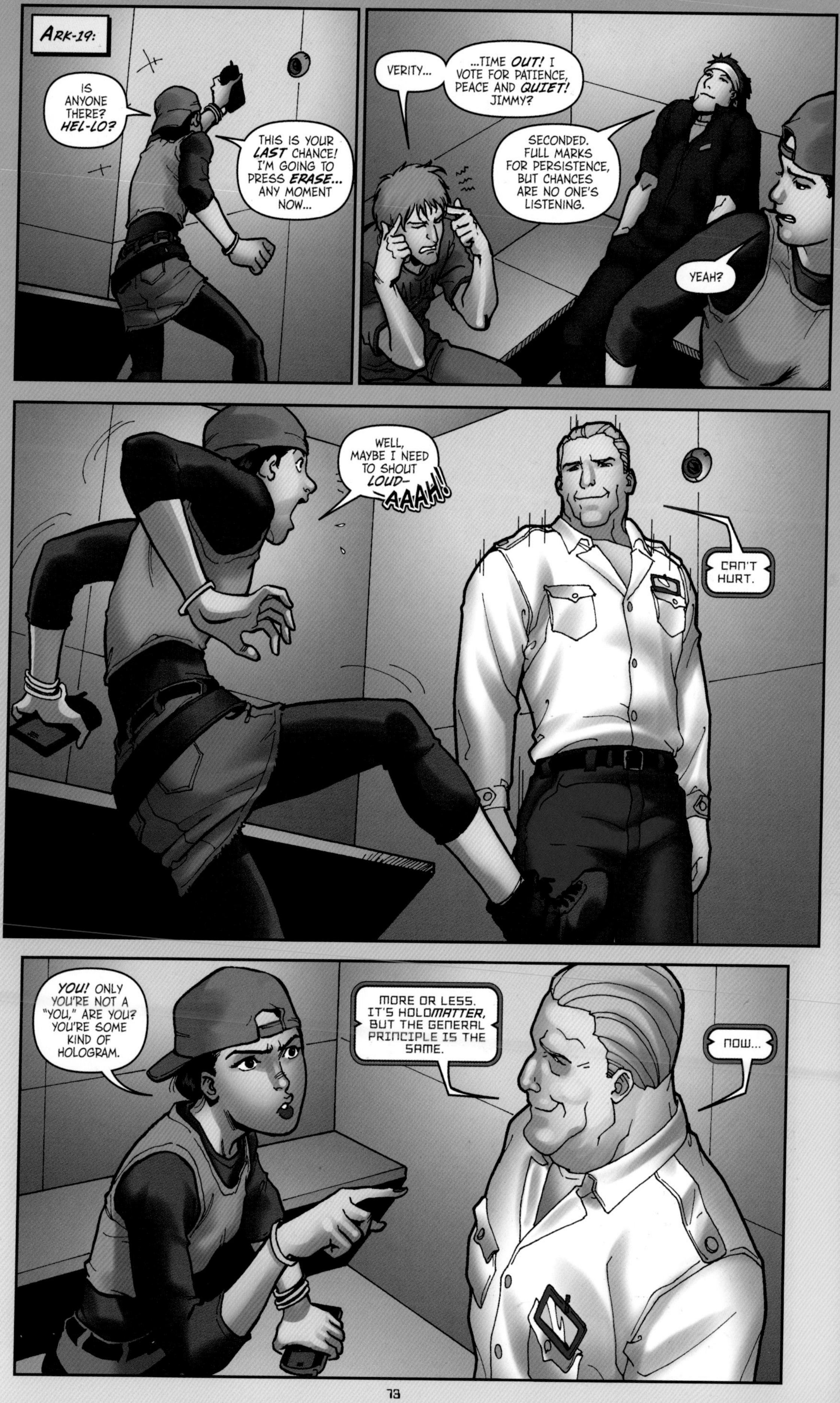

Ark-19:
IS ANYONE THERE? HEL-LO?
THIS IS YOUR LAST CHANCE! I'M GOING TO PRESS ERASE... ANY MOMENT NOW...
VERITY...
...TIME OUT! I VOTE FOR PATIENCE, PEACE AND QUIET! JIMMY?
SECONDED. FULL MARKS FOR PERSISTENCE, BUT CHANCES ARE NO ONE'S LISTENING.
YEAH?
WELL, MAYBE I NEED TO SHOUT LOUD-AAAH!
CAN'T HURT.
YOU! ONLY YOU'RE NOT A "YOU," ARE YOU? YOU'RE SOME KIND OF HOLOGRAM.
MORE OR LESS. IT'S HOLOMATTER, BUT THE GENERAL PRINCIPLE IS THE SAME.
NOW...

WHOA!

..WHAT SAY WE GET YOU *OUT* OF HERE?

A BIGGER BOX. NICE.

AN UNFORTUNATE NECESSITY. YOUR BEING HERE AT ALL...

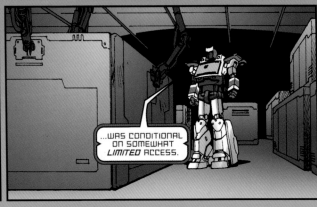

...WAS CONDITIONAL ON SOMEWHAT *LIMITED* ACCESS.

AND WHERE IS HERE... *EXACTLY?*

THIS IS *ARK-19*—OUR, UH, SPACECRAFT.

BITCHIN'.

WE'RE IN *OUTER SPACE?!* BUT... WE *DROVE* HERE, DIDN'T WE? *ALL THE WAY!*

WE DID. AND YOU'RE *NOT*... IN OUTER SPACE, THAT IS.

"YOU'RE ON THE BOTTOM OF *LAKE MICHIGAN,* ABOUT TEN MILES NORTHEAST OF CHICAGO."

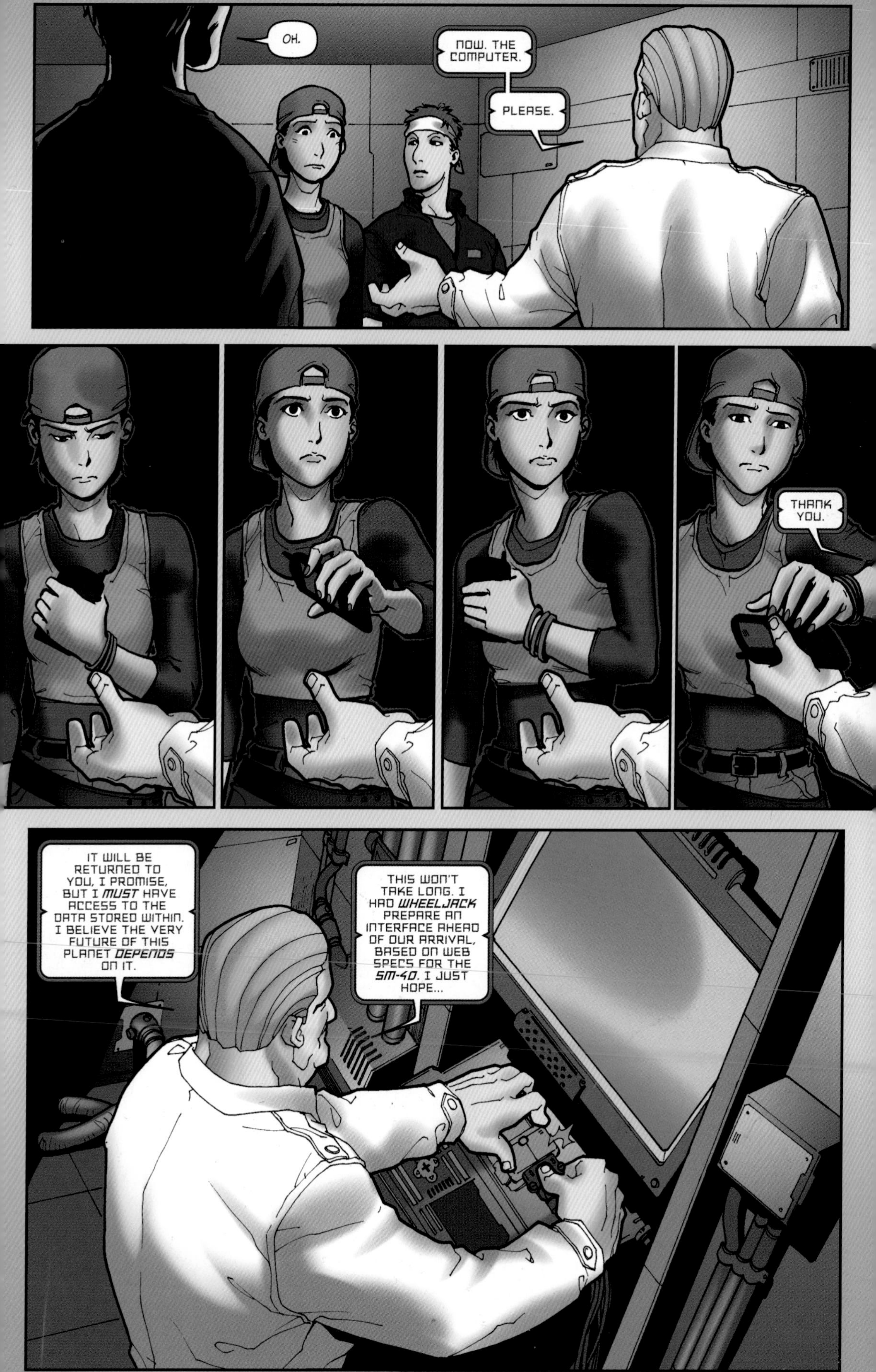
OH.
NOW. THE COMPUTER.
PLEASE.
THANK YOU.
IT WILL BE RETURNED TO YOU, I PROMISE, BUT I MUST HAVE ACCESS TO THE DATA STORED WITHIN. I BELIEVE THE VERY FUTURE OF THIS PLANET DEPENDS ON IT.
THIS WON'T TAKE LONG. I HAD WHEELJACK PREPARE AN INTERFACE AHEAD OF OUR ARRIVAL, BASED ON WEB SPECS FOR THE SM-40. I JUST HOPE...

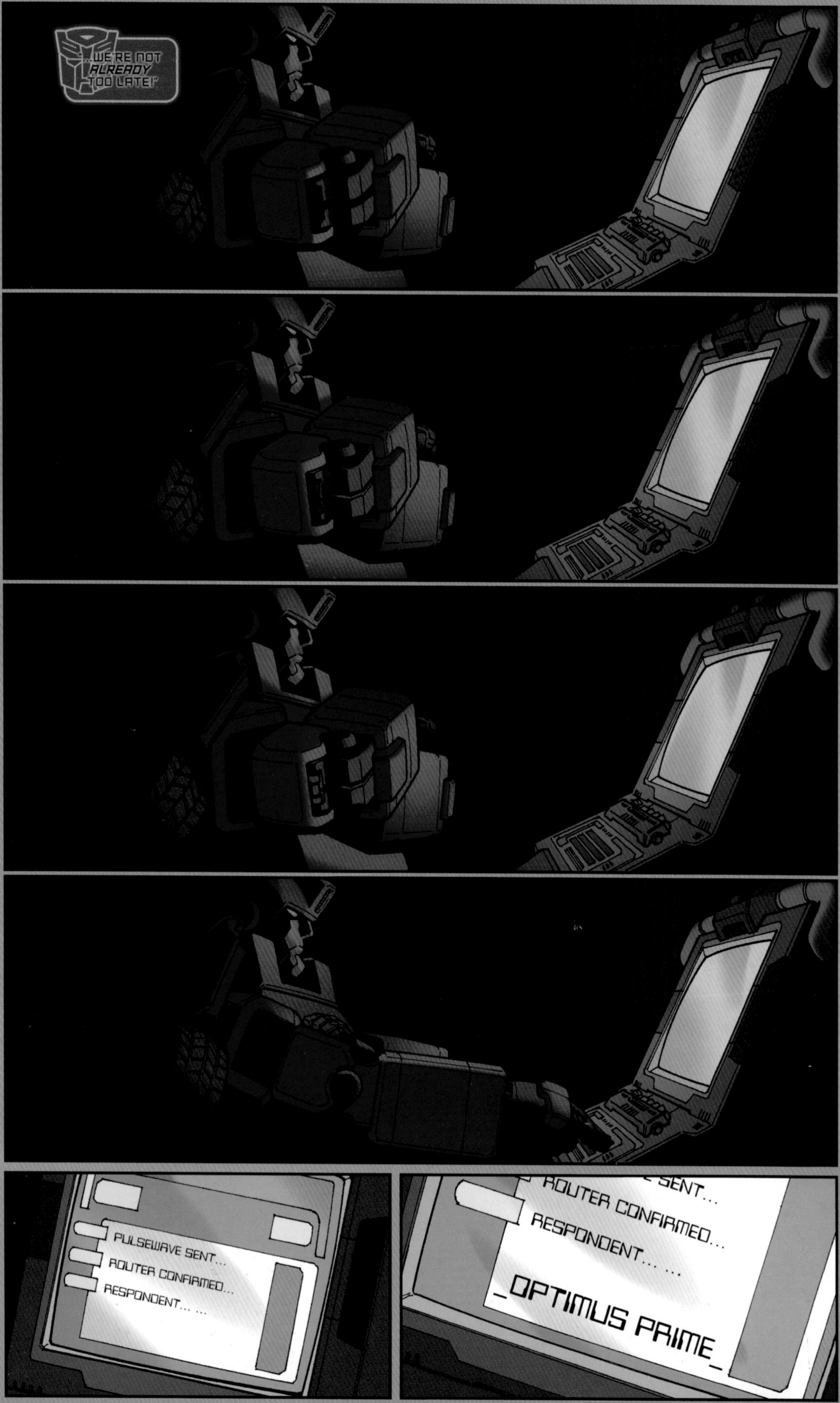

"...WE'RE NOT ALREADY TOO LATE!"
PULSEWAVE SENT...
ROUTER CONFIRMED...
RESPONDENT... ...
...SENT...
ROUTER CONFIRMED...
RESPONDENT... ...
OPTIMUS PRIME

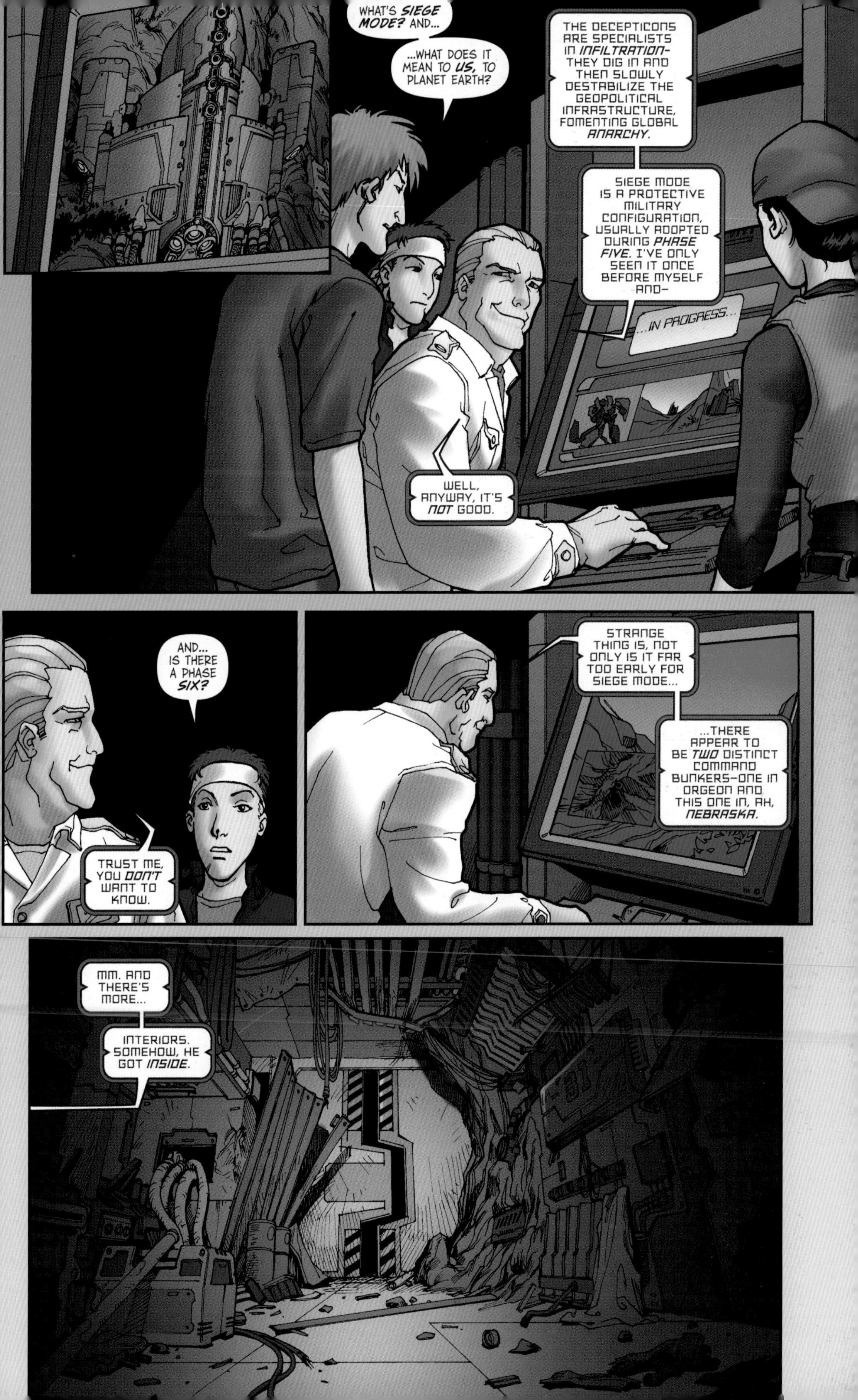
WHAT'S SIEGE MODE? AND...
...WHAT DOES IT MEAN TO US, TO PLANET EARTH?
THE DECEPTICONS ARE SPECIALISTS IN INFILTRATION–THEY DIG IN AND THEN SLOWLY DESTABILIZE THE GEOPOLITICAL INFRASTRUCTURE, FOMENTING GLOBAL ANARCHY.
SIEGE MODE IS A PROTECTIVE MILITARY CONFIGURATION, USUALLY ADOPTED DURING PHASE FIVE. I'VE ONLY SEEN IT ONCE BEFORE MYSELF AND–
...IN PROGRESS...
WELL, ANYWAY, IT'S NOT GOOD.
AND... IS THERE A PHASE SIX?
TRUST ME, YOU DON'T WANT TO KNOW.
STRANGE THING IS, NOT ONLY IS IT FAR TOO EARLY FOR SIEGE MODE...
...THERE APPEAR TO BE TWO DISTINCT COMMAND BUNKERS–ONE IN ORGEON AND THIS ONE IN, AH, NEBRASKA.
MM. AND THERE'S MORE...
INTERIORS. SOMEHOW, HE GOT INSIDE.

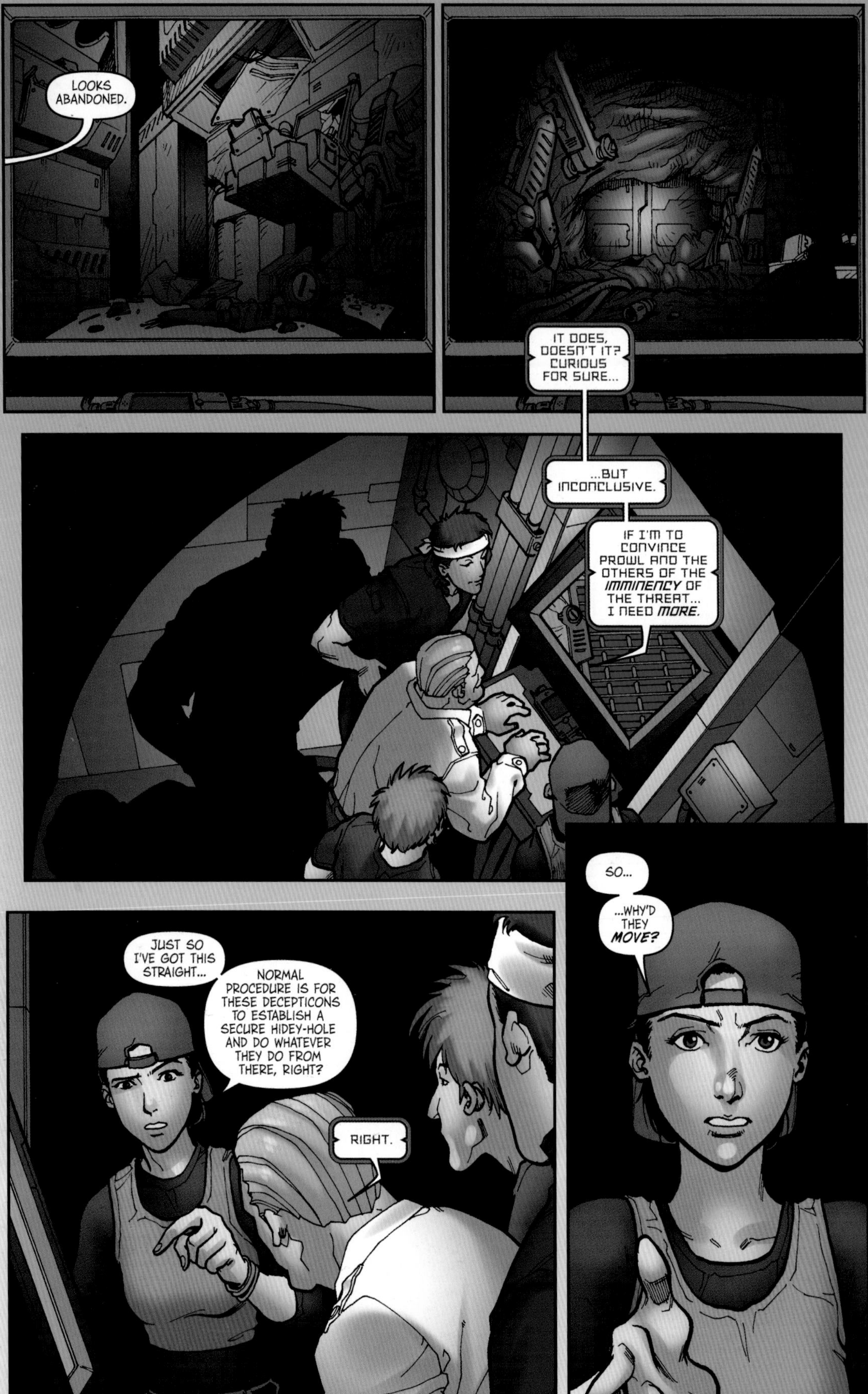
LOOKS ABANDONED.
IT DOES, DOESN'T IT? CURIOUS FOR SURE...
...BUT INCONCLUSIVE.
IF I'M TO CONVINCE PROWL AND THE OTHERS OF THE *IMMINENCY* OF THE THREAT... I NEED *MORE*.
JUST SO I'VE GOT THIS STRAIGHT...
NORMAL PROCEDURE IS FOR THESE DECEPTICONS TO ESTABLISH A SECURE HIDEY-HOLE AND DO WHATEVER THEY DO FROM THERE, RIGHT?
RIGHT.
SO...
...WHY'D THEY *MOVE?*

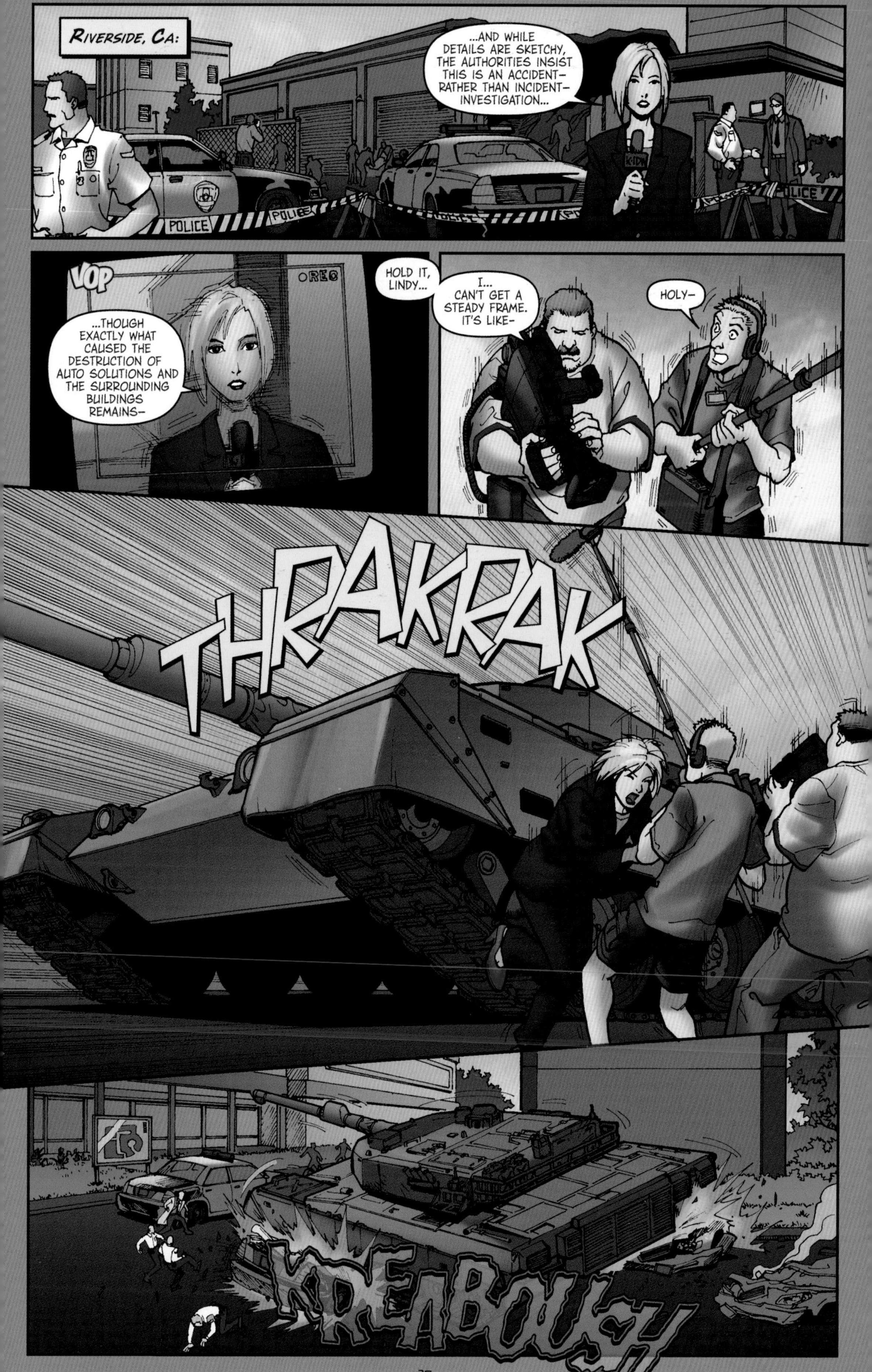
RIVERSIDE, CA:
...AND WHILE DETAILS ARE SKETCHY, THE AUTHORITIES INSIST THIS IS AN ACCIDENT-RATHER THAN INCIDENT-INVESTIGATION...
POLICE
POLICE
VOP
REC
...THOUGH EXACTLY WHAT CAUSED THE DESTRUCTION OF AUTO SOLUTIONS AND THE SURROUNDING BUILDINGS REMAINS-
HOLD IT, LINDY...
I... CAN'T GET A STEADY FRAME. IT'S LIKE-
HOLY-
THRAKRAK
KREABOUSH

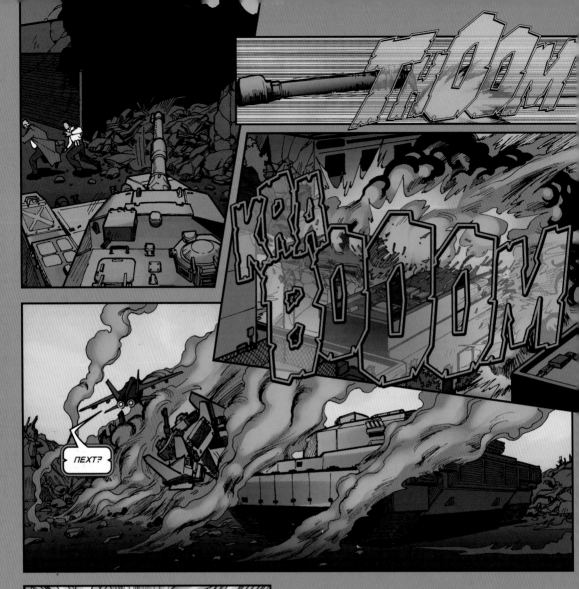

THOOM

KRAA-BOOOM

NEXT?

DID YOU *GET* THAT?

TELL ME YOU *GOT* THAT!

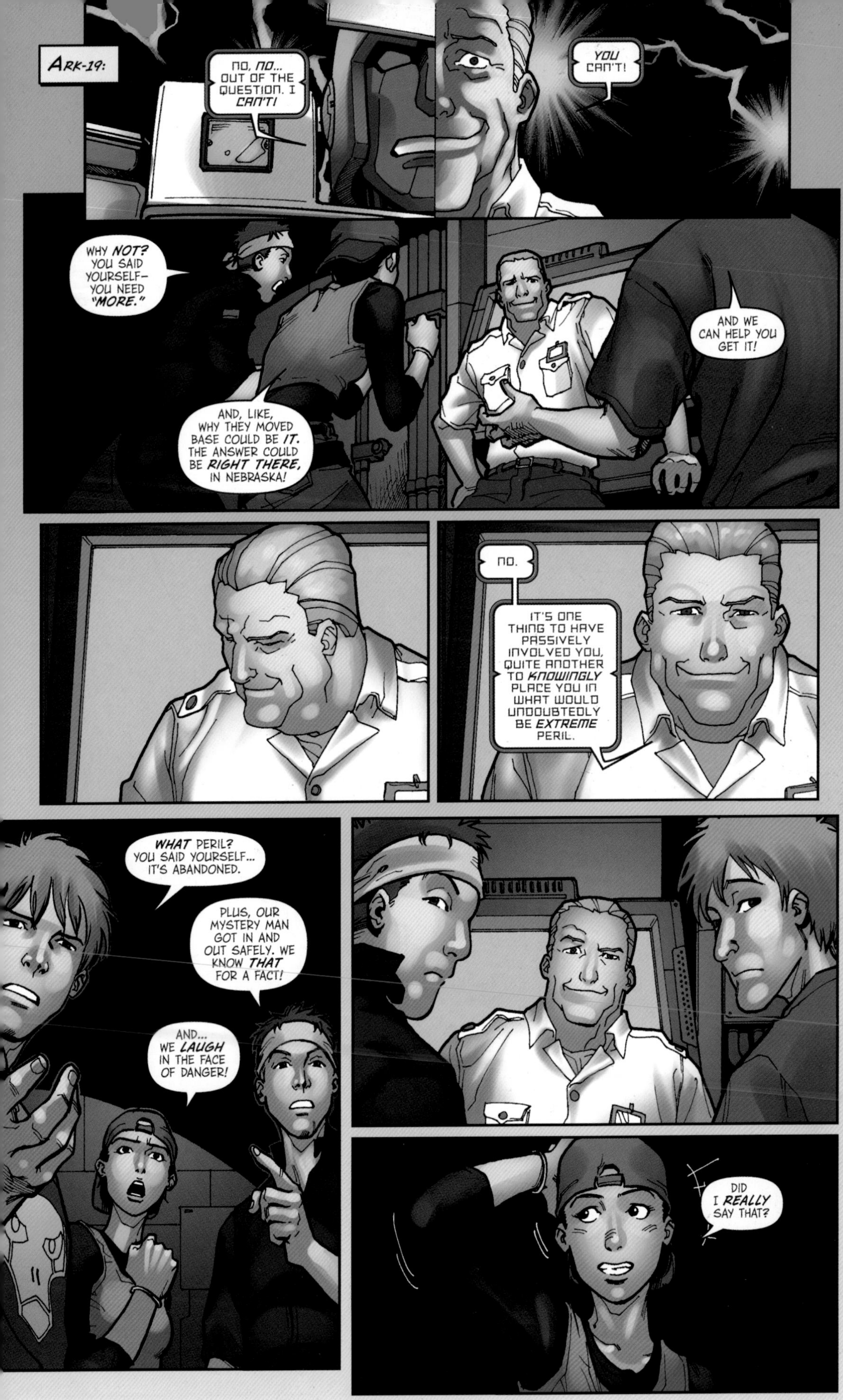
Ark-19:
NO, NO... OUT OF THE QUESTION. I CAN'T!
YOU CAN'T!
WHY NOT? YOU SAID YOURSELF— YOU NEED "MORE."
AND, LIKE, WHY THEY MOVED BASE COULD BE IT. THE ANSWER COULD BE RIGHT THERE, IN NEBRASKA!
AND WE CAN HELP YOU GET IT!
NO.
IT'S ONE THING TO HAVE PASSIVELY INVOLVED YOU, QUITE ANOTHER TO KNOWINGLY PLACE YOU IN WHAT WOULD UNDOUBTEDLY BE EXTREME PERIL.
WHAT PERIL? YOU SAID YOURSELF... IT'S ABANDONED.
PLUS, OUR MYSTERY MAN GOT IN AND OUT SAFELY. WE KNOW THAT FOR A FACT!
AND... WE LAUGH IN THE FACE OF DANGER!
DID I REALLY SAY THAT?

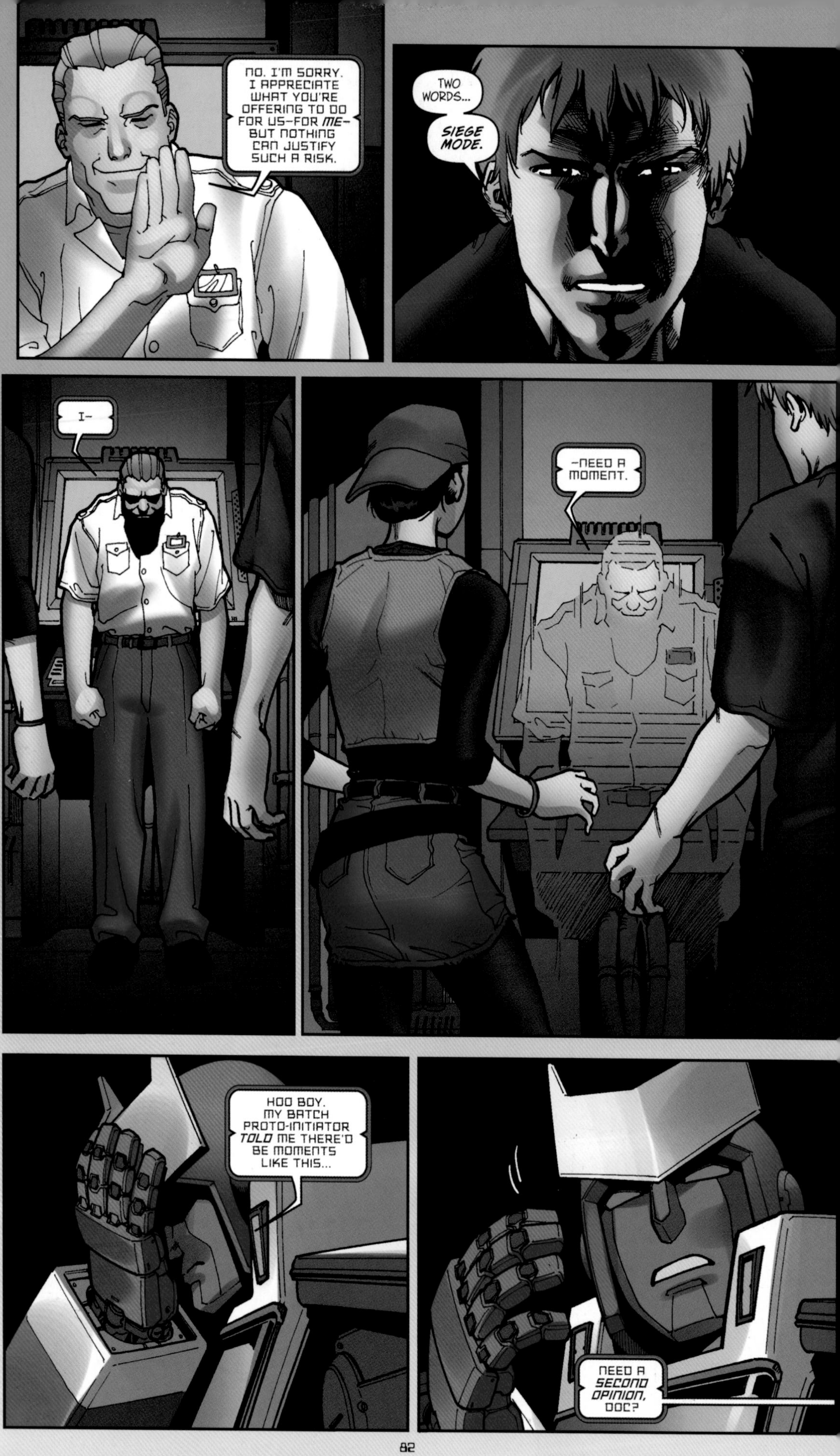
NO. I'M SORRY. I APPRECIATE WHAT YOU'RE OFFERING TO DO FOR US—FOR ME—BUT NOTHING CAN JUSTIFY SUCH A RISK.
TWO WORDS...
SIEGE MODE.
I—
—NEED A MOMENT.
HOO BOY. MY BATCH PROTO-INITIATOR TOLD ME THERE'D BE MOMENTS LIKE THIS...
NEED A SECOND OPINION, DOC?

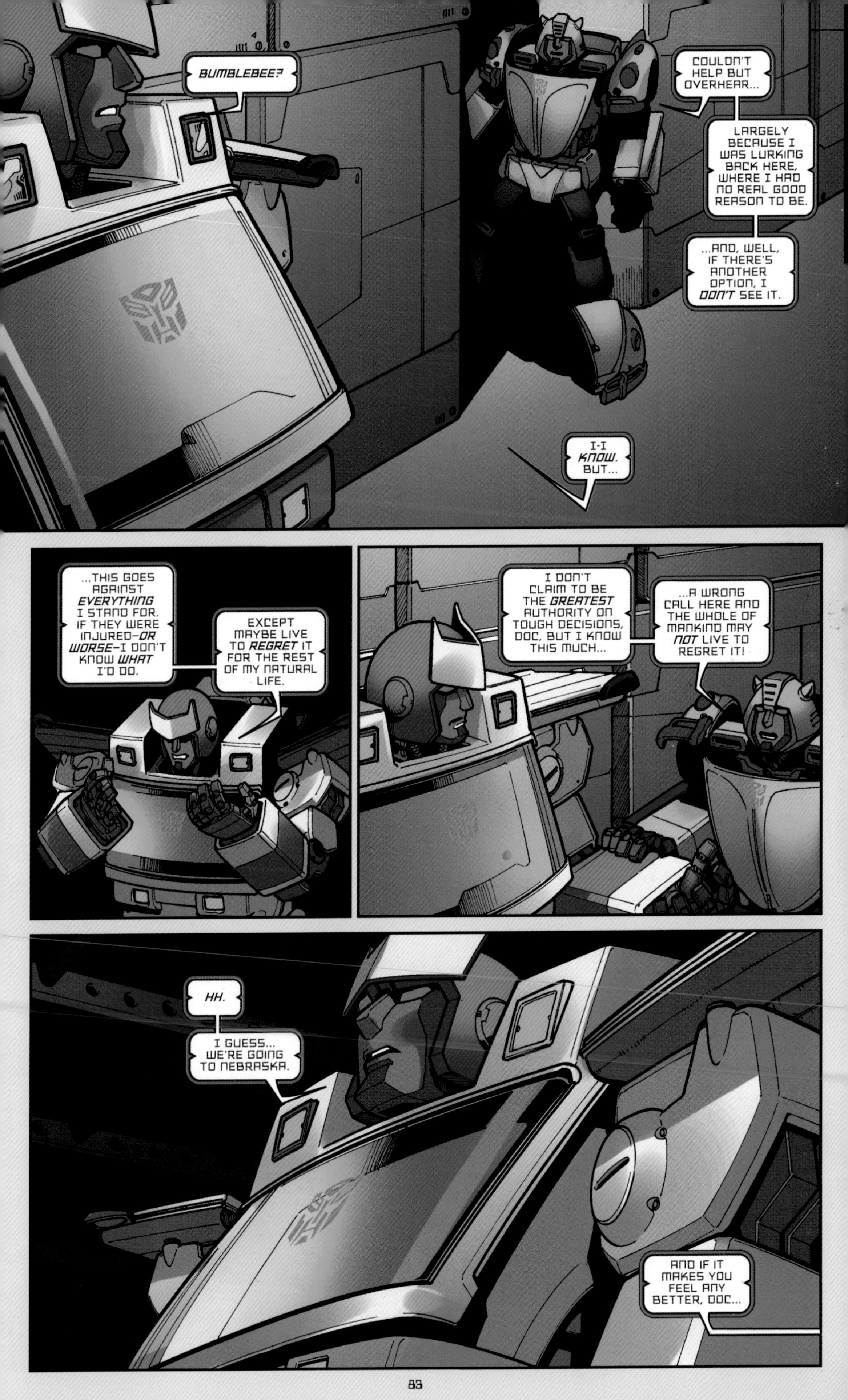
BUMBLEBEE?
COULDN'T HELP BUT OVERHEAR...
LARGELY BECAUSE I WAS LURKING BACK HERE, WHERE I HAD NO REAL GOOD REASON TO BE.
...AND, WELL, IF THERE'S ANOTHER OPTION, I DON'T SEE IT.
I-I KNOW. BUT...
...THIS GOES AGAINST EVERYTHING I STAND FOR. IF THEY WERE INJURED—OR WORSE—I DON'T KNOW WHAT I'D DO.
EXCEPT MAYBE LIVE TO REGRET IT FOR THE REST OF MY NATURAL LIFE.
I DON'T CLAIM TO BE THE GREATEST AUTHORITY ON TOUGH DECISIONS, DOC, BUT I KNOW THIS MUCH...
...A WRONG CALL HERE AND THE WHOLE OF MANKIND MAY NOT LIVE TO REGRET IT!
HH.
I GUESS... WE'RE GOING TO NEBRASKA.
AND IF IT MAKES YOU FEEL ANY BETTER, DOC...

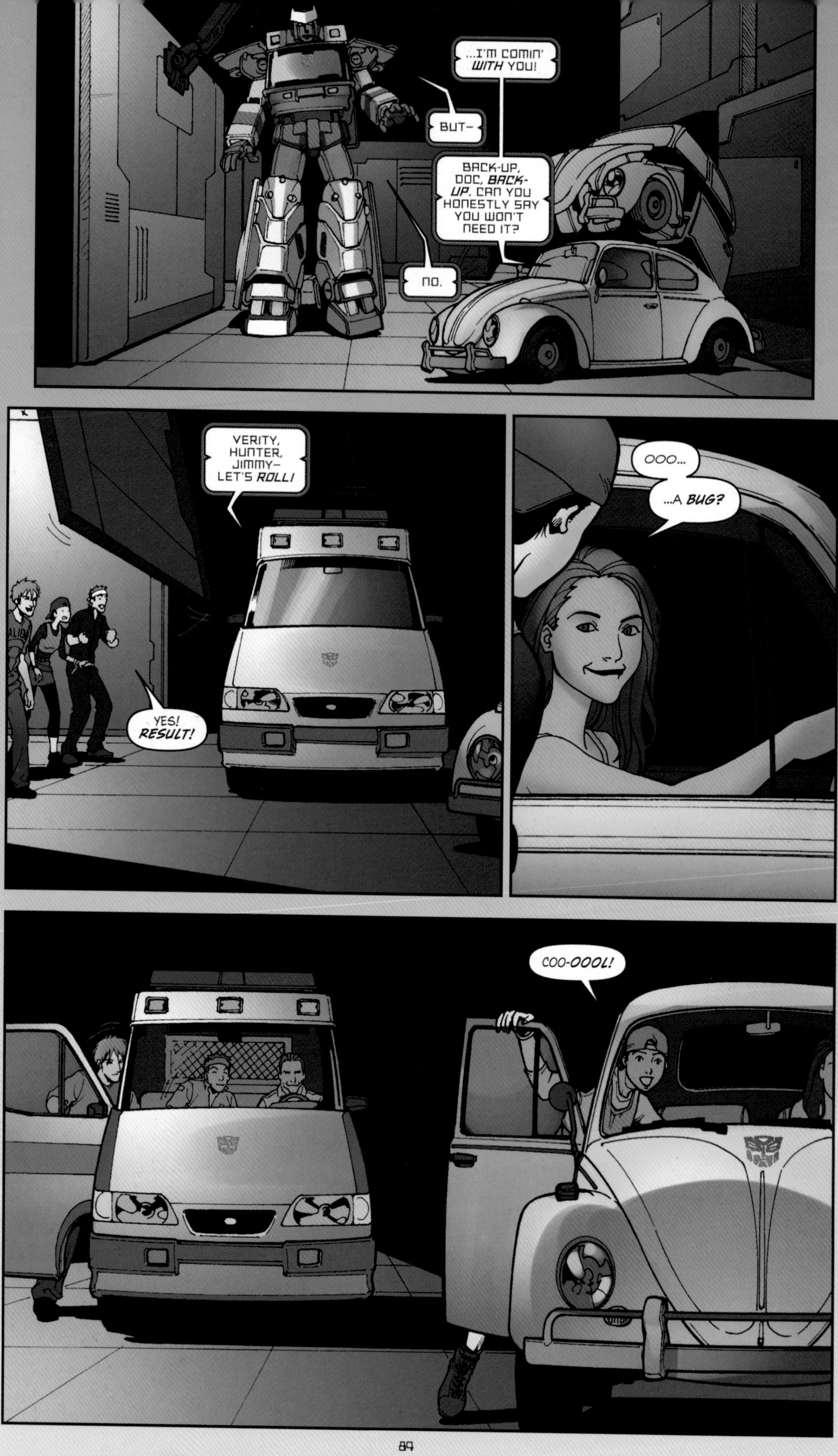
...I'M COMIN' WITH YOU!
BUT–
BACK-UP, DOC, BACK-UP. CAN YOU HONESTLY SAY YOU WON'T NEED IT?
NO.
VERITY, HUNTER, JIMMY– LET'S ROLL!
YES! RESULT!
OOO...
...A BUG?
COO-OOOL!

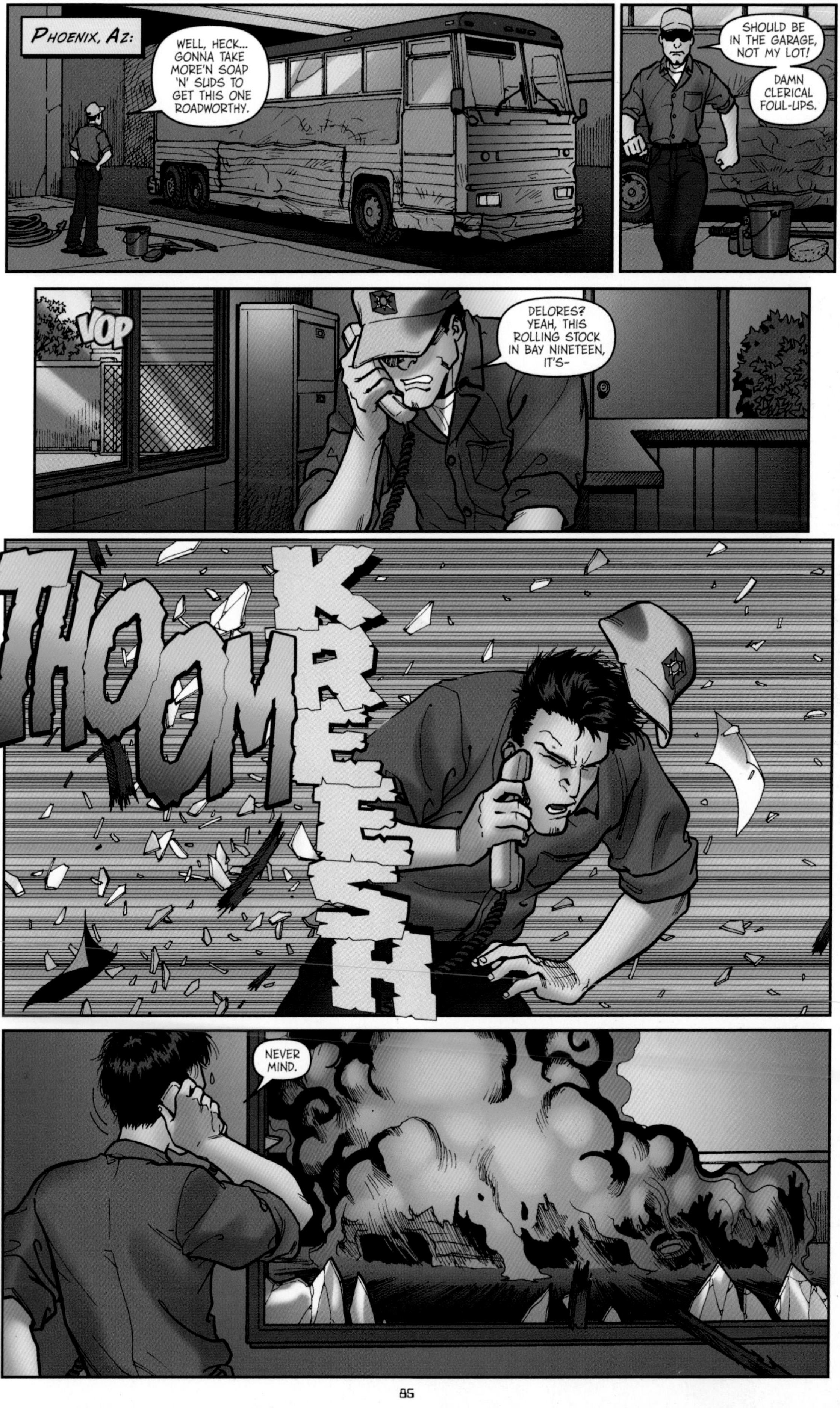

PHOENIX, AZ:
WELL, HECK... GONNA TAKE MORE'N SOAP 'N' SUDS TO GET THIS ONE ROADWORTHY.
SHOULD BE IN THE GARAGE, NOT MY LOT!
DAMN CLERICAL FOUL-UPS.
VOP
DELORES? YEAH, THIS ROLLING STOCK IN BAY NINETEEN, IT'S-
THOOM
KRRESSH
NEVER MIND.

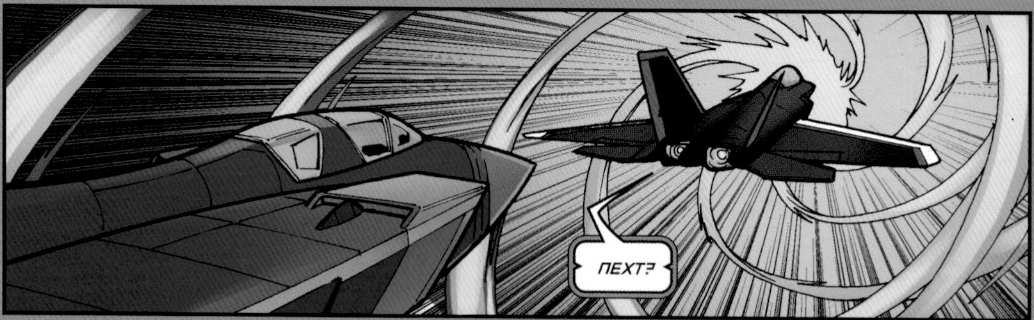
NEXT?

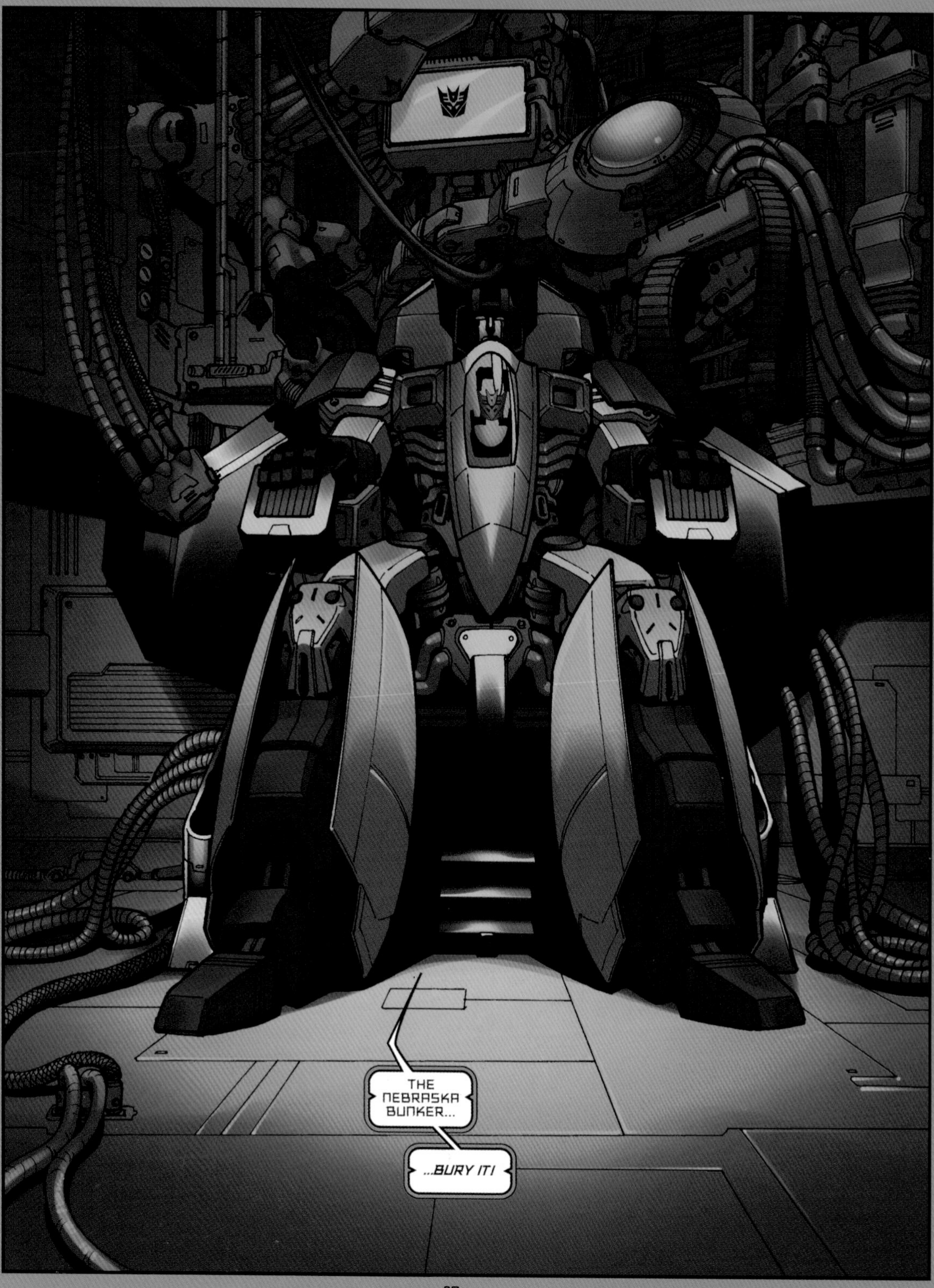
THE NEBRASKA BUNKER...
...BURY IT!

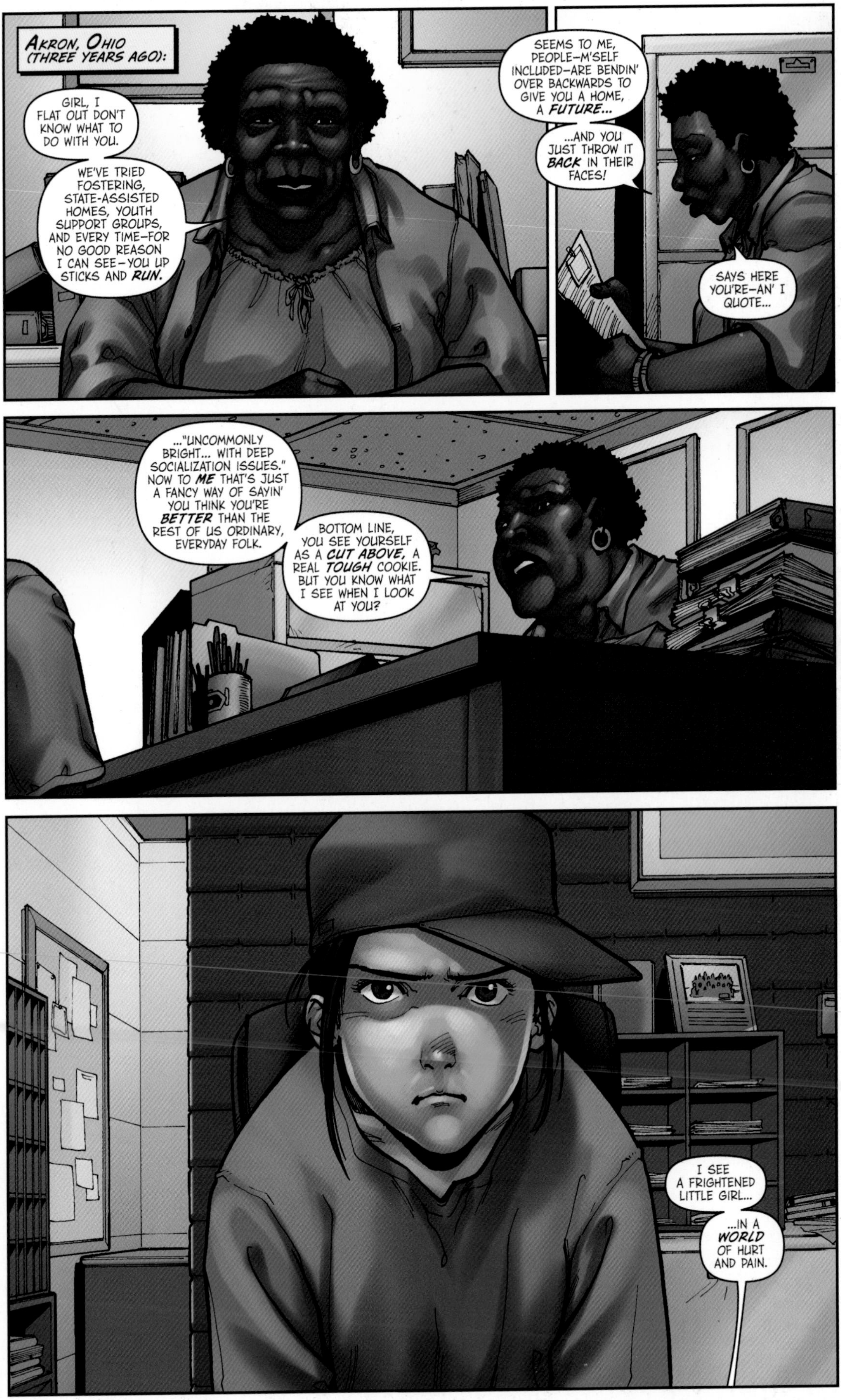

AKRON, OHIO (THREE YEARS AGO):
GIRL, I FLAT OUT DON'T KNOW WHAT TO DO WITH YOU.
WE'VE TRIED FOSTERING, STATE-ASSISTED HOMES, YOUTH SUPPORT GROUPS, AND EVERY TIME—FOR NO GOOD REASON I CAN SEE—YOU UP STICKS AND RUN.
SEEMS TO ME, PEOPLE—M'SELF INCLUDED—ARE BENDIN' OVER BACKWARDS TO GIVE YOU A HOME, A FUTURE...
...AND YOU JUST THROW IT BACK IN THEIR FACES!
SAYS HERE YOU'RE—AN' I QUOTE...
..."UNCOMMONLY BRIGHT... WITH DEEP SOCIALIZATION ISSUES." NOW TO ME THAT'S JUST A FANCY WAY OF SAYIN' YOU THINK YOU'RE BETTER THAN THE REST OF US ORDINARY, EVERYDAY FOLK.
BOTTOM LINE, YOU SEE YOURSELF AS A CUT ABOVE, A REAL TOUGH COOKIE. BUT YOU KNOW WHAT I SEE WHEN I LOOK AT YOU?
I SEE A FRIGHTENED LITTLE GIRL...
...IN A WORLD OF HURT AND PAIN.

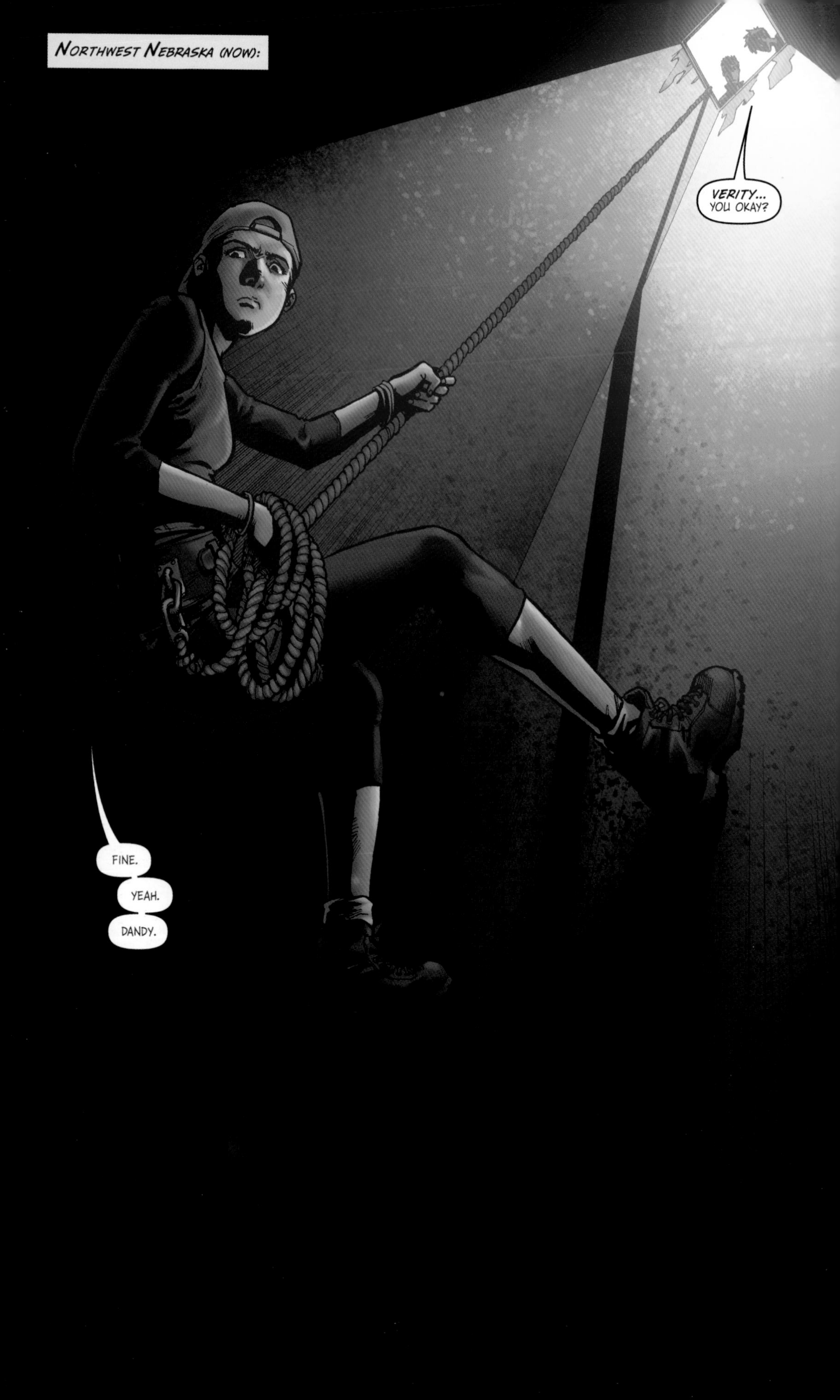
NORTHWEST NEBRASKA (NOW):
VERITY... YOU OKAY?
FINE.
YEAH.
DANDY.

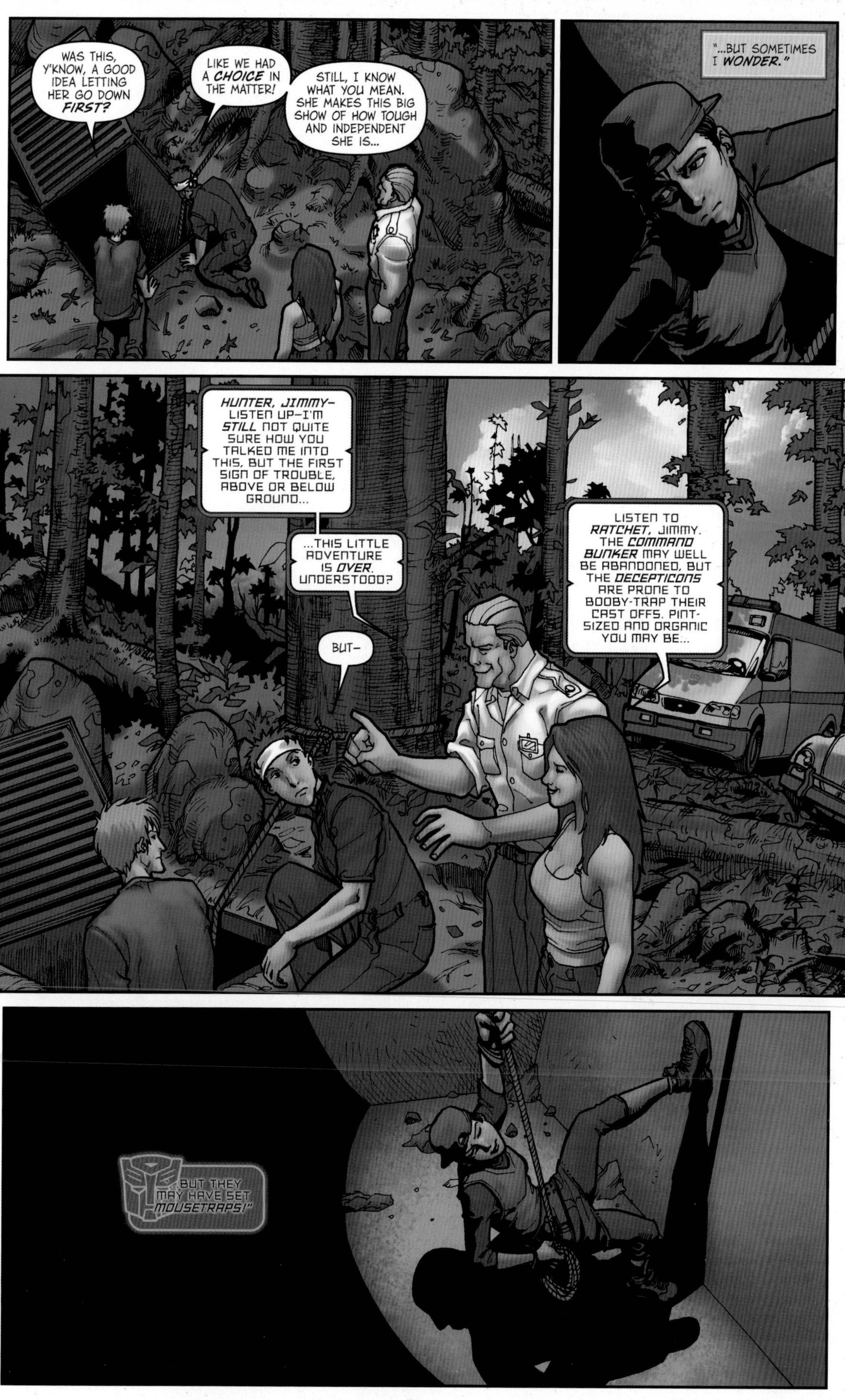

WAS THIS, Y'KNOW, A GOOD IDEA LETTING HER GO DOWN *FIRST?*
LIKE WE HAD A *CHOICE* IN THE MATTER!
STILL, I KNOW WHAT YOU MEAN. SHE MAKES THIS BIG SHOW OF HOW TOUGH AND INDEPENDENT SHE IS...
"...BUT SOMETIMES I *WONDER.*"
HUNTER, JIMMY– LISTEN UP–I'M *STILL* NOT QUITE SURE HOW YOU TALKED ME INTO THIS, BUT THE FIRST SIGN OF TROUBLE, ABOVE OR BELOW GROUND...
...THIS LITTLE ADVENTURE IS *OVER*. UNDERSTOOD?
BUT–
LISTEN TO *RATCHET,* JIMMY. THE *COMMAND BUNKER* MAY WELL BE ABANDONED, BUT THE *DECEPTICONS* ARE PRONE TO BOOBY-TRAP THEIR CAST OFFS. PINT-SIZED AND ORGANIC YOU MAY BE...
"...BUT THEY MAY HAVE SET *MOUSETRAPS!*"

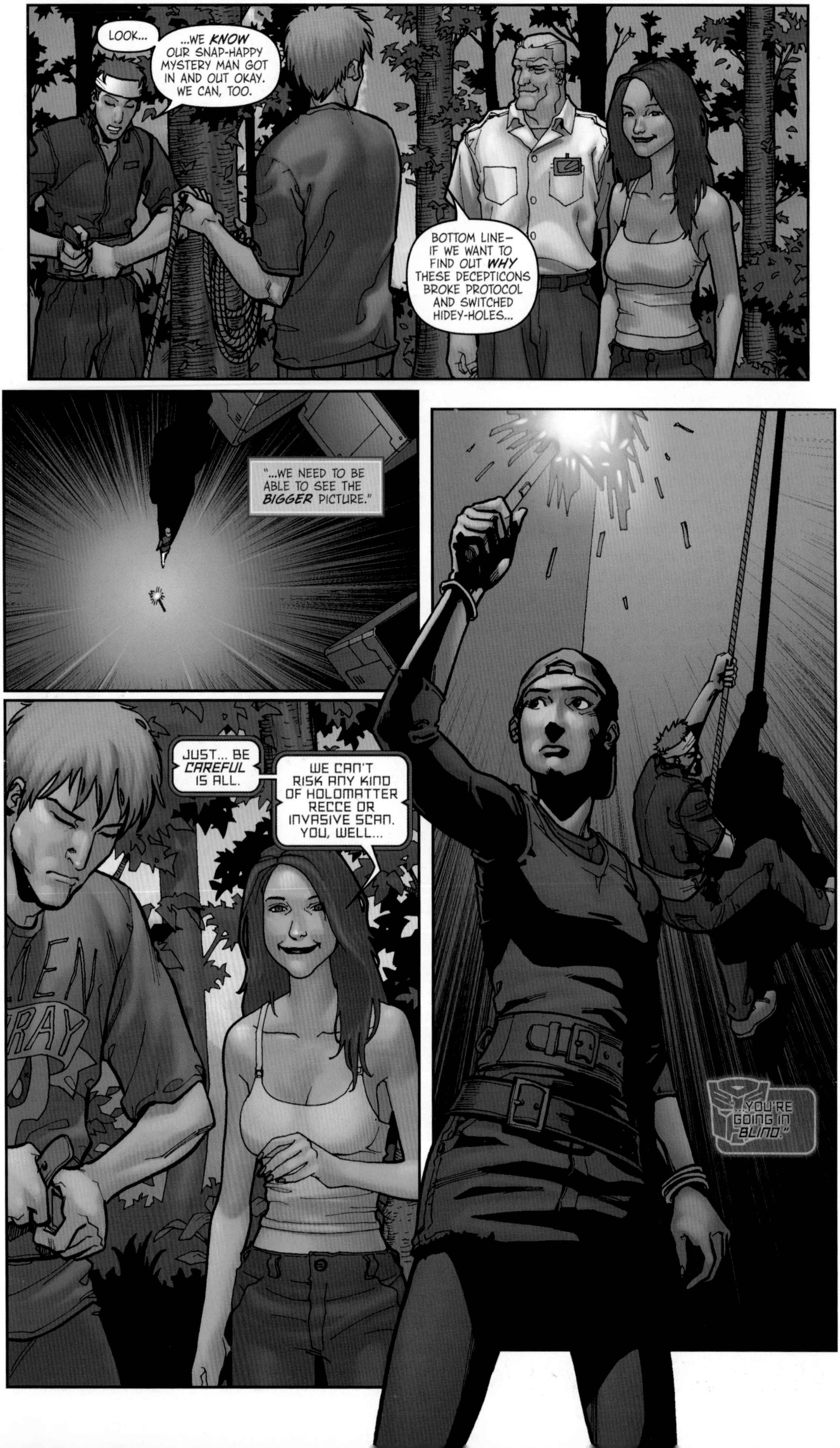
LOOK...
...WE KNOW OUR SNAP-HAPPY MYSTERY MAN GOT IN AND OUT OKAY. WE CAN, TOO.
BOTTOM LINE— IF WE WANT TO FIND OUT WHY THESE DECEPTICONS BROKE PROTOCOL AND SWITCHED HIDEY-HOLES...
"...WE NEED TO BE ABLE TO SEE THE BIGGER PICTURE."
JUST... BE CAREFUL IS ALL.
WE CAN'T RISK ANY KIND OF HOLOMATTER RECCE OR INVASIVE SCAN. YOU, WELL...
"...YOU'RE GOING IN BLIND."

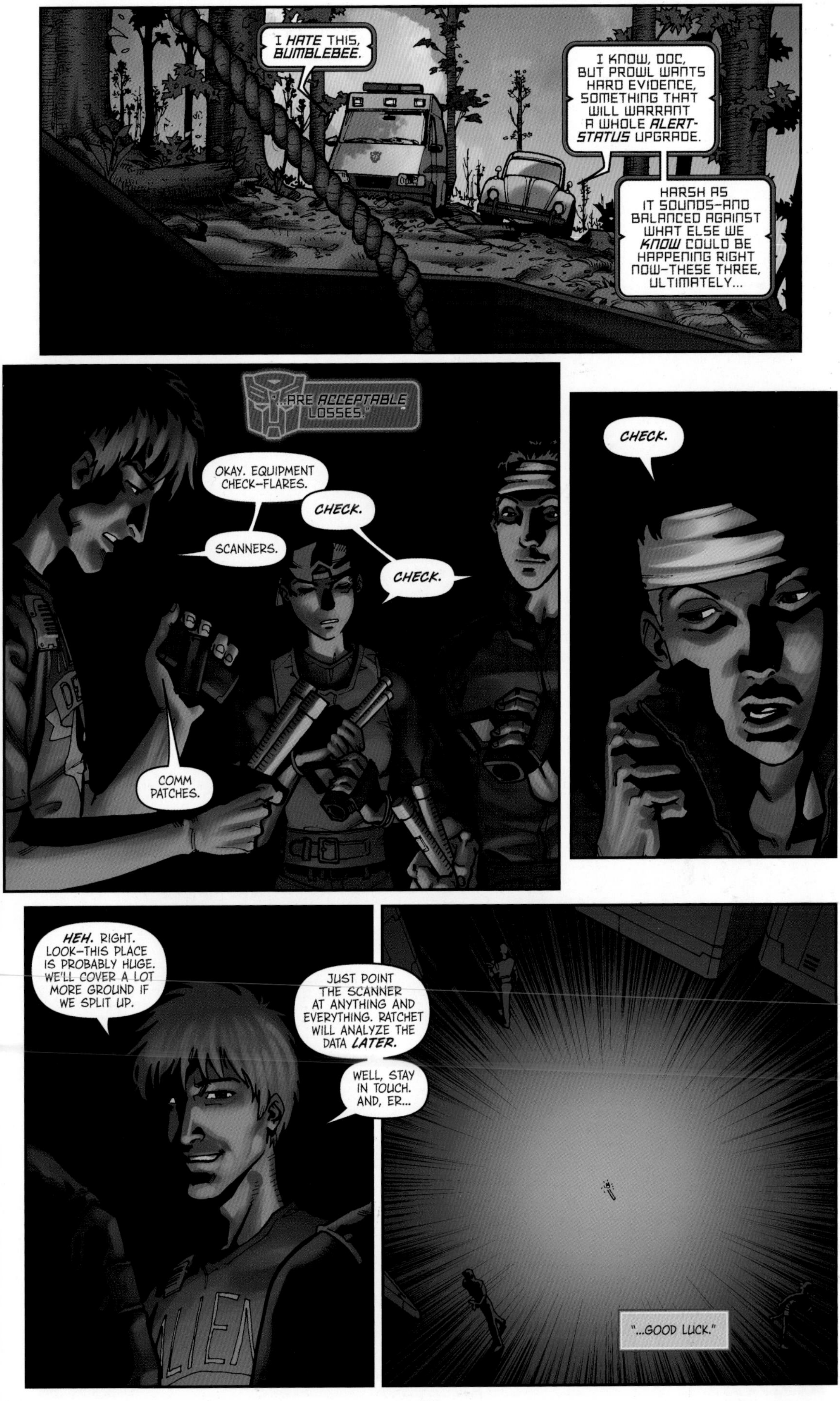

I *HATE* THIS, *BUMBLEBEE.*
I KNOW, DOC, BUT PROWL WANTS HARD EVIDENCE, SOMETHING THAT WILL WARRANT A WHOLE *ALERT-STATUS* UPGRADE.
HARSH AS IT SOUNDS—AND BALANCED AGAINST WHAT ELSE WE *KNOW* COULD BE HAPPENING RIGHT NOW—THESE THREE, ULTIMATELY...
"...ARE *ACCEPTABLE* LOSSES."
OKAY. EQUIPMENT CHECK—FLARES.
CHECK.
SCANNERS.
CHECK.
COMM PATCHES.
CHECK.
HEH. RIGHT. LOOK—THIS PLACE IS PROBABLY HUGE. WE'LL COVER A LOT MORE GROUND IF WE SPLIT UP.
JUST POINT THE SCANNER AT ANYTHING AND EVERYTHING. RATCHET WILL ANALYZE THE DATA *LATER.*
WELL, STAY IN TOUCH. AND, ER...
"...GOOD LUCK."

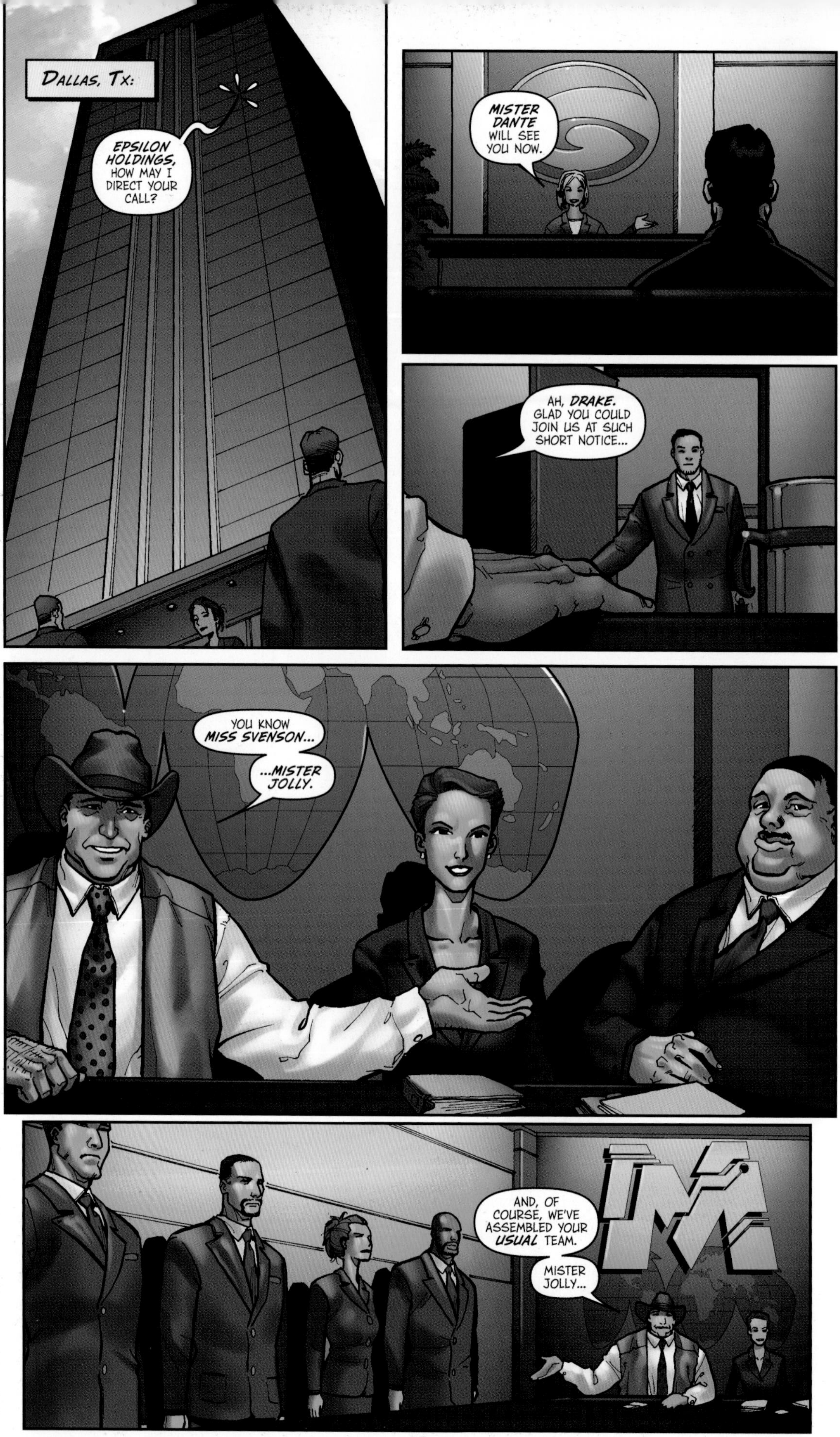
DALLAS, TX:
EPSILON HOLDINGS, HOW MAY I DIRECT YOUR CALL?
MISTER DANTE WILL SEE YOU NOW.
AH, DRAKE. GLAD YOU COULD JOIN US AT SUCH SHORT NOTICE...
YOU KNOW MISS SVENSON...
...MISTER JOLLY.
AND, OF COURSE, WE'VE ASSEMBLED YOUR USUAL TEAM.
MISTER JOLLY...

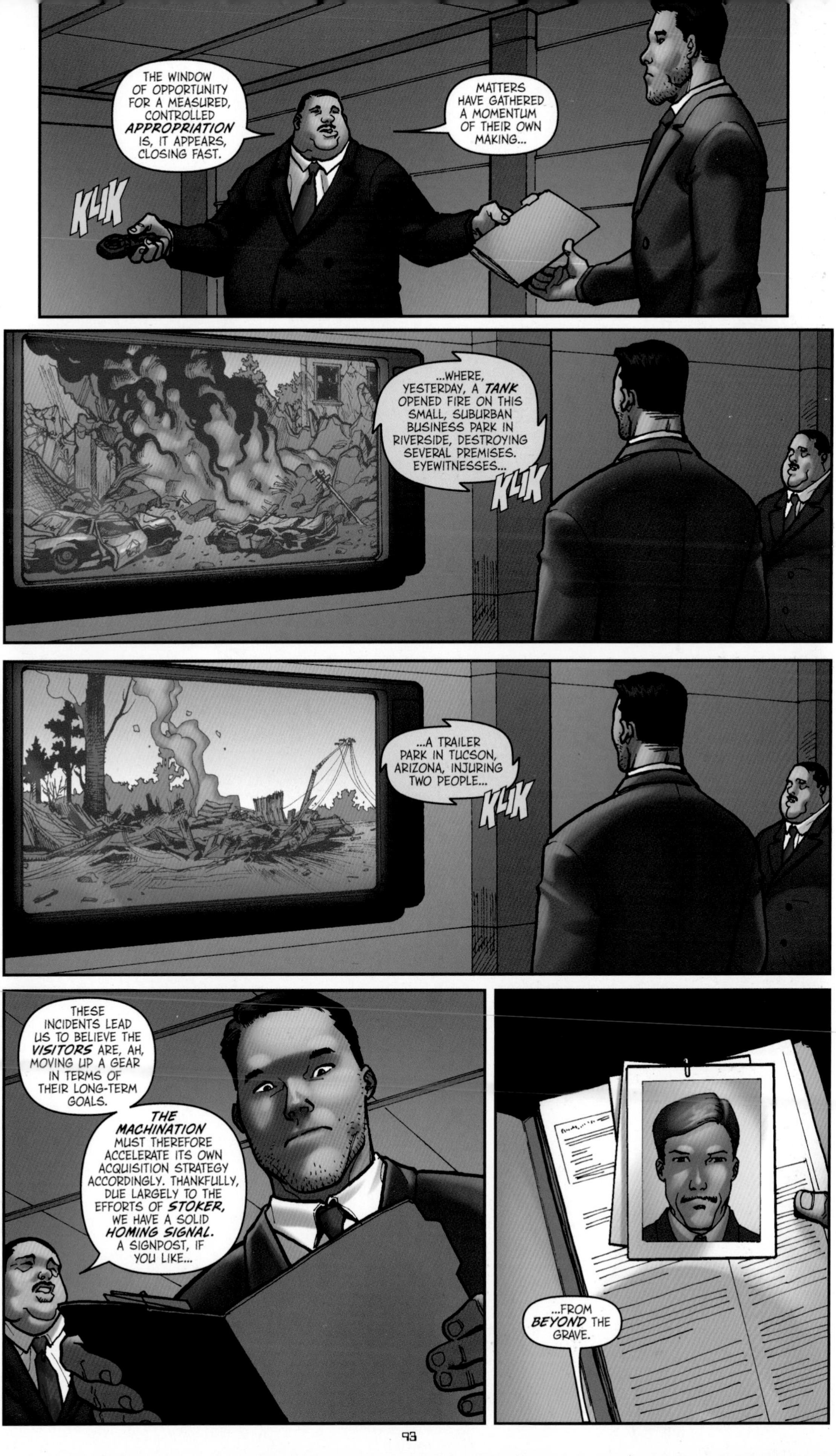
THE WINDOW OF OPPORTUNITY FOR A MEASURED, CONTROLLED APPROPRIATION IS, IT APPEARS, CLOSING FAST.
MATTERS HAVE GATHERED A MOMENTUM OF THEIR OWN MAKING...
KLIK
...WHERE, YESTERDAY, A TANK OPENED FIRE ON THIS SMALL, SUBURBAN BUSINESS PARK IN RIVERSIDE, DESTROYING SEVERAL PREMISES. EYEWITNESSES...
KLIK
...A TRAILER PARK IN TUCSON, ARIZONA, INJURING TWO PEOPLE...
KLIK
THESE INCIDENTS LEAD US TO BELIEVE THE VISITORS ARE, AH, MOVING UP A GEAR IN TERMS OF THEIR LONG-TERM GOALS.
THE MACHINATION MUST THEREFORE ACCELERATE ITS OWN ACQUISITION STRATEGY ACCORDINGLY. THANKFULLY, DUE LARGELY TO THE EFFORTS OF STOKER, WE HAVE A SOLID HOMING SIGNAL. A SIGNPOST, IF YOU LIKE...
...FROM BEYOND THE GRAVE.

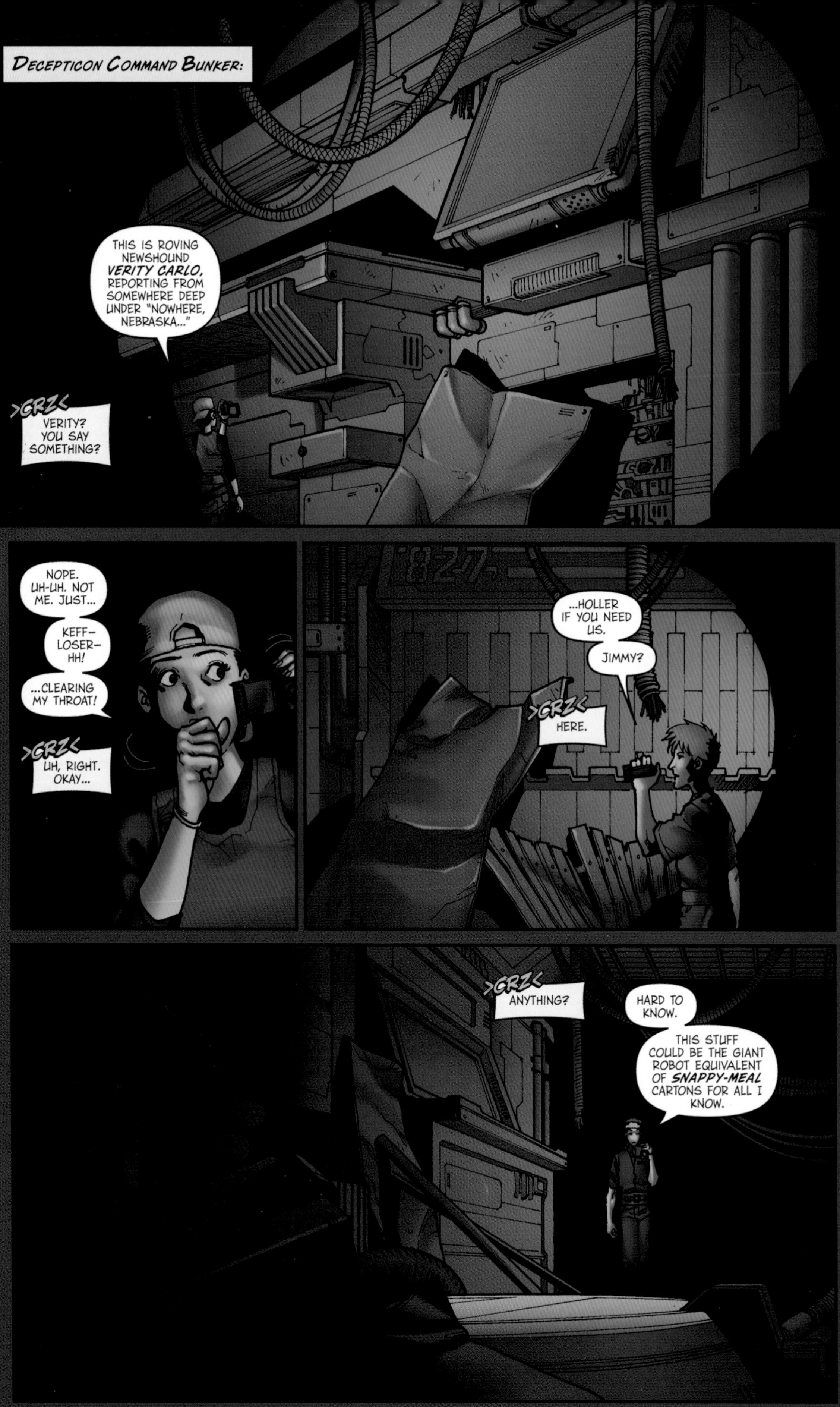
DECEPTICON COMMAND BUNKER:
THIS IS ROVING NEWSHOUND VERITY CARLO, REPORTING FROM SOMEWHERE DEEP UNDER "NOWHERE, NEBRASKA..."
>CRZ<
VERITY? YOU SAY SOMETHING?
NOPE. UH-UH. NOT ME. JUST...
KEFF-LOSER-HH!
...CLEARING MY THROAT!
>CRZ<
UH, RIGHT. OKAY...
...HOLLER IF YOU NEED US.
JIMMY?
>CRZ<
HERE.
>CRZ<
ANYTHING?
HARD TO KNOW.
THIS STUFF COULD BE THE GIANT ROBOT EQUIVALENT OF SNAPPY-MEAL CARTONS FOR ALL I KNOW.

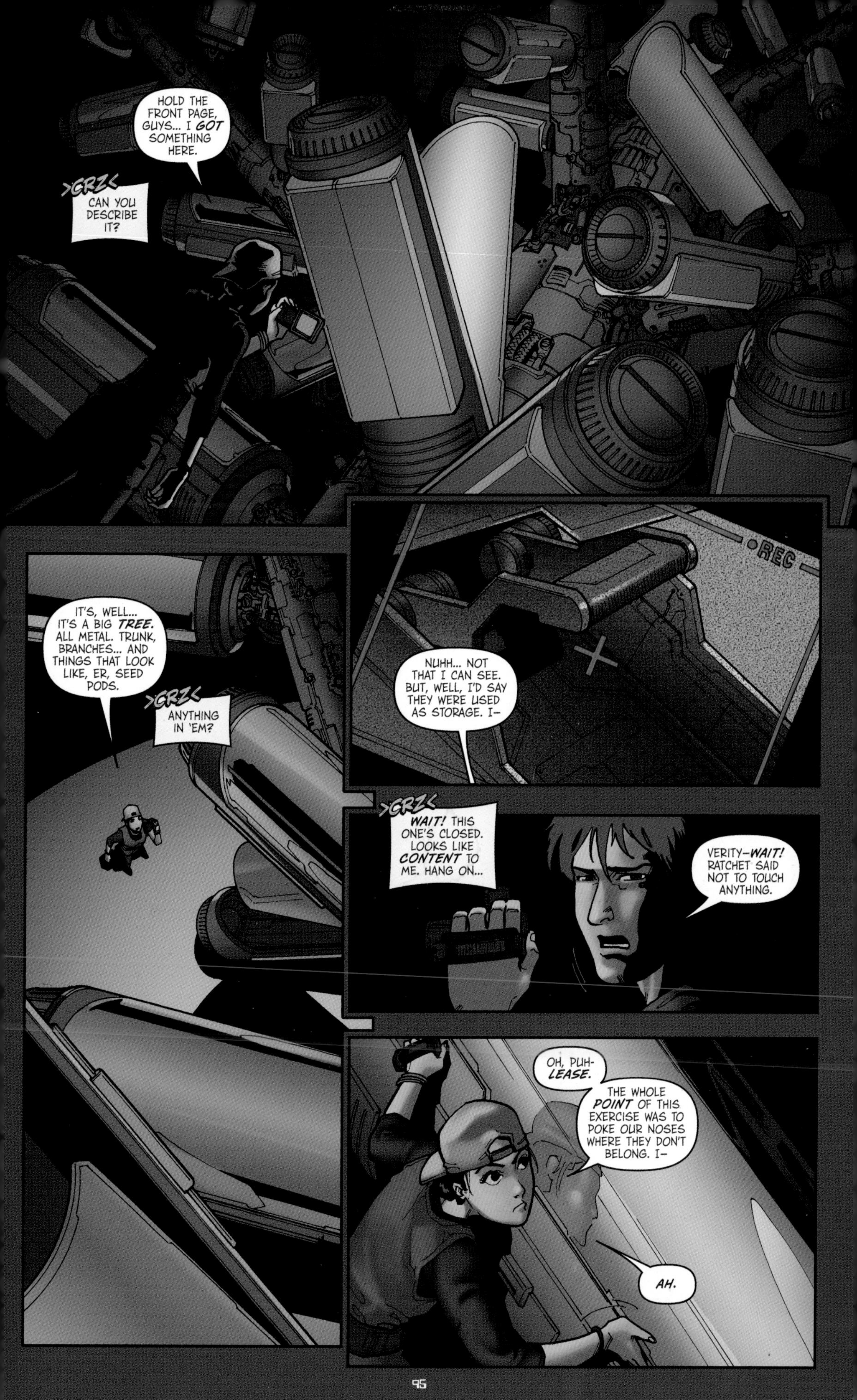
HOLD THE FRONT PAGE, GUYS... I GOT SOMETHING HERE.
>CRZ<
CAN YOU DESCRIBE IT?
IT'S, WELL... IT'S A BIG TREE. ALL METAL. TRUNK, BRANCHES... AND THINGS THAT LOOK LIKE, ER, SEED PODS.
>CRZ<
ANYTHING IN 'EM?
REC
NUHH... NOT THAT I CAN SEE. BUT, WELL, I'D SAY THEY WERE USED AS STORAGE. I–
>CRZ<
WAIT! THIS ONE'S CLOSED. LOOKS LIKE CONTENT TO ME. HANG ON...
VERITY–WAIT! RATCHET SAID NOT TO TOUCH ANYTHING.
OH, PUH-LEASE.
THE WHOLE POINT OF THIS EXERCISE WAS TO POKE OUR NOSES WHERE THEY DON'T BELONG. I–
AH.

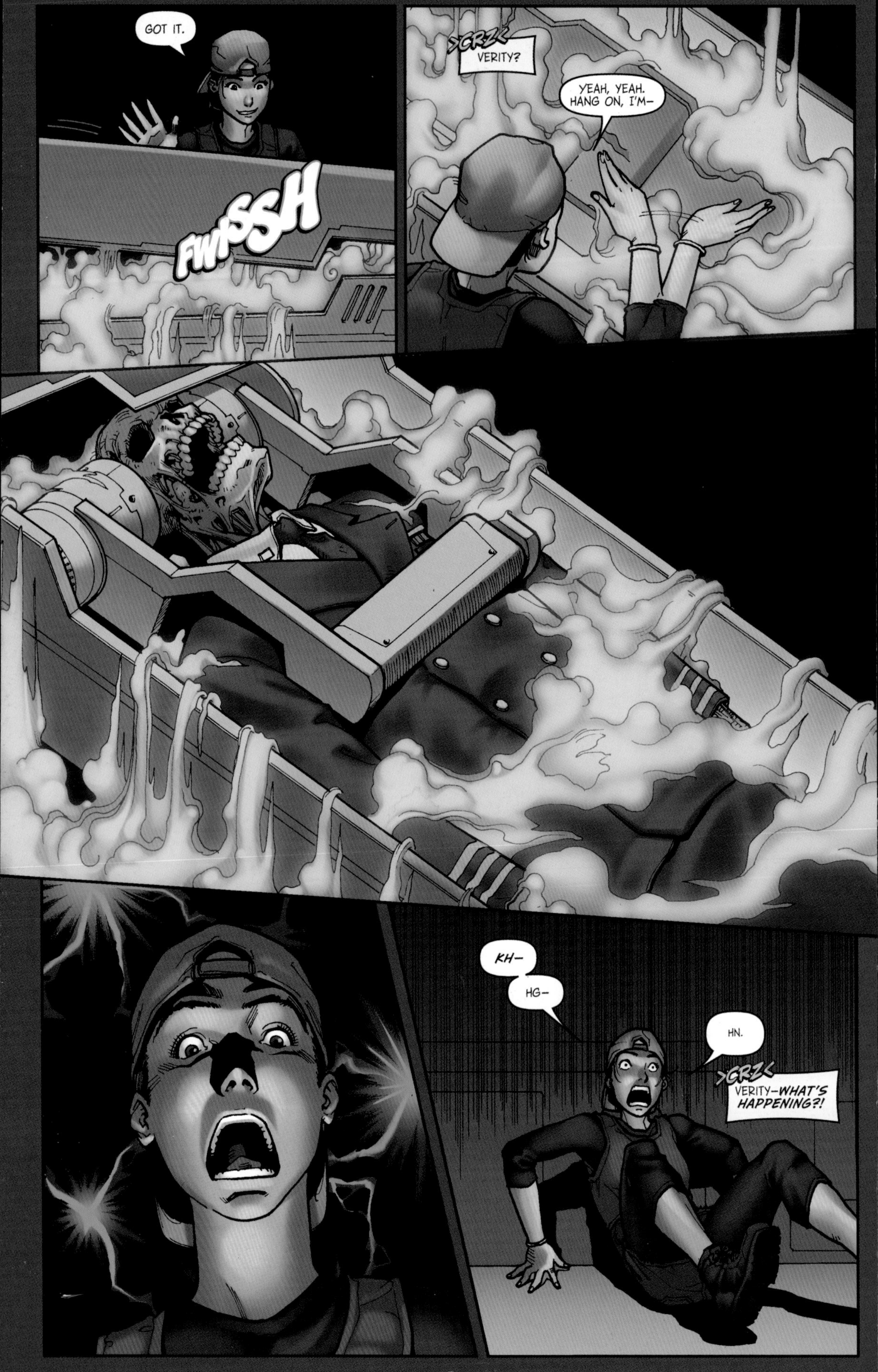
GOT IT.
FWISSH
>CRZ<
VERITY?
YEAH, YEAH. HANG ON, I'M–
KH–
HG–
HN.
>CRZ<
VERITY–WHAT'S HAPPENING?!

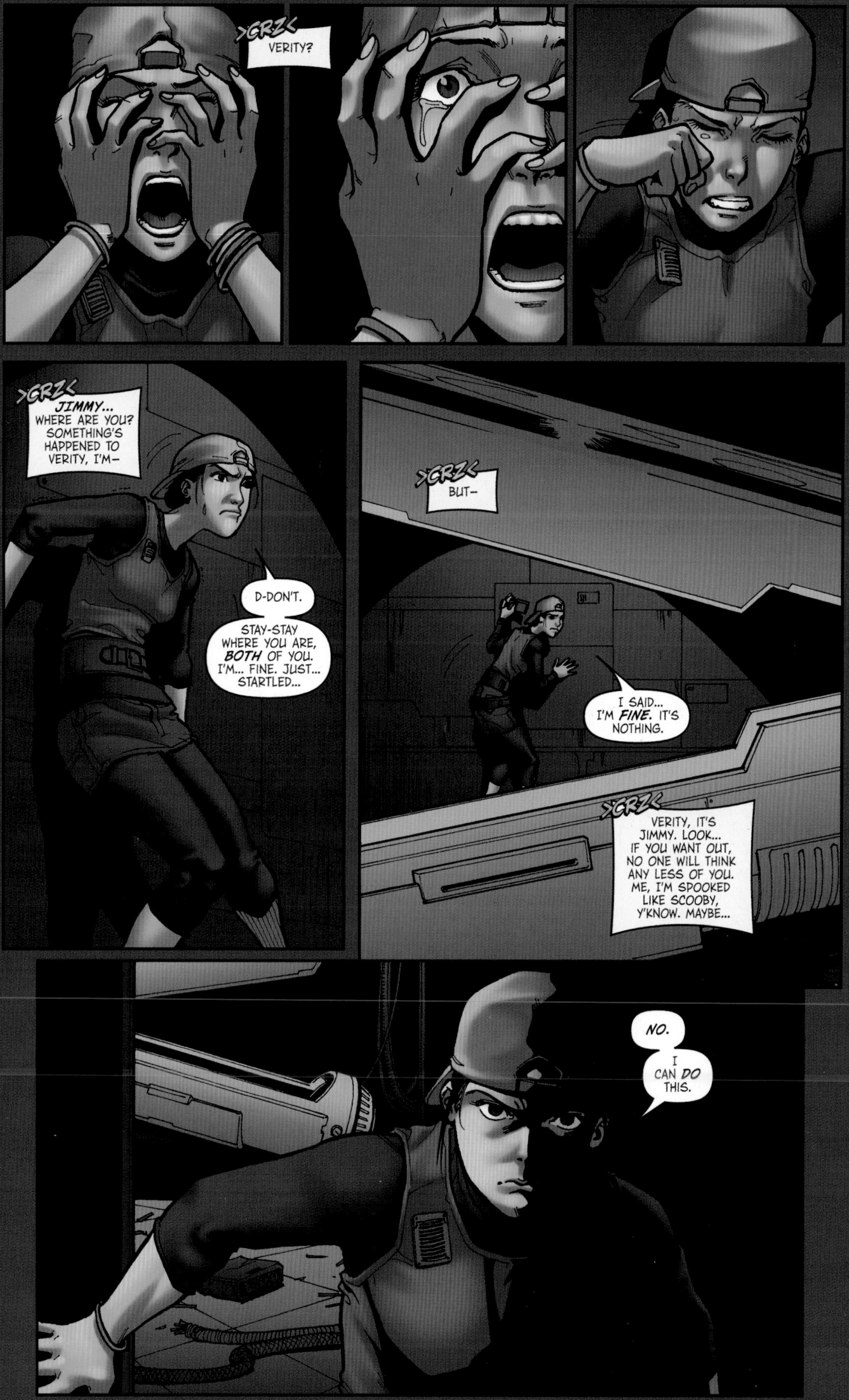

>CRZ<
VERITY?
>CRZ<
JIMMY... WHERE ARE YOU? SOMETHING'S HAPPENED TO VERITY, I'M–
D-DON'T.
STAY-STAY WHERE YOU ARE, BOTH OF YOU. I'M... FINE. JUST... STARTLED...
>CRZ<
BUT–
I SAID... I'M FINE. IT'S NOTHING.
>CRZ<
VERITY, IT'S JIMMY. LOOK... IF YOU WANT OUT, NO ONE WILL THINK ANY LESS OF YOU. ME, I'M SPOOKED LIKE SCOOBY, Y'KNOW. MAYBE...
NO.
I CAN DO THIS.

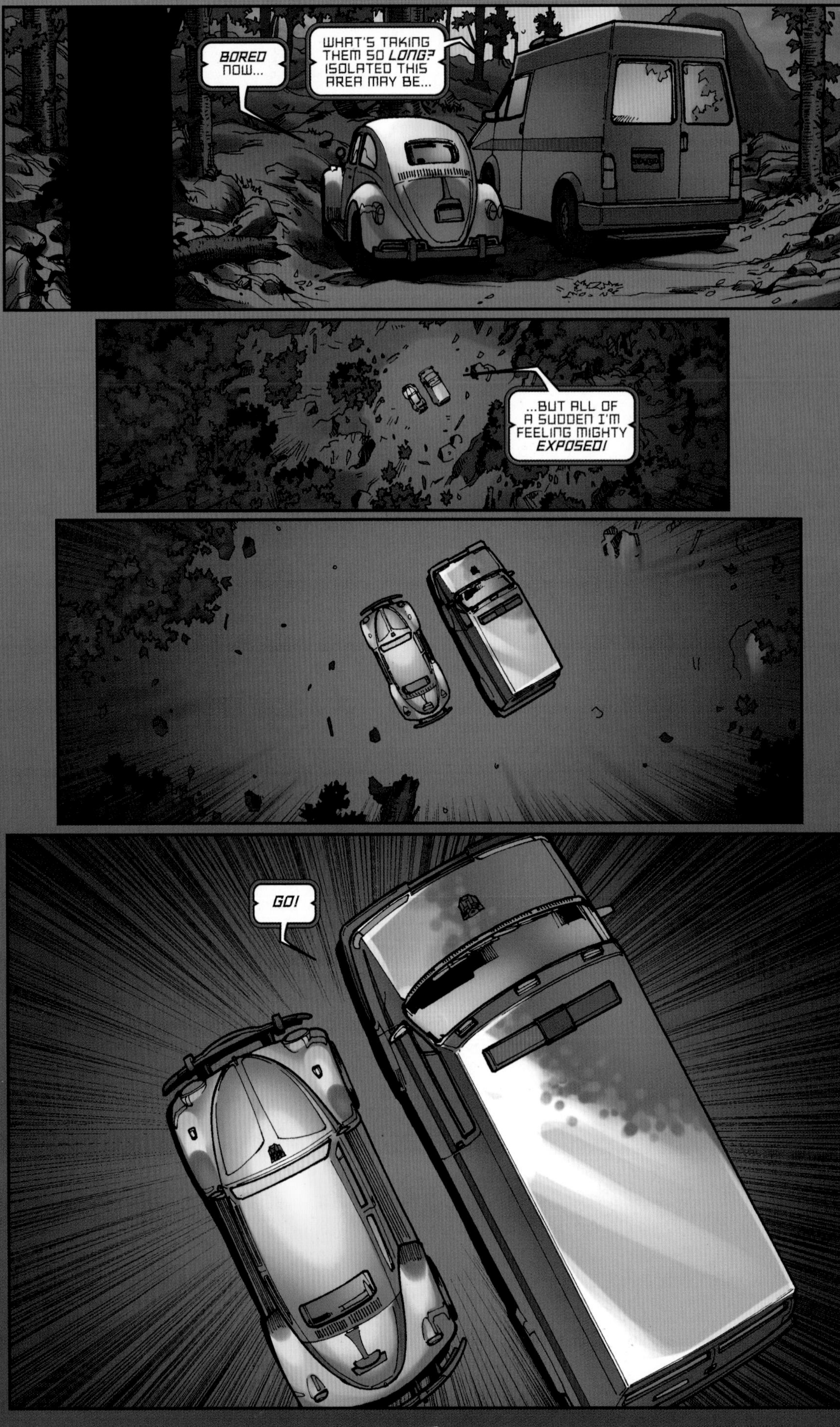
BORED NOW...
WHAT'S TAKING THEM SO LONG? ISOLATED THIS AREA MAY BE...
...BUT ALL OF A SUDDEN I'M FEELING MIGHTY EXPOSED!
GO!

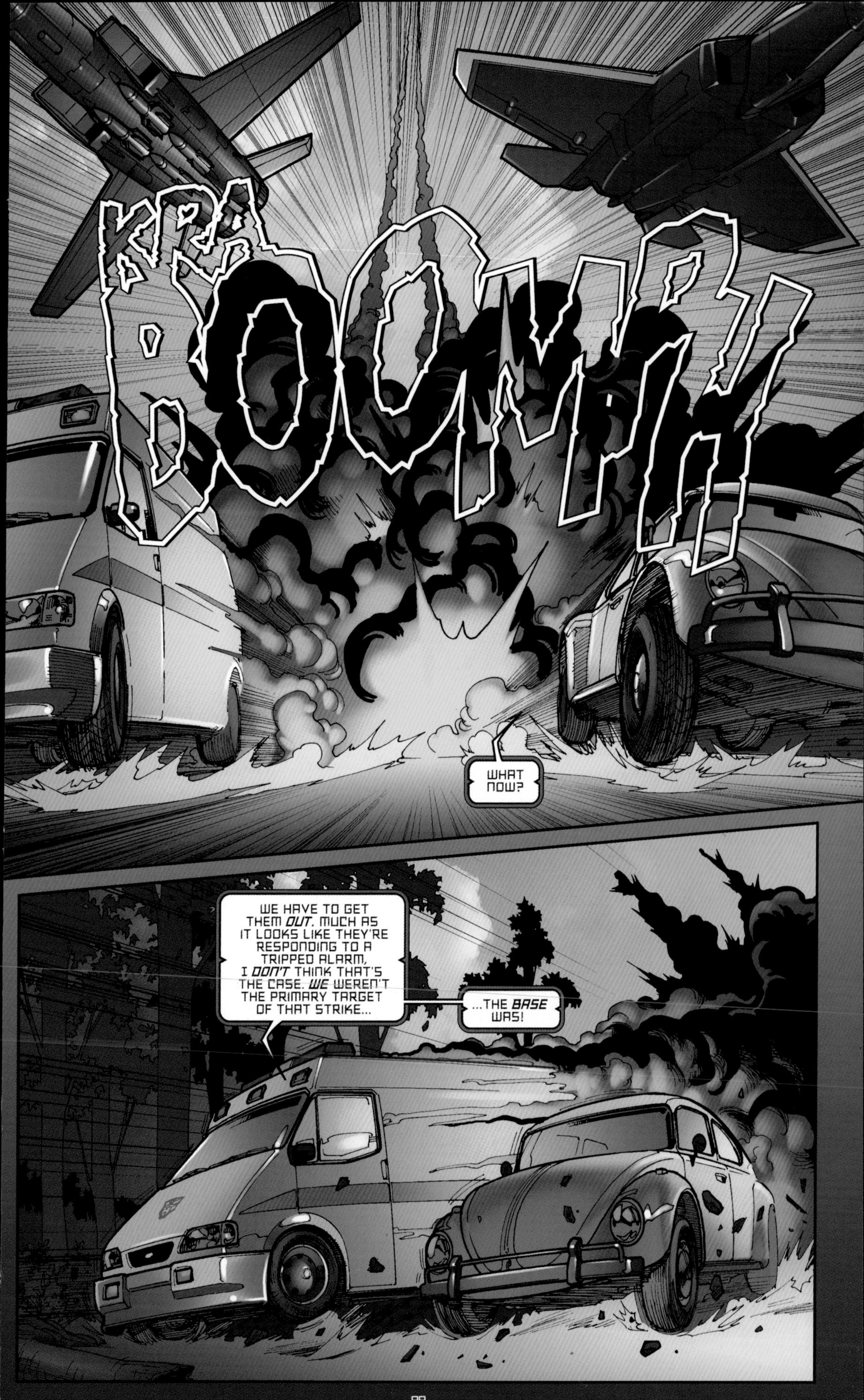

KRA BOOMM
WHAT NOW?
WE HAVE TO GET THEM *OUT*. MUCH AS IT LOOKS LIKE THEY'RE RESPONDING TO A TRIPPED ALARM, I *DON'T* THINK THAT'S THE CASE. *WE* WEREN'T THE PRIMARY TARGET OF THAT STRIKE...
...THE *BASE* WAS!

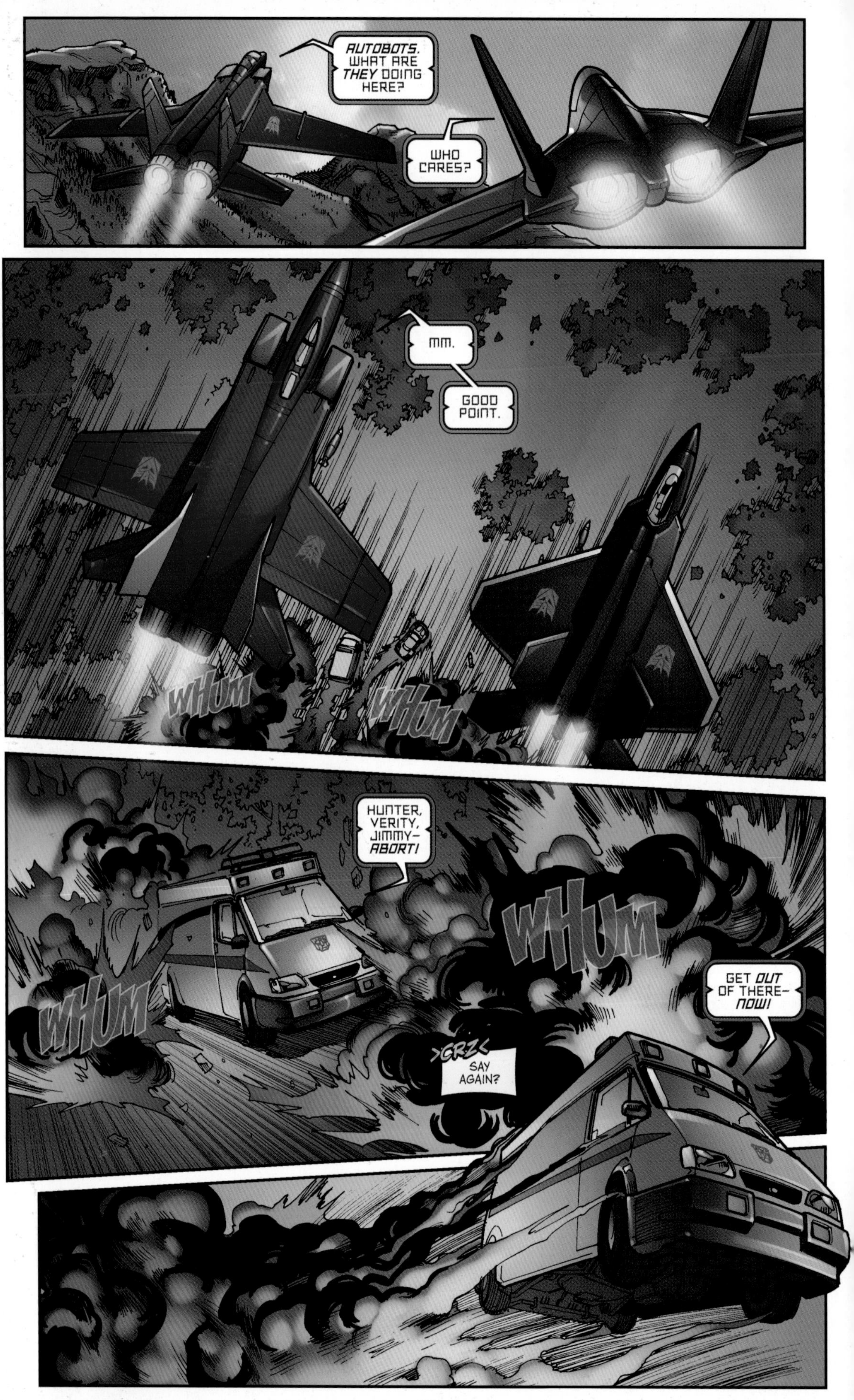
AUTOBOTS. WHAT ARE THEY DOING HERE?
WHO CARES?
MM.
GOOD POINT.
WHUM
WHUM
HUNTER, VERITY, JIMMY--ABORT!
WHUM
WHUM
GET OUT OF THERE--NOW!
>CRZ<
SAY AGAIN?

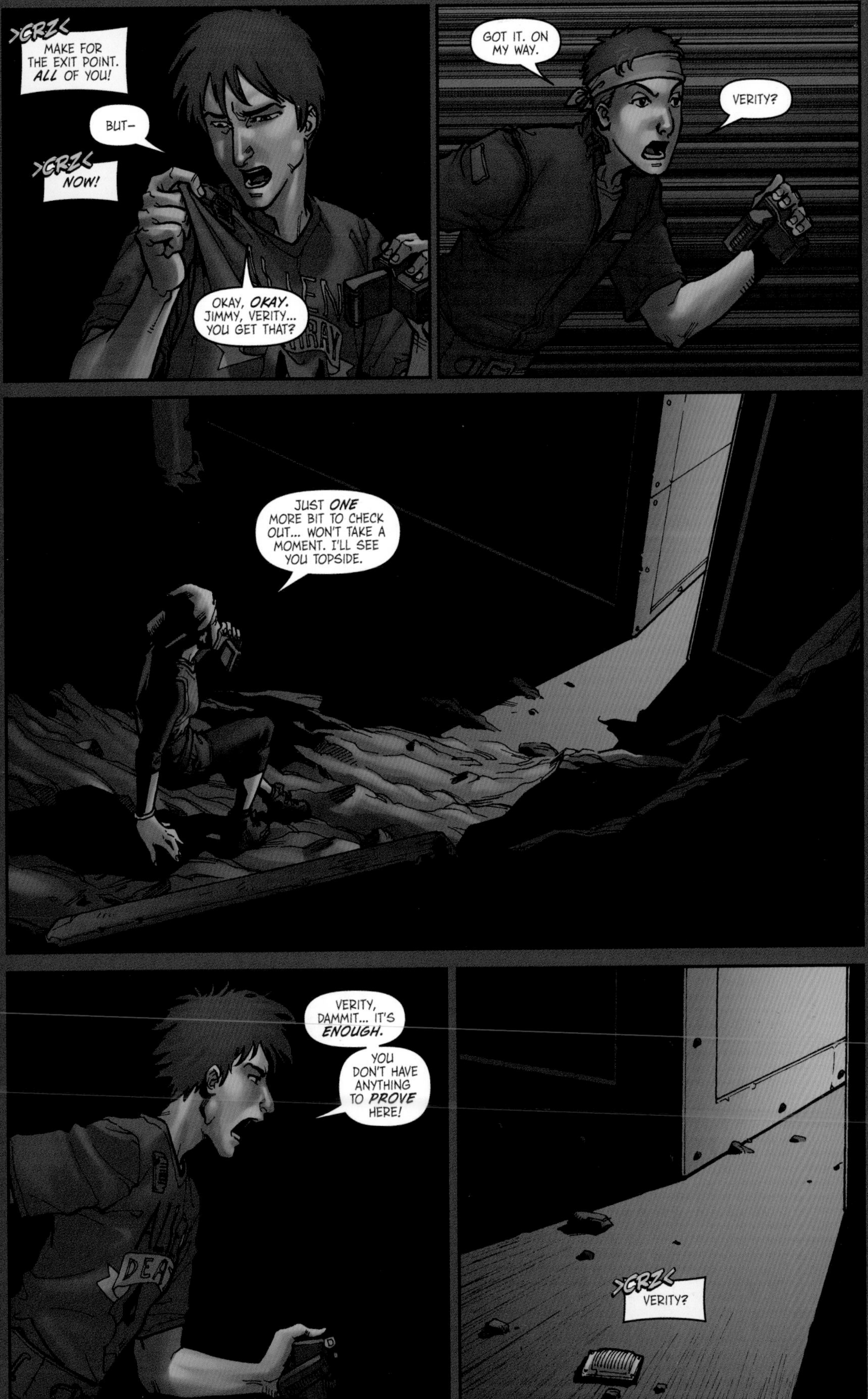
>GRZ<
MAKE FOR THE EXIT POINT. ALL OF YOU!
BUT–
>GRZ<
NOW!
OKAY, OKAY. JIMMY, VERITY... YOU GET THAT?
GOT IT. ON MY WAY.
VERITY?
JUST ONE MORE BIT TO CHECK OUT... WON'T TAKE A MOMENT. I'LL SEE YOU TOPSIDE.
VERITY, DAMMIT... IT'S ENOUGH.
YOU DON'T HAVE ANYTHING TO PROVE HERE!
>GRZ<
VERITY?

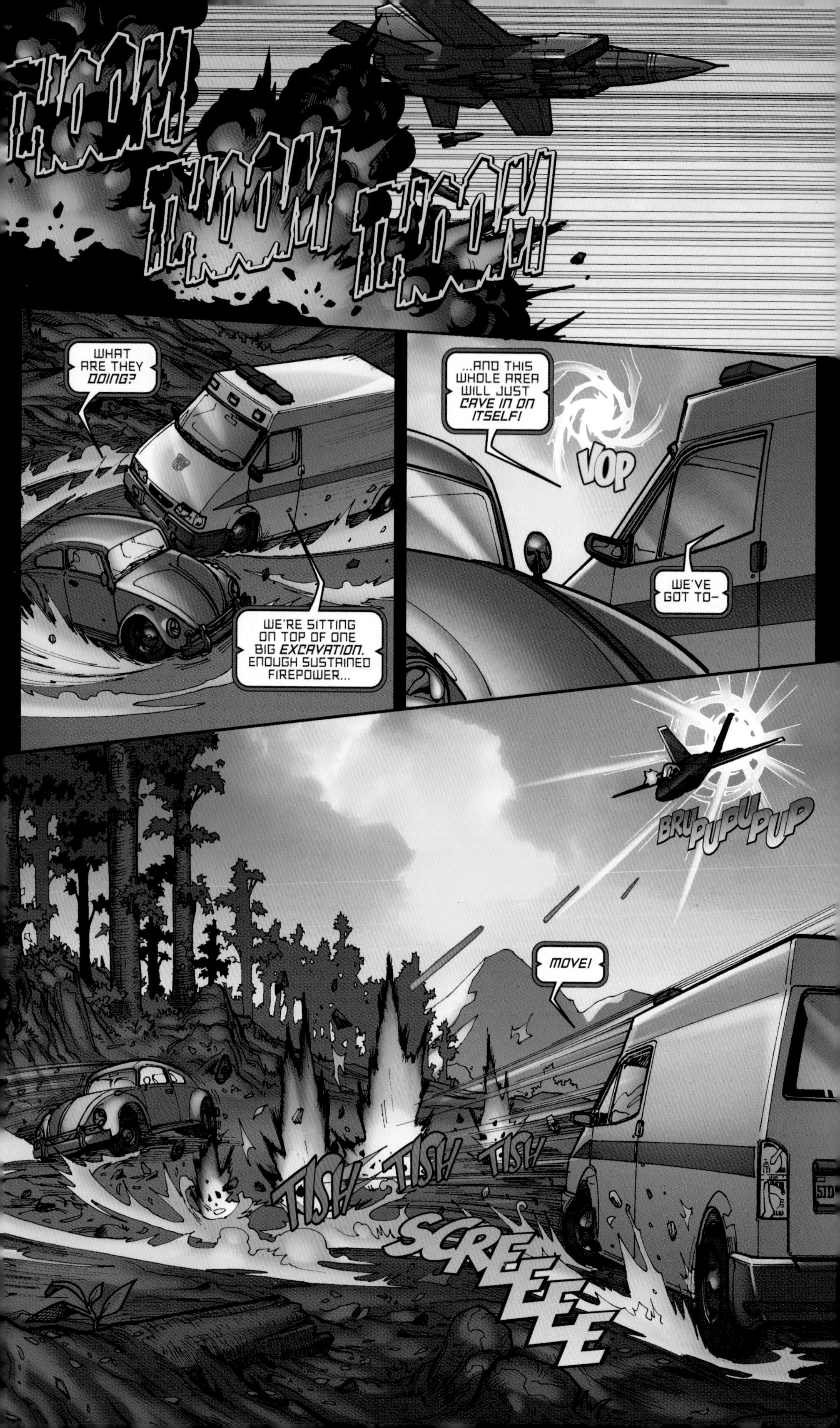
THOOM
THOOM
THOOM
WHAT ARE THEY *DOING?*
WE'RE SITTING ON TOP OF ONE BIG *EXCAVATION*. ENOUGH SUSTAINED FIREPOWER...
...AND THIS WHOLE AREA WILL JUST *CAVE IN ON ITSELF!*
VOP
WE'VE GOT TO–
BRUPUPUPUP
MOVE!
TISH
TISH
TISH
SCREEEEEE

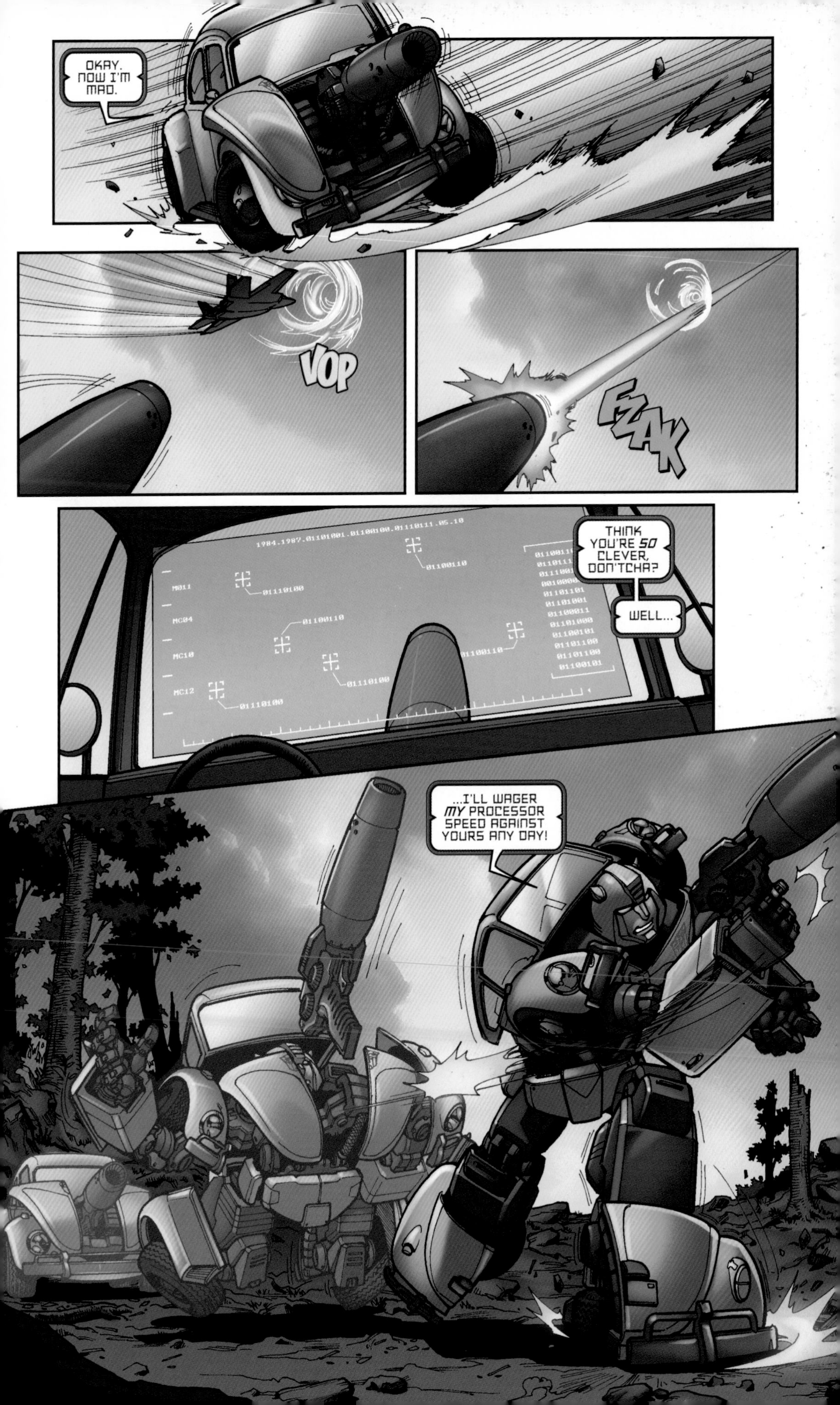
OKAY. NOW I'M MAD.
VOP
FZAK
THINK YOU'RE SO CLEVER, DON'TCHA?
WELL...
...I'LL WAGER MY PROCESSOR SPEED AGAINST YOURS ANY DAY!

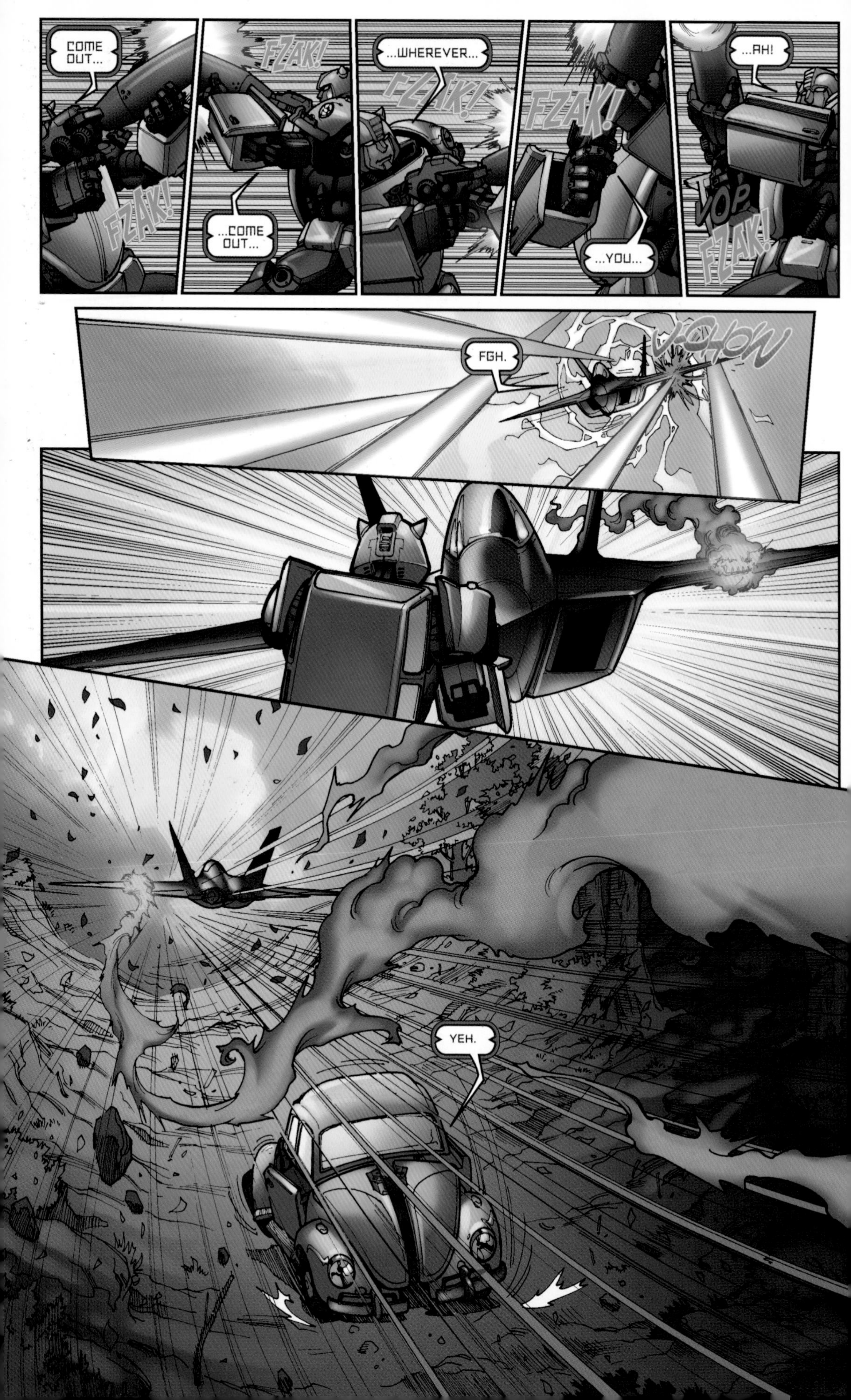

COME OUT...
FZAK!
FZAK!
...COME OUT...
...WHEREVER...
FZAK!
FZAK!
...YOU...
...AH!
VOP
FZAK!
FGH.
V-CHOW
YEH.

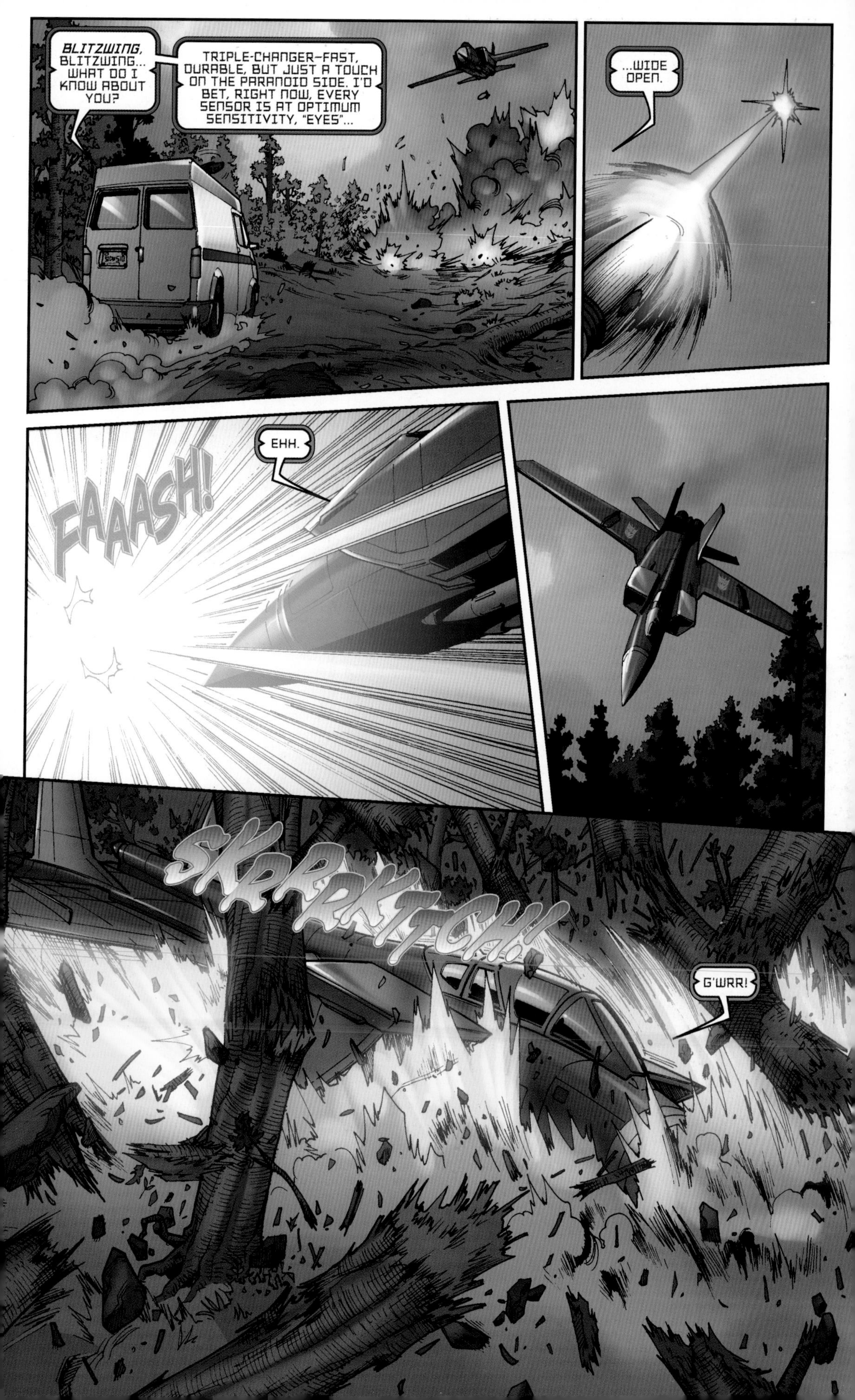
BLITZWING, BLITZWING... WHAT DO I KNOW ABOUT YOU?
TRIPLE-CHANGER—FAST, DURABLE, BUT JUST A TOUCH ON THE PARANOID SIDE. I'D BET, RIGHT NOW, EVERY SENSOR IS AT OPTIMUM SENSITIVITY, "EYES"...
...WIDE OPEN.
FAAASH!
EHH.
SKRRKTCH!
G'WRR!

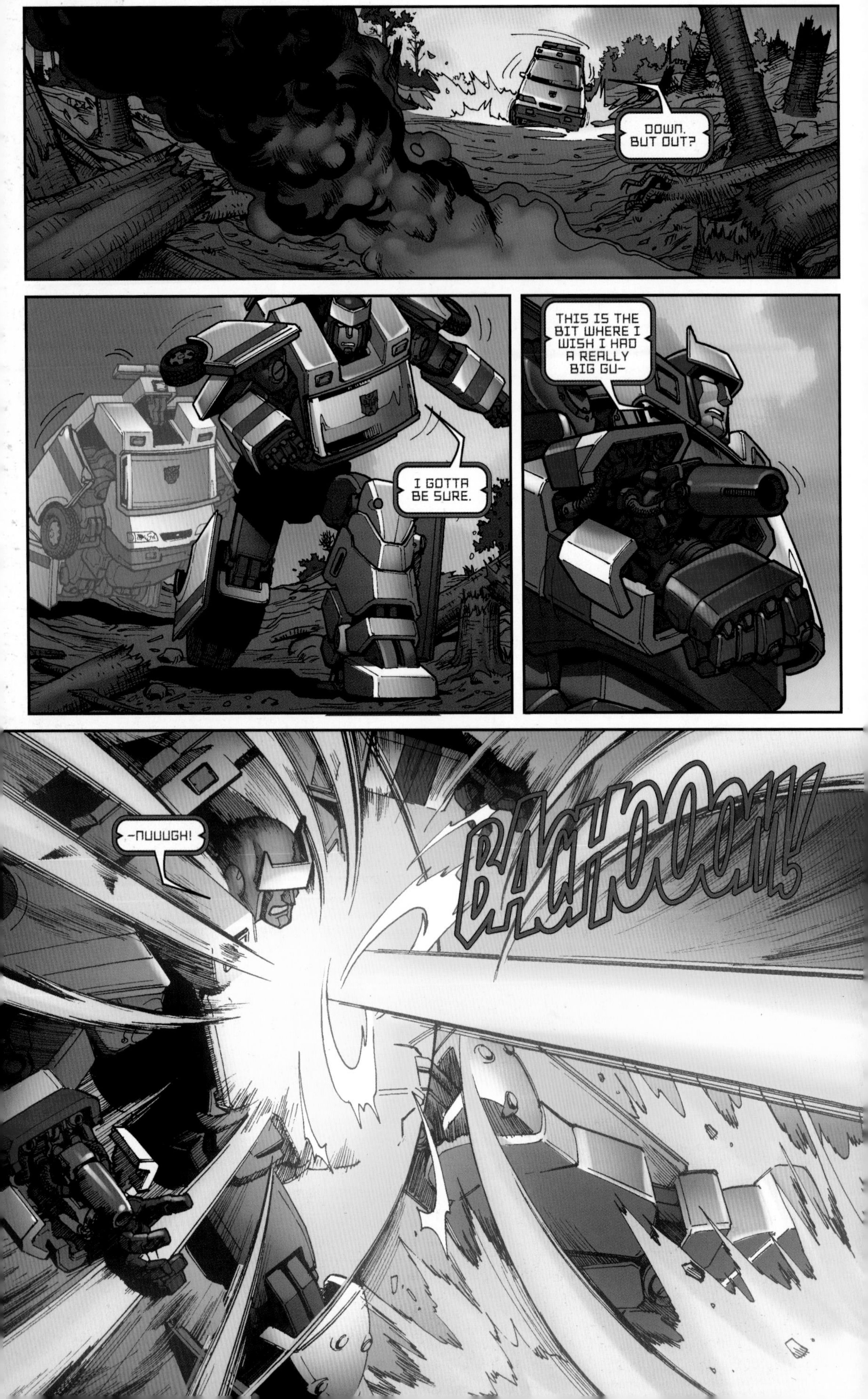
DOWN. BUT OUT?
I GOTTA BE SURE.
THIS IS THE BIT WHERE I WISH I HAD A REALLY BIG GU–
–NUUUGH!
BAKOOOM!

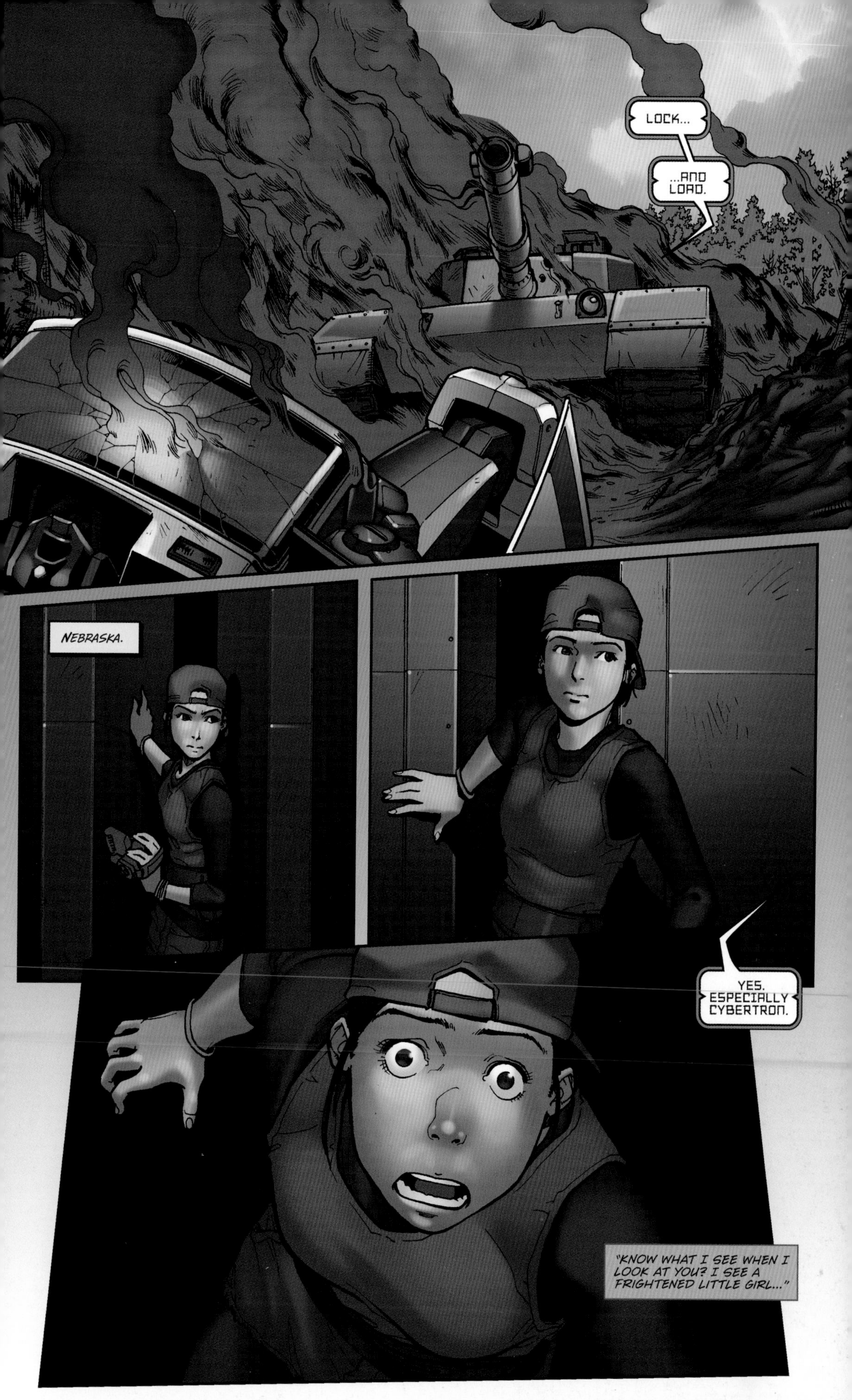
LOCK...
...AND LOAD.
NEBRASKA.
YES. ESPECIALLY CYBERTRON.
"KNOW WHAT I SEE WHEN I LOOK AT YOU? I SEE A FRIGHTENED LITTLE GIRL..."

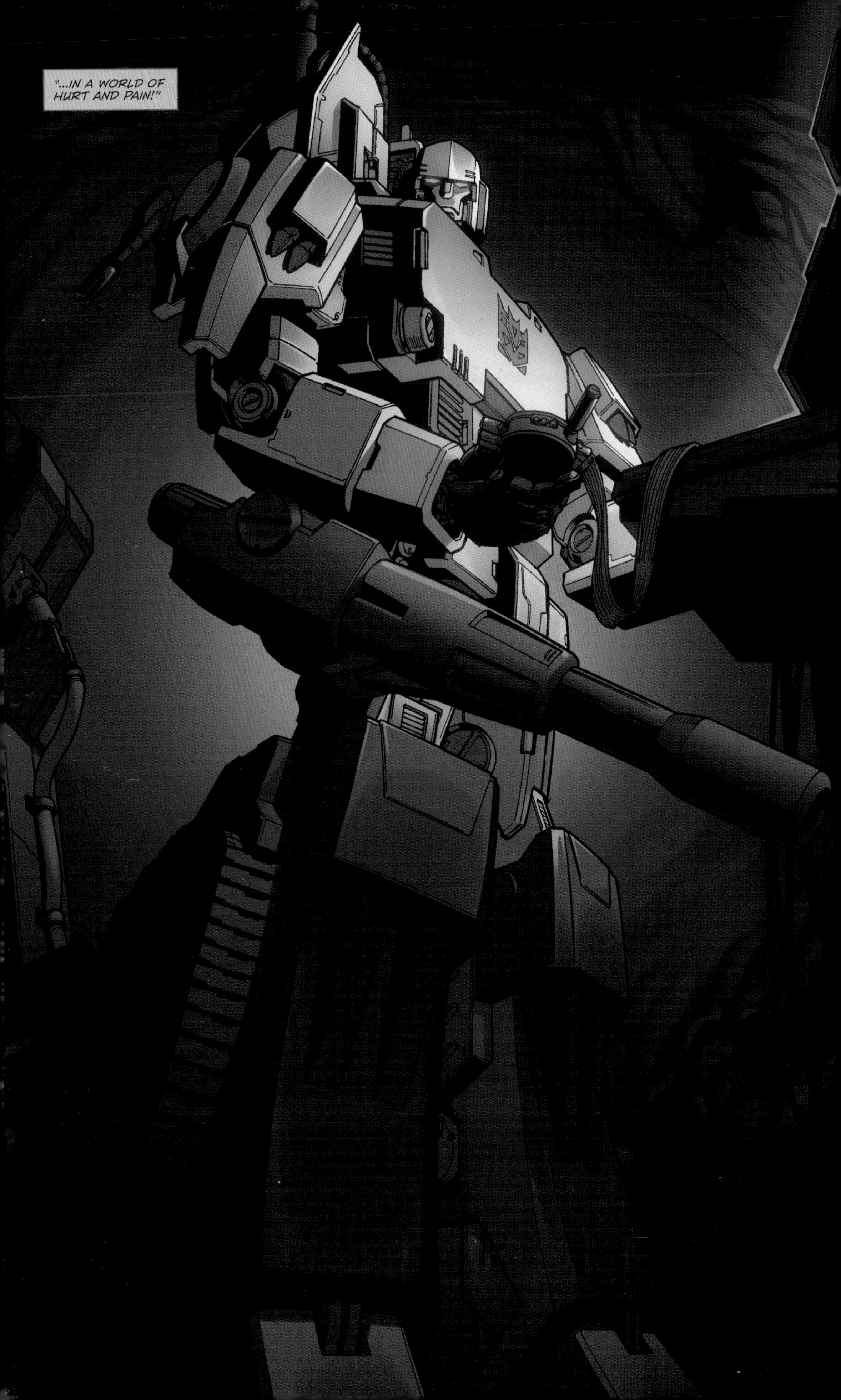
"...IN A WORLD OF HURT AND PAIN!"

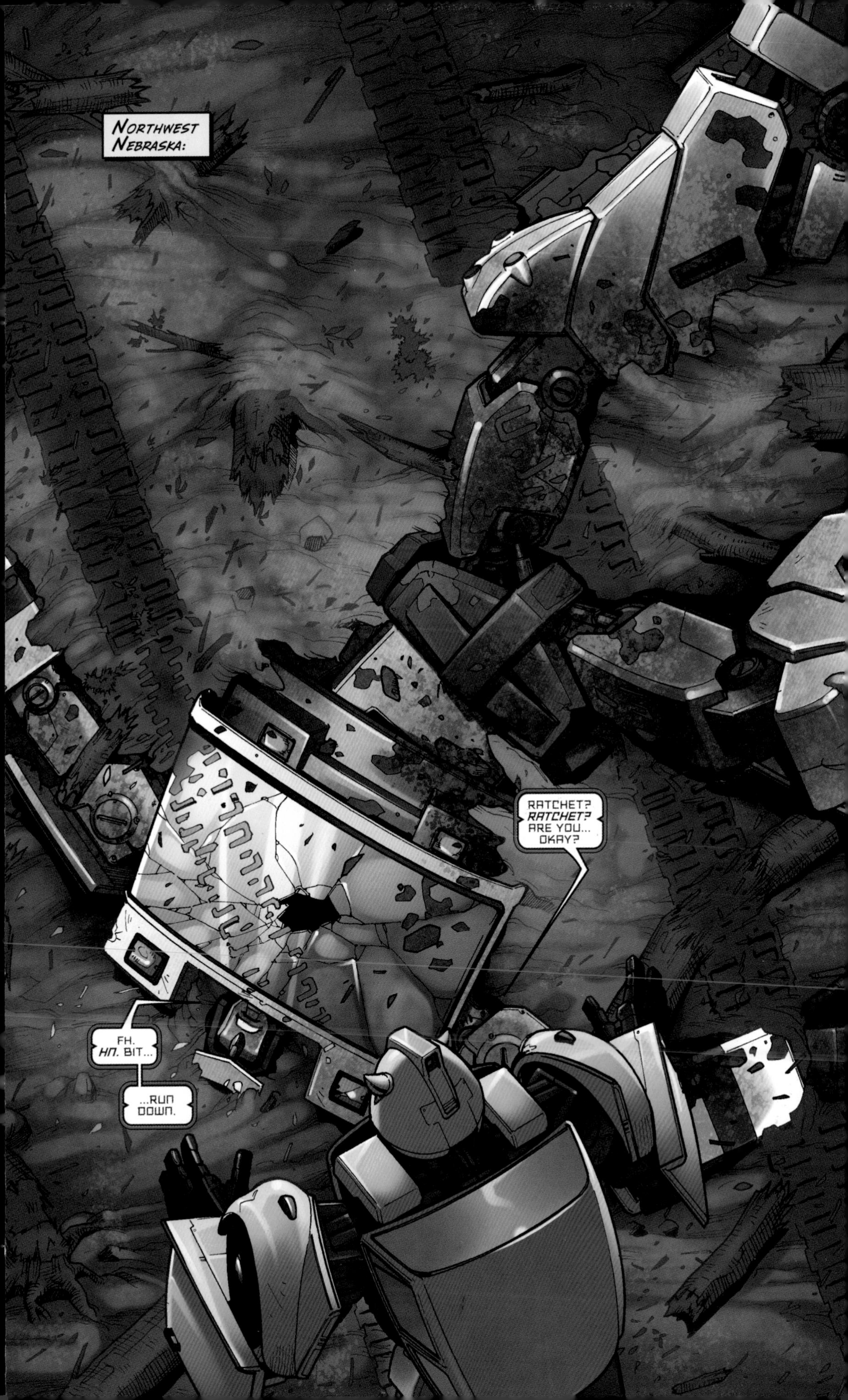
Northwest Nebraska:
RATCHET? RATCHET? ARE YOU... OKAY?
FH. HN. BIT...
...RUN DOWN.

UH? OH, YEAH, GOOD. HAVEN'T LOST YOUR SENSE OF HUMOR, THEN.

C'MON, DOC— UP AND *AT* 'EM.

EHH—NNN... THE *DECEPTICONS?*

IGNORING US. GUESS WE DON'T SCORE HIGH ON THEIR THREAT-O-METER.

THOOM THOOM THOOM

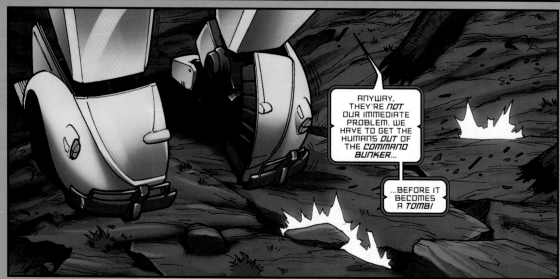

ANYWAY, THEY'RE *NOT* OUR IMMEDIATE PROBLEM. WE HAVE TO GET THE HUMANS *OUT* OF THE *COMMAND BUNKER...*

...BEFORE IT BECOMES A *TOMB!*

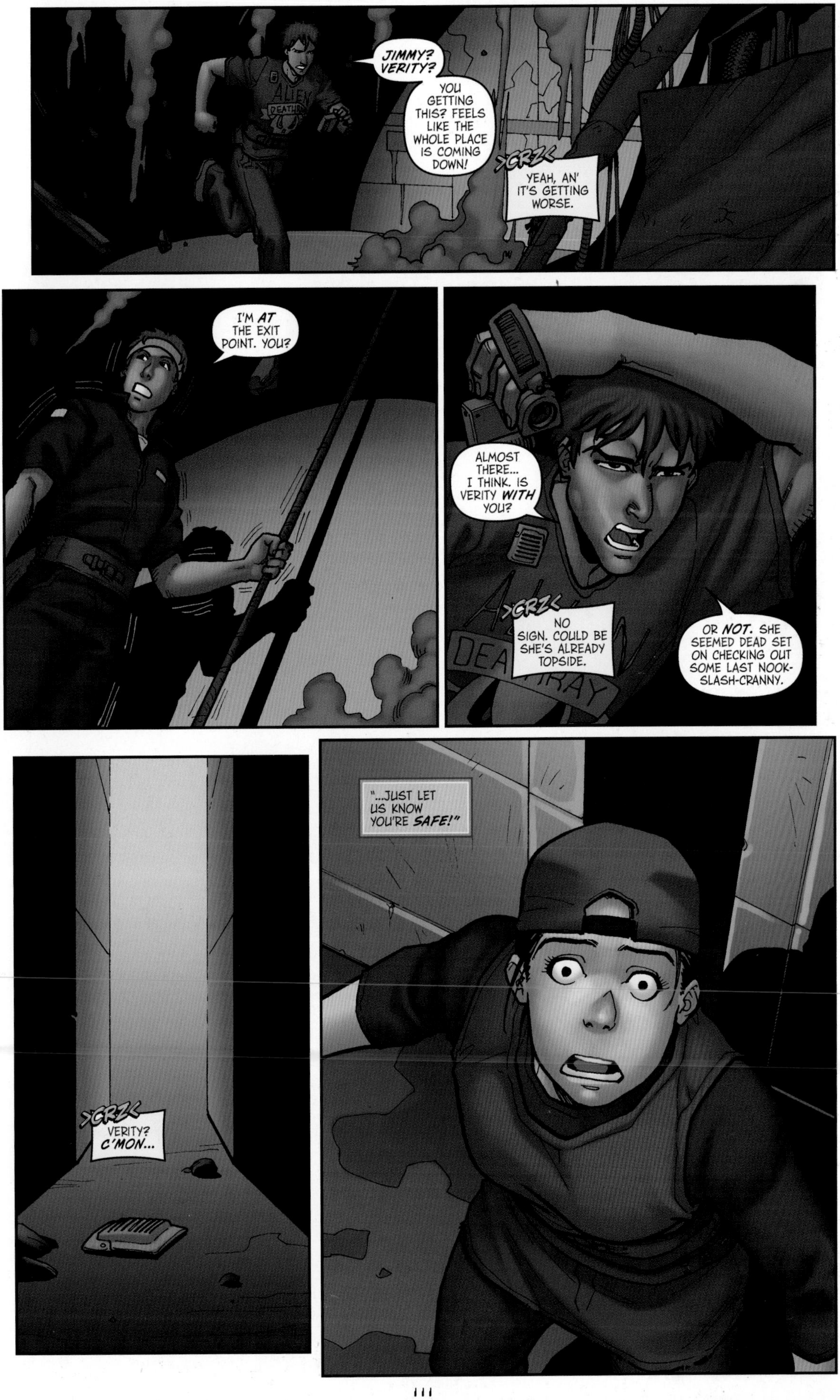
JIMMY? VERITY?
YOU GETTING THIS? FEELS LIKE THE WHOLE PLACE IS COMING DOWN!
>CRZ<
YEAH, AN' IT'S GETTING WORSE.
I'M AT THE EXIT POINT. YOU?
ALMOST THERE... I THINK. IS VERITY WITH YOU?
>CRZ<
NO SIGN. COULD BE SHE'S ALREADY TOPSIDE.
OR NOT. SHE SEEMED DEAD SET ON CHECKING OUT SOME LAST NOOK-SLASH-CRANNY.
>CRZ<
VERITY? C'MON...
"...JUST LET US KNOW YOU'RE SAFE!"

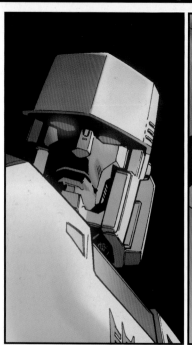

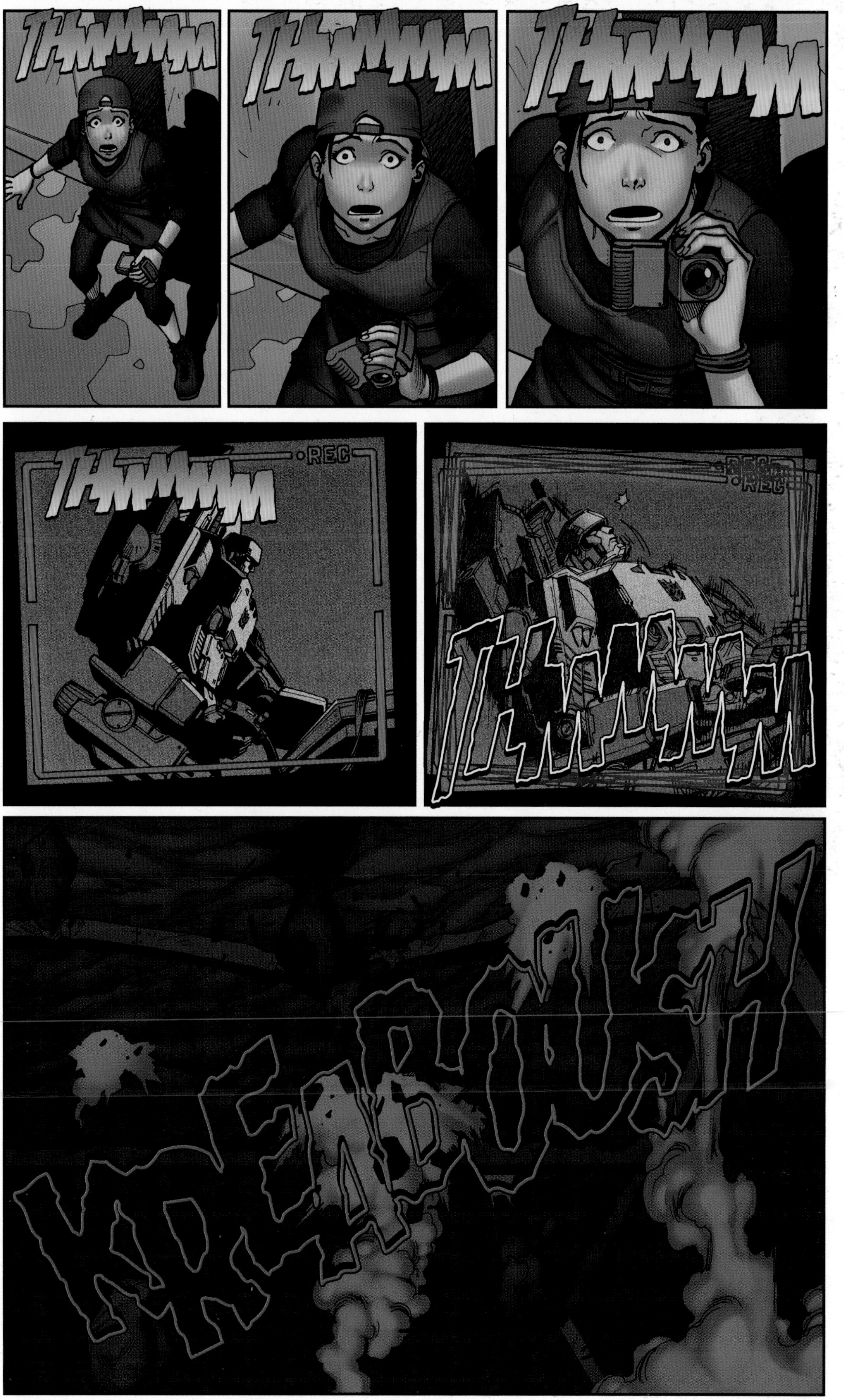
THMMMMM
THMMMMMMM
THMMMMMMMM
REC
THMMMMM
REC
THMMMMMM

KACHIOOM

GHA!

AH—
AH—
AH—

-AAAAAAAA!

CHOKT

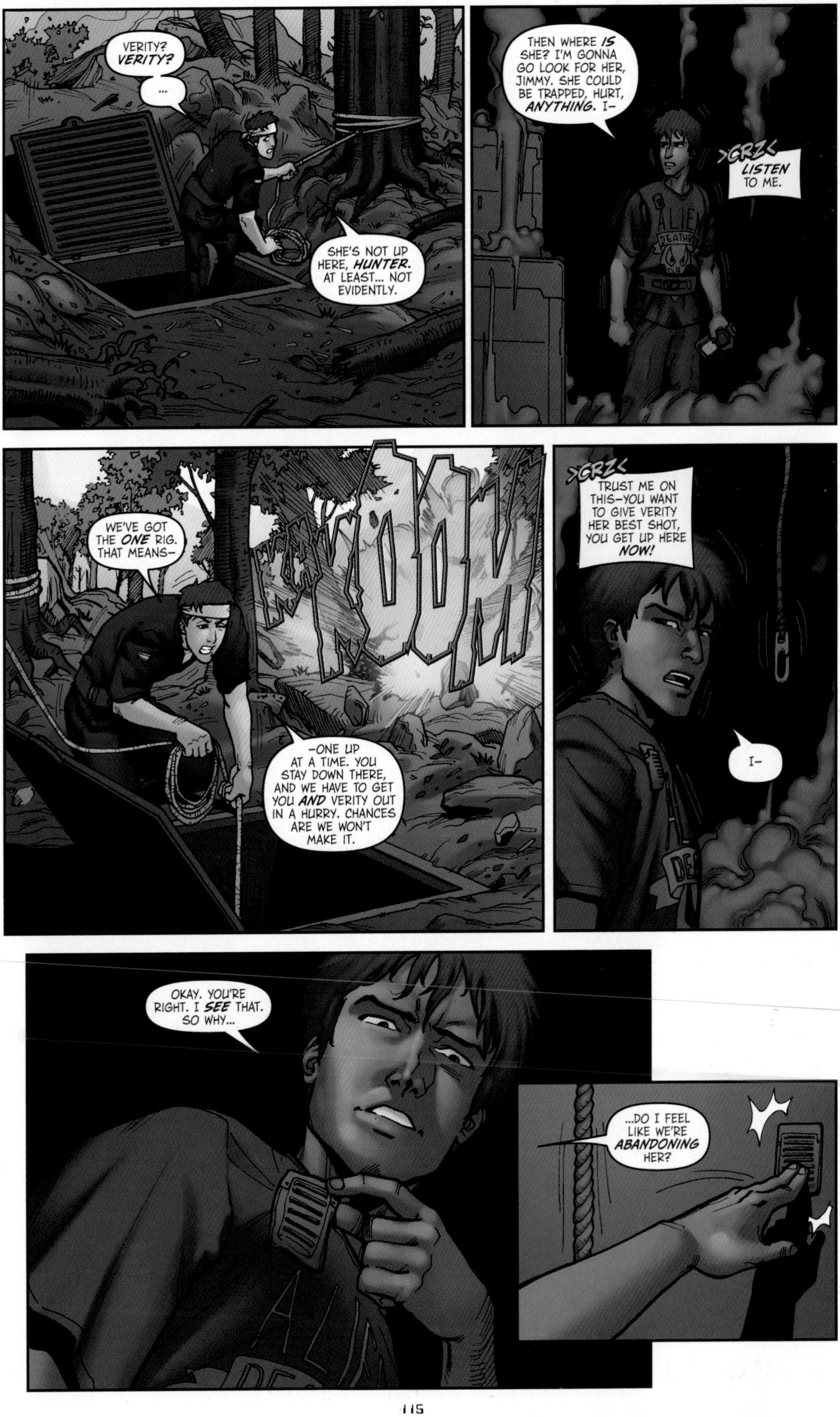
VERITY? VERITY?
...
SHE'S NOT UP HERE, HUNTER. AT LEAST... NOT EVIDENTLY.
THEN WHERE IS SHE? I'M GONNA GO LOOK FOR HER, JIMMY. SHE COULD BE TRAPPED, HURT, ANYTHING. I–
>GRZ< LISTEN TO ME.
WE'VE GOT THE ONE RIG. THAT MEANS–
KRA-KOOM
–ONE UP AT A TIME. YOU STAY DOWN THERE, AND WE HAVE TO GET YOU AND VERITY OUT IN A HURRY. CHANCES ARE WE WON'T MAKE IT.
>GRZ< TRUST ME ON THIS–YOU WANT TO GIVE VERITY HER BEST SHOT, YOU GET UP HERE NOW!
I–
OKAY. YOU'RE RIGHT. I SEE THAT. SO WHY...
...DO I FEEL LIKE WE'RE ABANDONING HER?

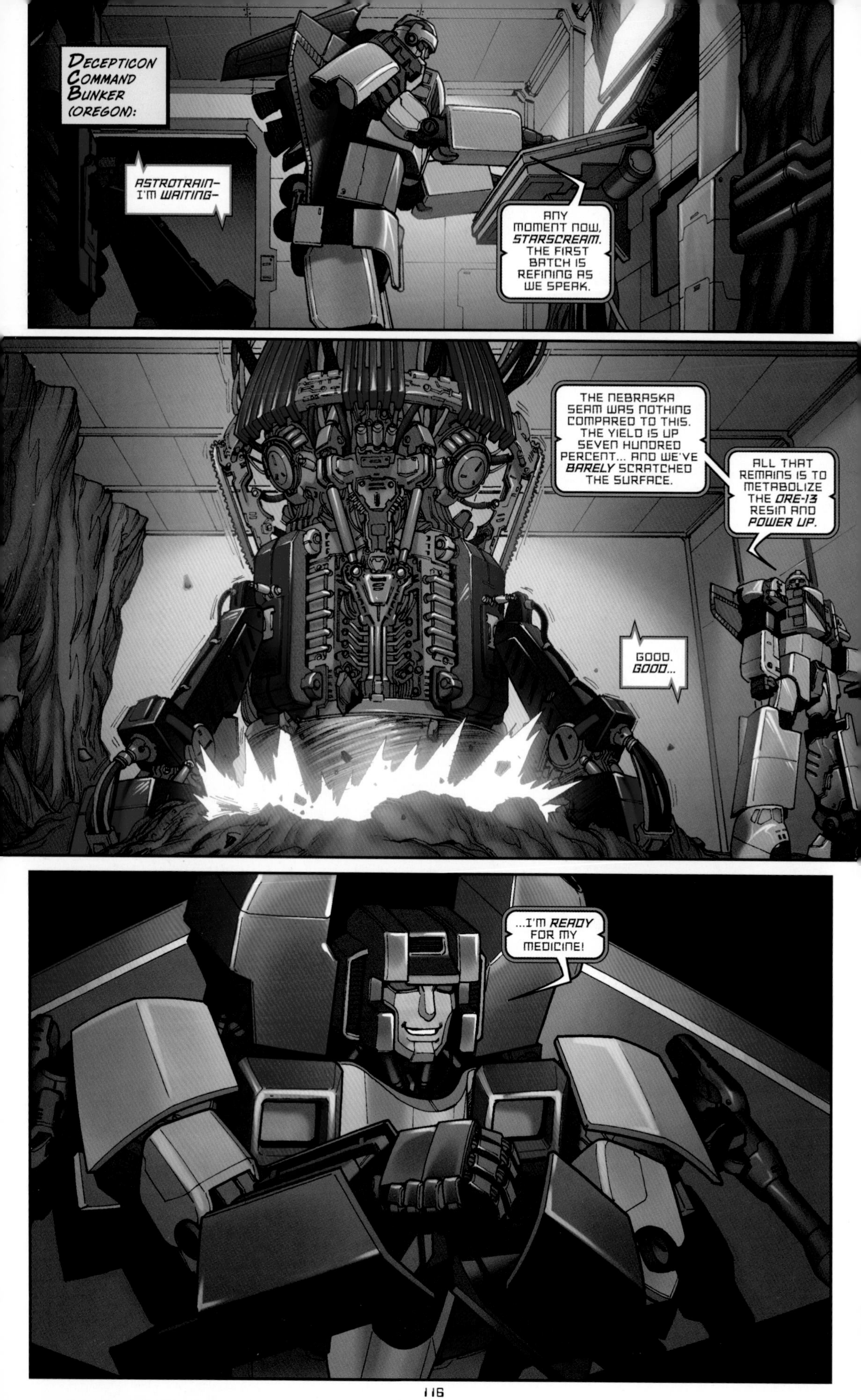
DECEPTICON COMMAND BUNKER (OREGON):
ASTROTRAIN— I'M WAITING—
ANY MOMENT NOW, STARSCREAM. THE FIRST BATCH IS REFINING AS WE SPEAK.
THE NEBRASKA SEAM WAS NOTHING COMPARED TO THIS. THE YIELD IS UP SEVEN HUNDRED PERCENT... AND WE'VE BARELY SCRATCHED THE SURFACE.
ALL THAT REMAINS IS TO METABOLIZE THE ORE-13 RESIN AND POWER UP.
GOOD. GOOD...
...I'M READY FOR MY MEDICINE!

NEBRASKA:

IT'S *GOING!*

AND TAKING US *WITH* IT!

HUNTER, JIMMY—LET'S *MOVE OUT!*

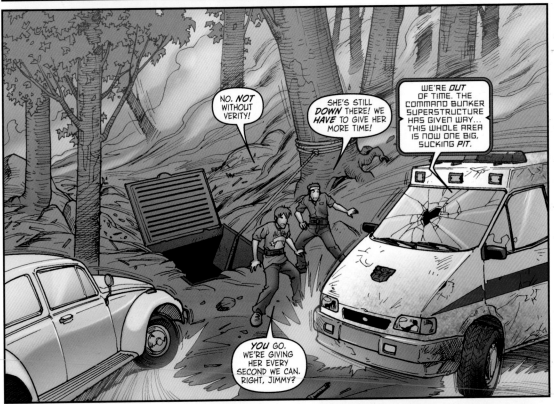

NO. *NOT WITHOUT* VERITY!

SHE'S STILL *DOWN* THERE! WE *HAVE* TO GIVE HER MORE TIME!

WE'RE *OUT* OF TIME. THE COMMAND BUNKER SUPERSTRUCTURE HAS GIVEN WAY... THIS WHOLE AREA IS NOW ONE BIG, SUCKING *PIT.*

YOU GO. WE'RE GIVING HER EVERY SECOND WE CAN. RIGHT, JIMMY?

RIGHT.

WE'RE IN THIS *TOGETHER.* VERITY'S... *SPECIAL.*

SCRZK

GUYS, GUYS...

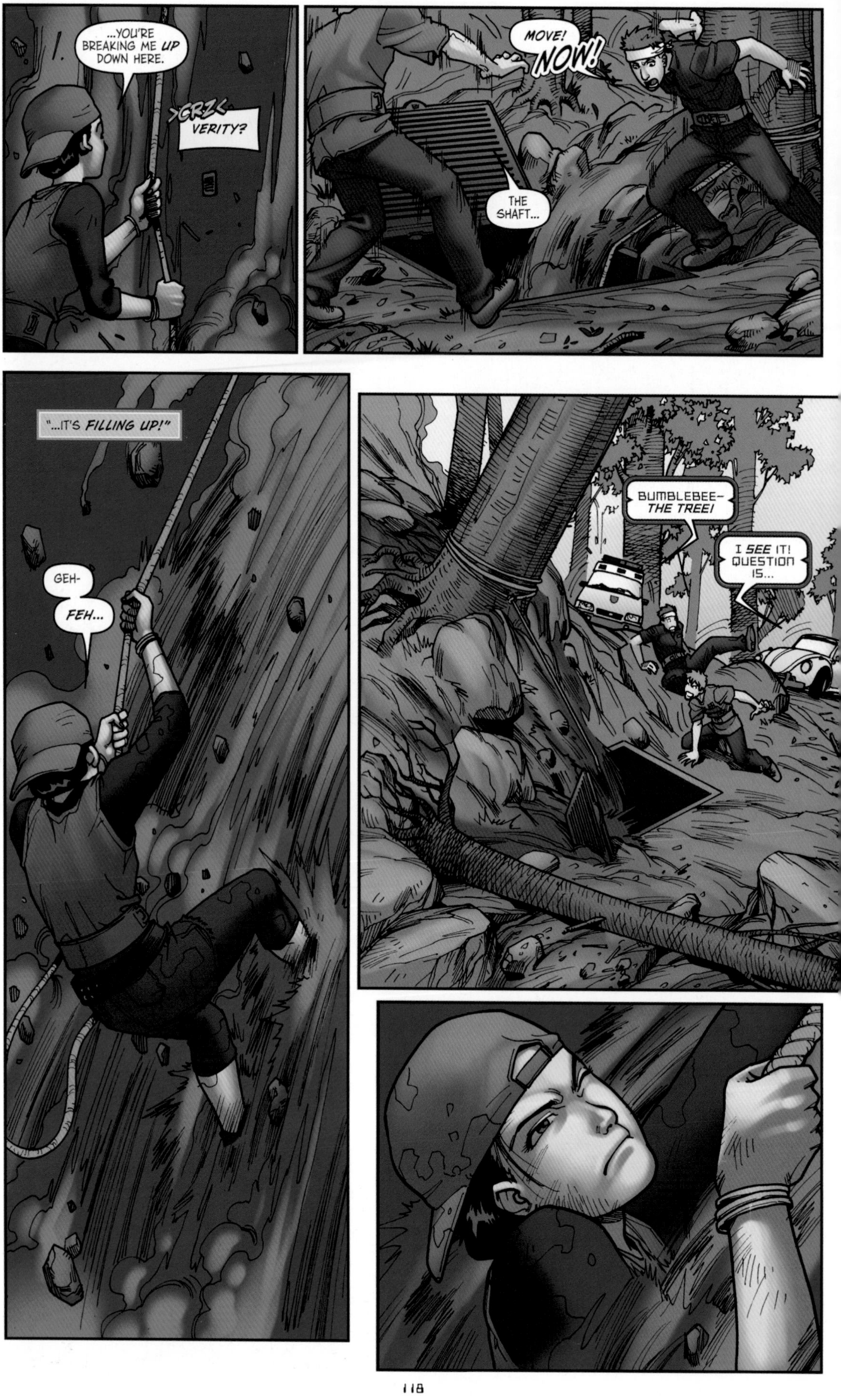
...YOU'RE BREAKING ME UP DOWN HERE.
>GRZ< VERITY?
MOVE! NOW!
THE SHAFT...
"...IT'S FILLING UP!"
GEH-
FEH...
BUMBLEBEE- THE TREE!
I SEE IT! QUESTION IS...

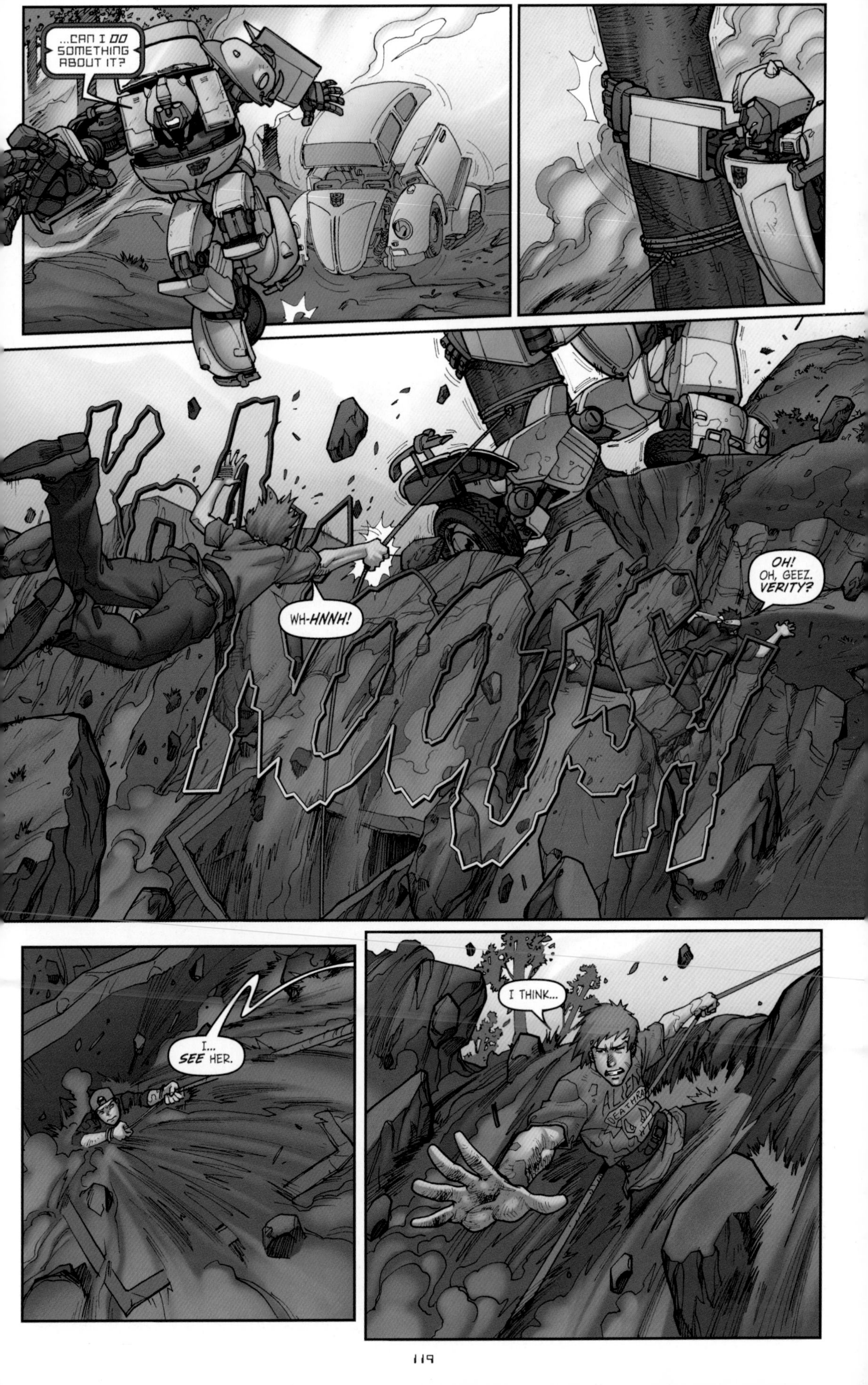
...CAN I *DO* SOMETHING ABOUT IT?
WH-*HNNH!*
OH! OH, GEEZ. *VERITY?*
I... *SEE* HER.
I THINK...

...I CAN *REACH* HER!

HUNTER! WHATEVER YOU'RE GOING TO DO...

...DO IT *NOW!*

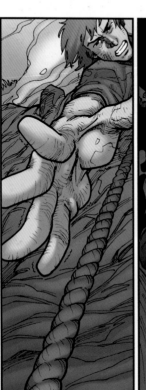

P-PULL...

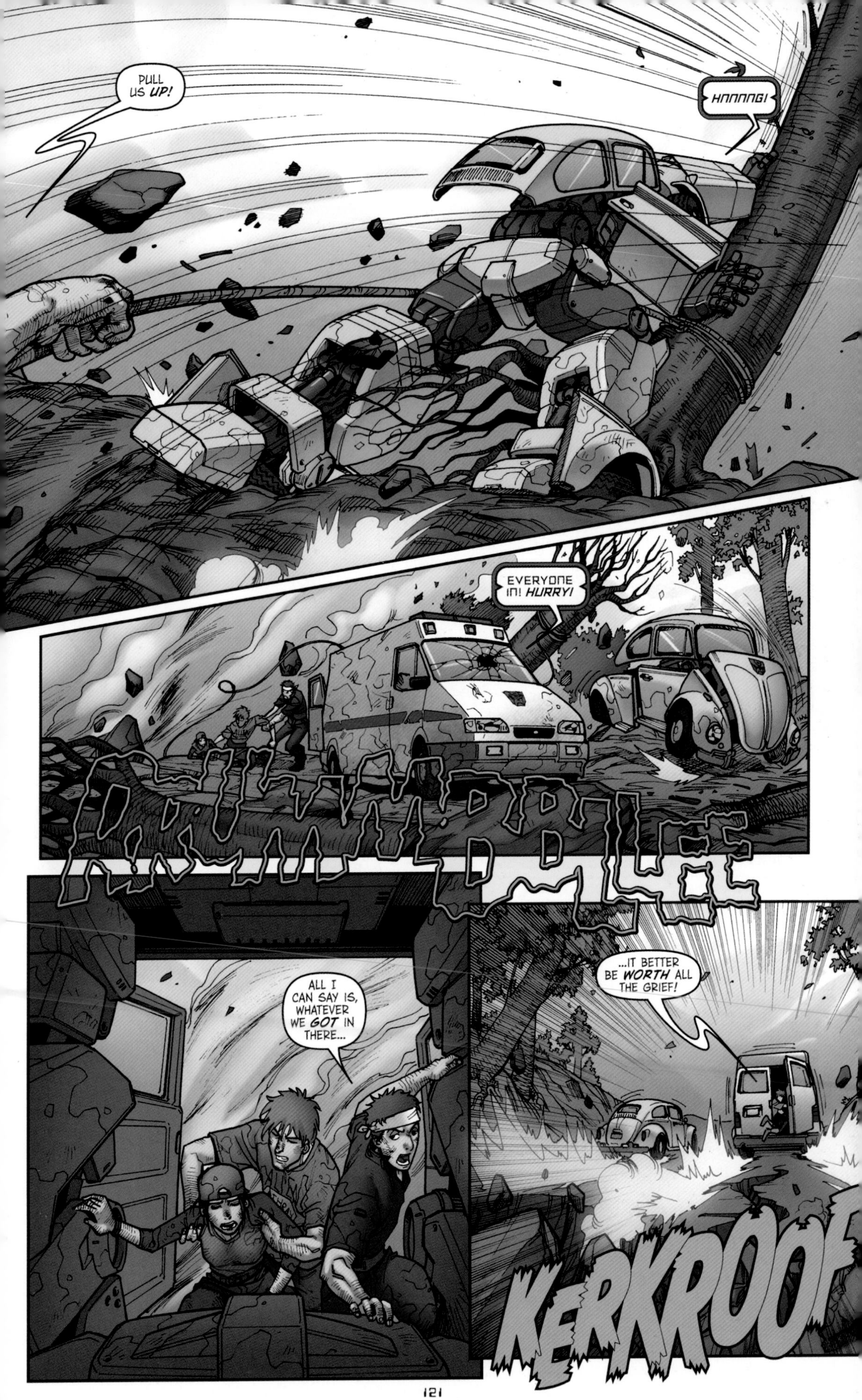
PULL US UP!
HNNNNG!
EVERYONE IN! HURRY!
ALL I CAN SAY IS, WHATEVER WE GOT IN THERE...
...IT BETTER BE WORTH ALL THE GRIEF!
KERKROOF

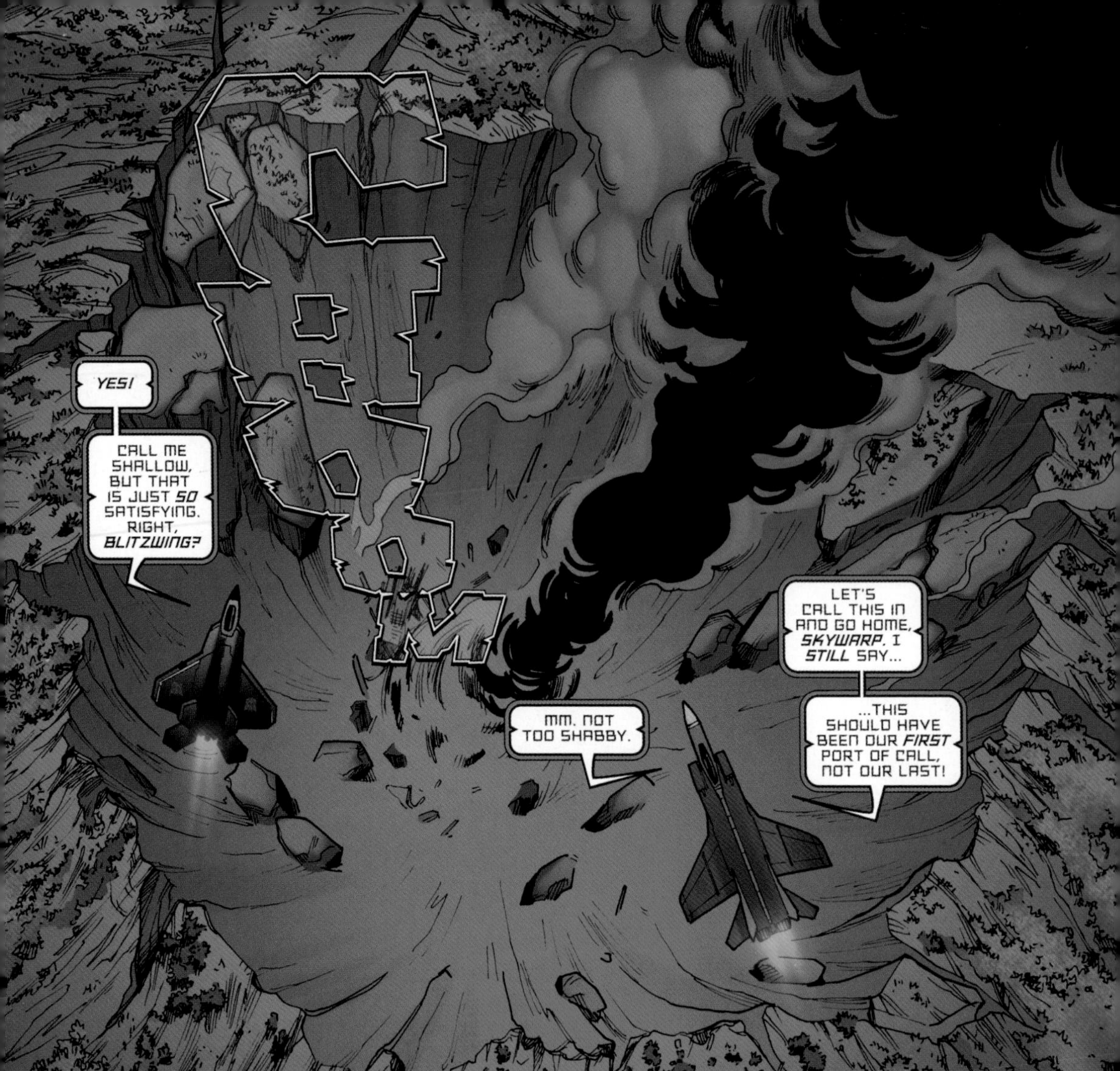
YES!
CALL ME SHALLOW, BUT THAT IS JUST SO SATISFYING. RIGHT, BLITZWING?
MM. NOT TOO SHABBY.
LET'S CALL THIS IN AND GO HOME, SKYWARP. I STILL SAY...
...THIS SHOULD HAVE BEEN OUR FIRST PORT OF CALL, NOT OUR LAST!

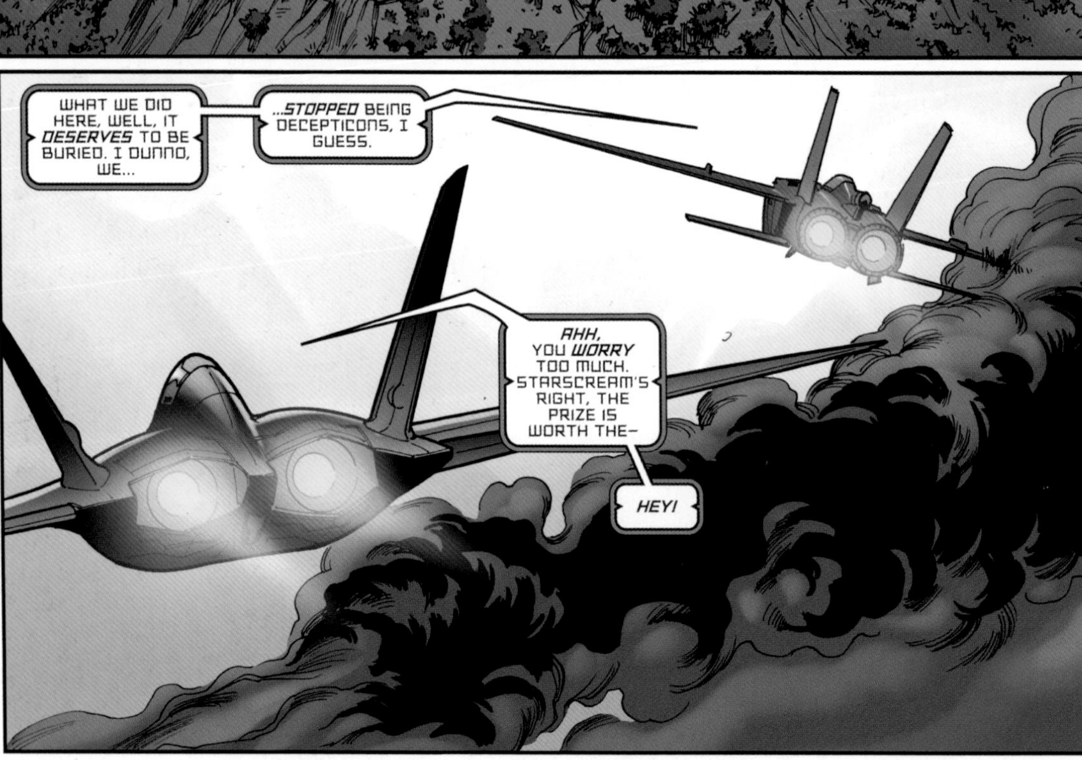
WHAT WE DID HERE, WELL, IT DESERVES TO BE BURIED. I DUNNO, WE...
...STOPPED BEING DECEPTICONS, I GUESS.
AHH, YOU WORRY TOO MUCH. STARSCREAM'S RIGHT, THE PRIZE IS WORTH THE–
HEY!

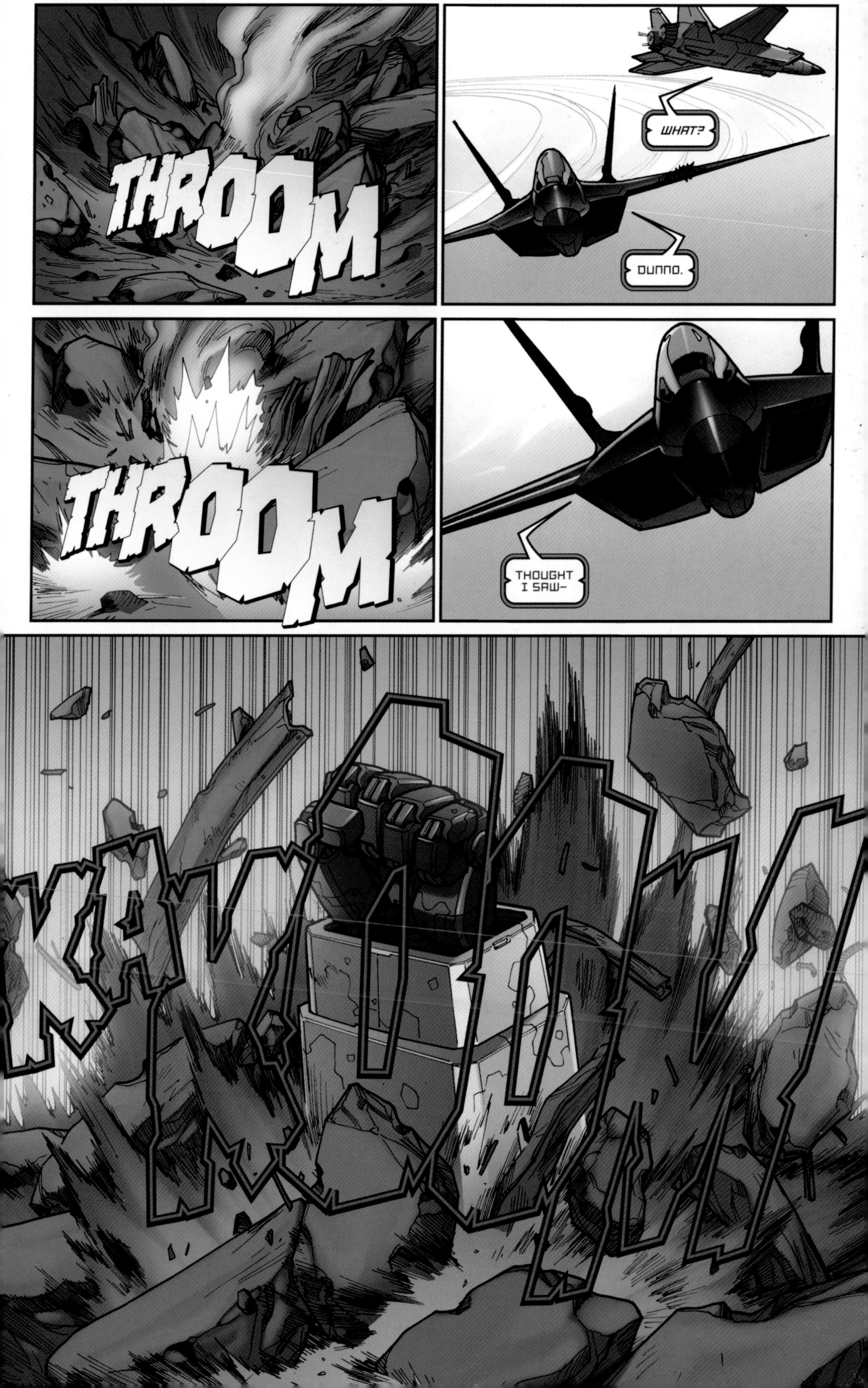
THROOM
WHAT?
DUNNO.
THROOM
THOUGHT I SAW–

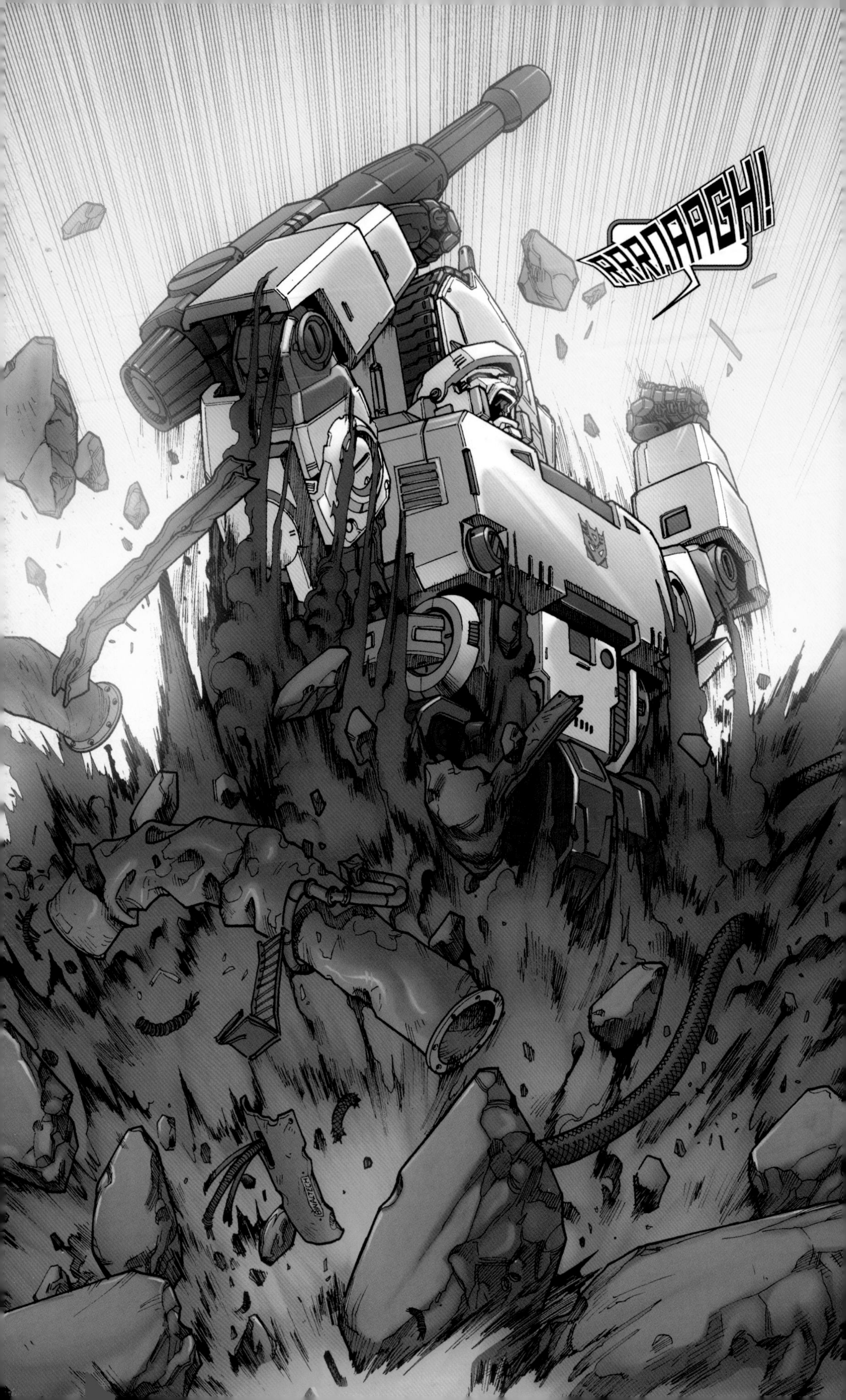
RRRNAAGH!

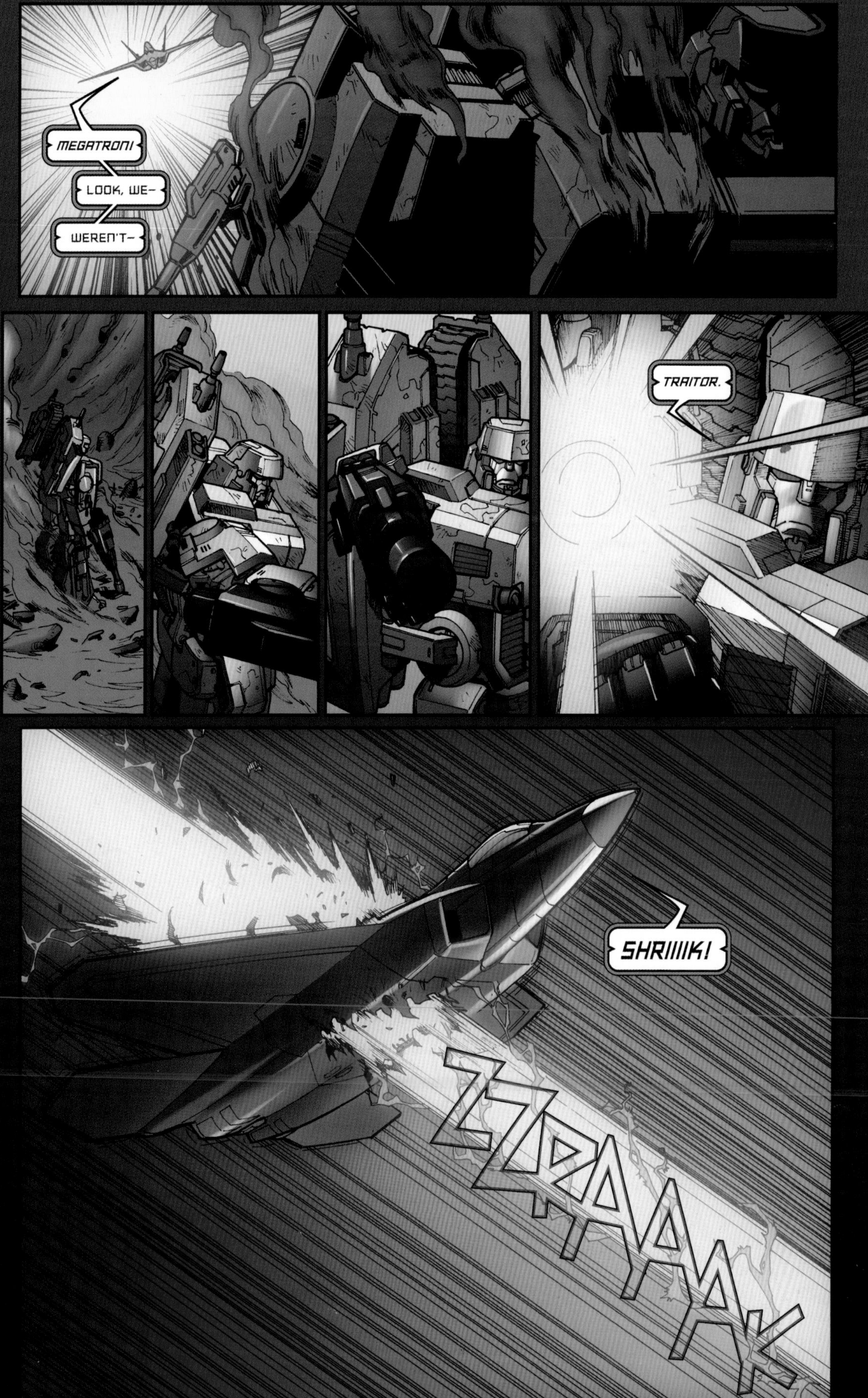
MEGATRON!
LOOK, WE–
WEREN'T–
TRAITOR.
SHRIIIIK!
ZZRAAAAK

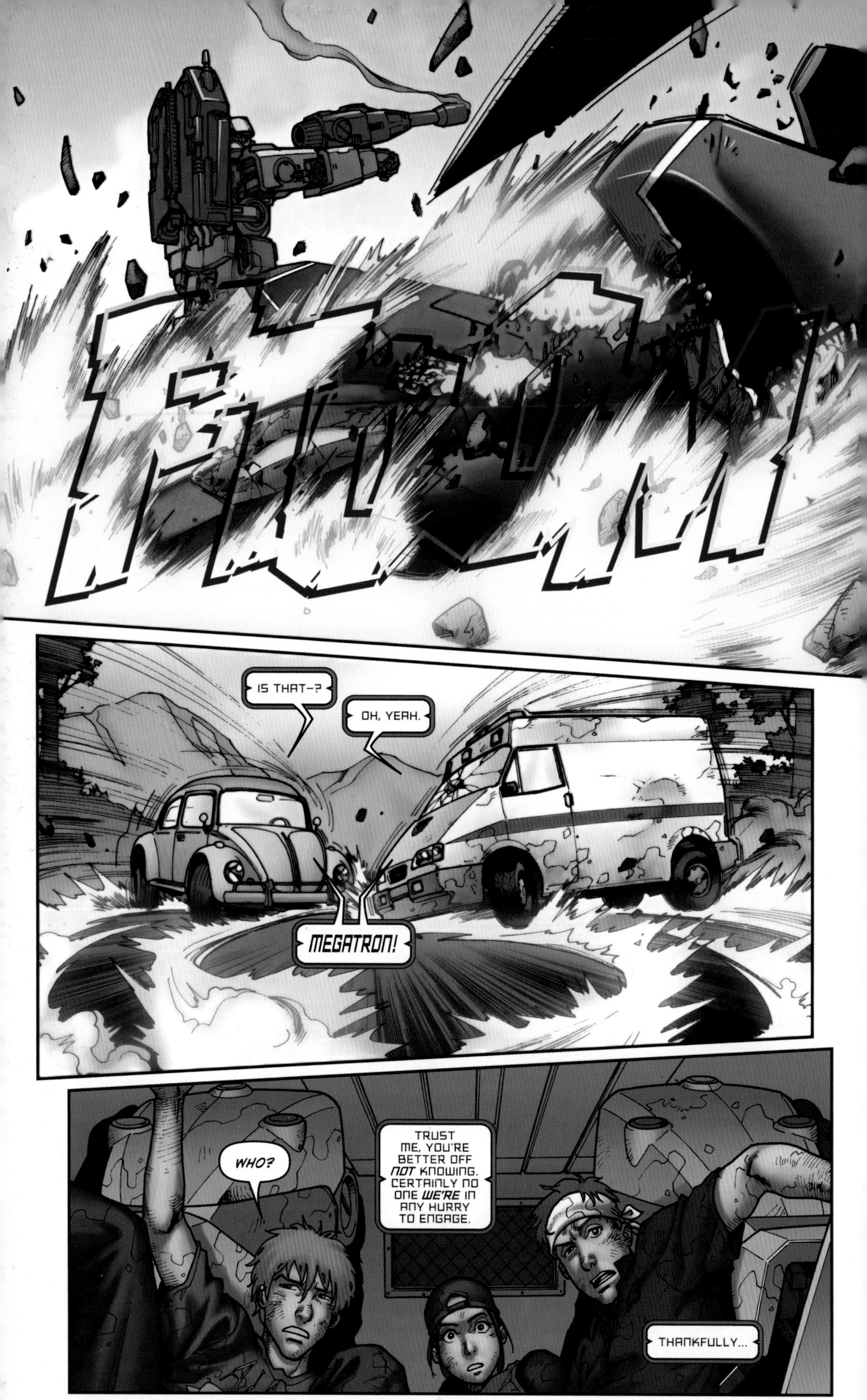

IS THAT–?
OH, YEAH.
MEGATRON!
WHO?
TRUST ME, YOU'RE BETTER OFF NOT KNOWING. CERTAINLY NO ONE WE'RE IN ANY HURRY TO ENGAGE.
THANKFULLY...

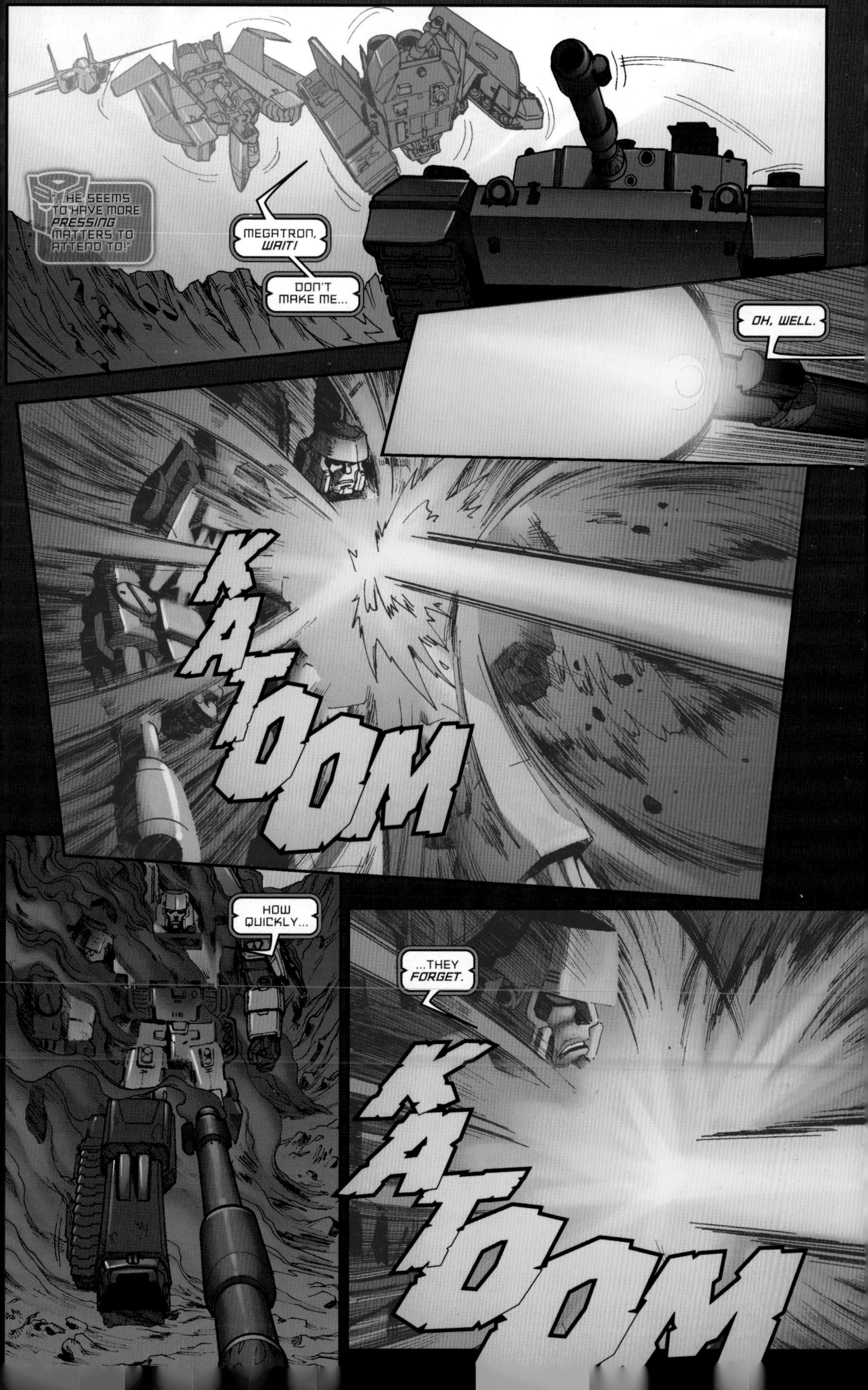
"...HE SEEMS TO HAVE MORE *PRESSING* MATTERS TO ATTEND TO!"
MEGATRON, *WAIT!*
DON'T MAKE ME...
OH, WELL.
KATOOM
HOW QUICKLY...
...THEY *FORGET.*
KATOOM

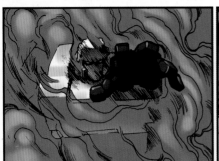

AK—

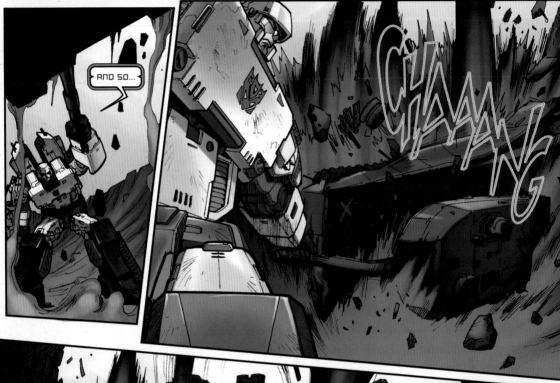

AND SO...

CHAAANG

...I MUST *REMIND* THEM.

CHAAANG

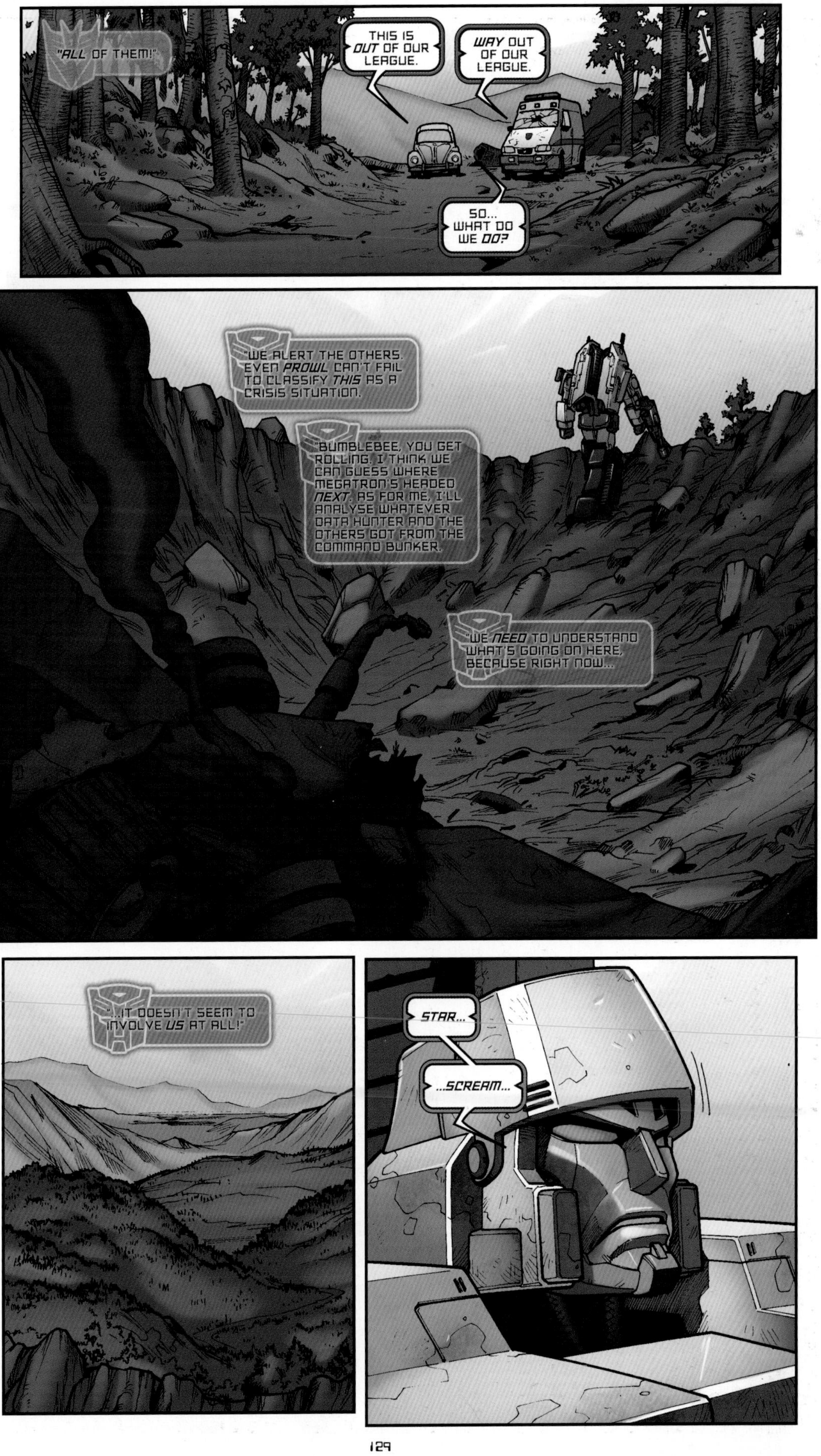
"ALL OF THEM!"
THIS IS OUT OF OUR LEAGUE.
WAY OUT OF OUR LEAGUE.
SO... WHAT DO WE DO?
"WE ALERT THE OTHERS. EVEN PROWL CAN'T FAIL TO CLASSIFY THIS AS A CRISIS SITUATION.
"BUMBLEBEE, YOU GET ROLLING. I THINK WE CAN GUESS WHERE MEGATRON'S HEADED NEXT. AS FOR ME, I'LL ANALYSE WHATEVER DATA HUNTER AND THE OTHERS GOT FROM THE COMMAND BUNKER.
"WE NEED TO UNDERSTAND WHAT'S GOING ON HERE, BECAUSE RIGHT NOW...
"...IT DOESN'T SEEM TO INVOLVE US AT ALL!"
STAR...
...SCREAM...

IT'S KIND OF *PIECEMEAL*, BUT HERE'S WHAT WE HAVE...

A GEOLOGICAL SURVEY SHAFT AND SOME VARIETY OF UPGRADED REFINING APPARATUS. MEGATRON WAS *VERY* INTERESTED IN THAT.

EVIDENCE THROUGHOUT THE COMMAND BUNKER OF MODIFIED *DELIVERY* CAPSULES. TRACE READINGS INDICATE BASELINE *ENERGON*, BUT WITH A *TWIST*. I CAN FIND NOTHING LIKE IT IN ANY DATATRACK.

80 EAST

MY THEORY IS THIS—THE DECEPTICONS FOUND SOME KIND OF *UNCLASSIFIED* ORE, ONE THAT THEY WERE ABLE TO PURIFY AND APPLY *DIRECTLY* TO THEIR SYSTEMS.

THE SEAM WAS SOON EXHAUSTED, NECESSITATING THE MOVE TO OREGON. ONCE THERE, THEY ENGAGED *SIEGE MODE*, PROBABLY TO PROTECT WHAT THEY HAD, AND IN SO DOING BROKE PROTOCOL.

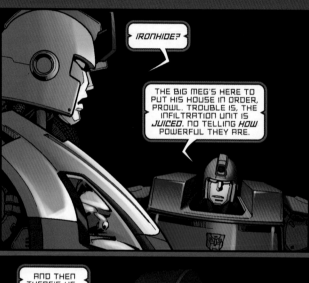

IRONHIDE?

THE BIG MEG'S HERE TO PUT HIS HOUSE IN ORDER, PROWL. TROUBLE IS, THE INFILTRATION UNIT IS *JUICED*. NO TELLING *HOW* POWERFUL THEY ARE.

AND THEN THERE'S US...

...STUCK IN THE *MIDDLE!*

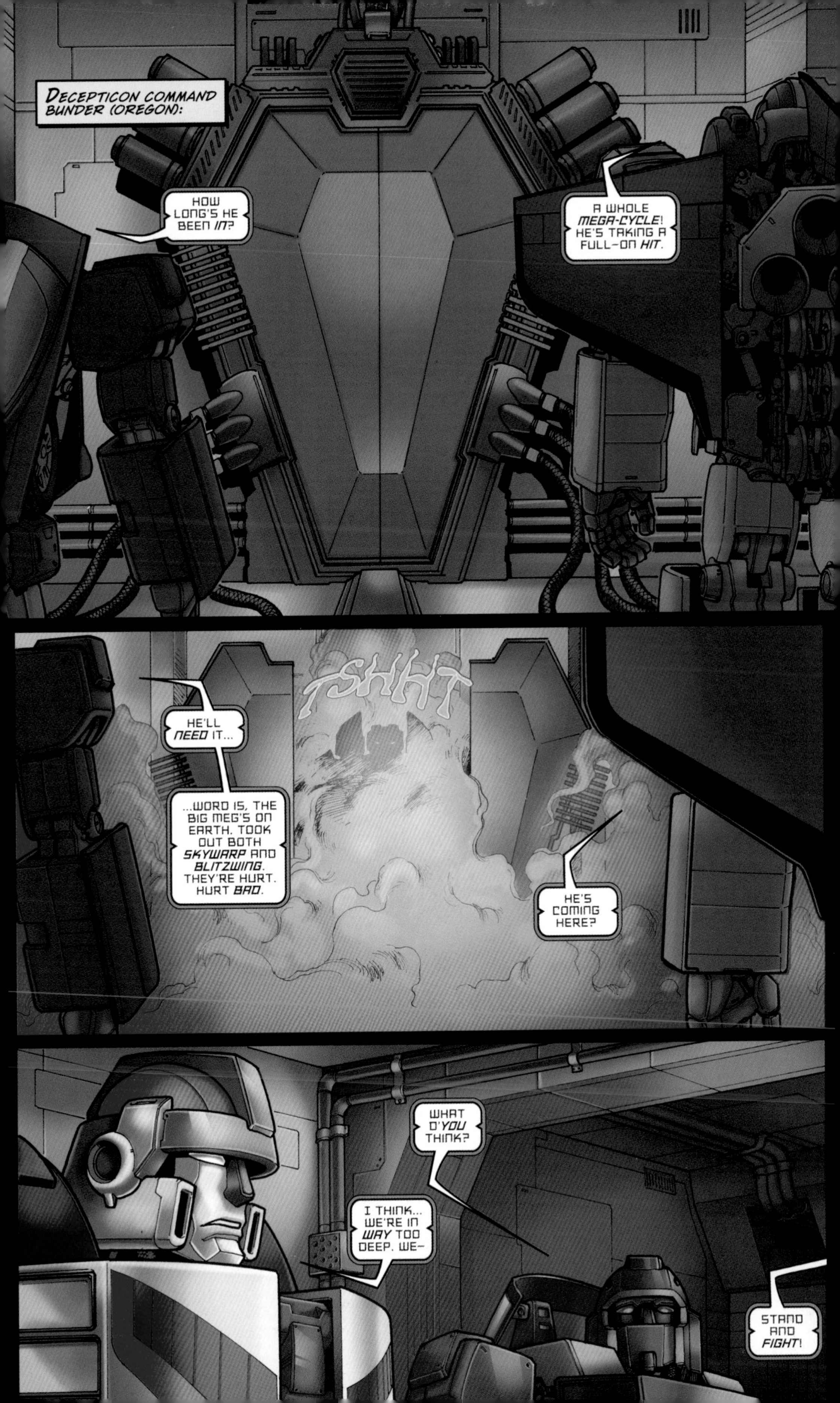

DECEPTICON COMMAND BUNDER (OREGON):
HOW LONG'S HE BEEN *IN*?
A WHOLE *MEGA-CYCLE*! HE'S TAKING A FULL-ON *HIT*.
TSHHT
HE'LL *NEED* IT...
...WORD IS, THE BIG MEG'S ON EARTH. TOOK OUT BOTH *SKYWARP* AND *BLITZWING*. THEY'RE HURT. HURT *BAD*.
HE'S COMING HERE?
WHAT D'*YOU* THINK?
I THINK... WE'RE IN *WAY* TOO DEEP. WE–
STAND AND *FIGHT*!

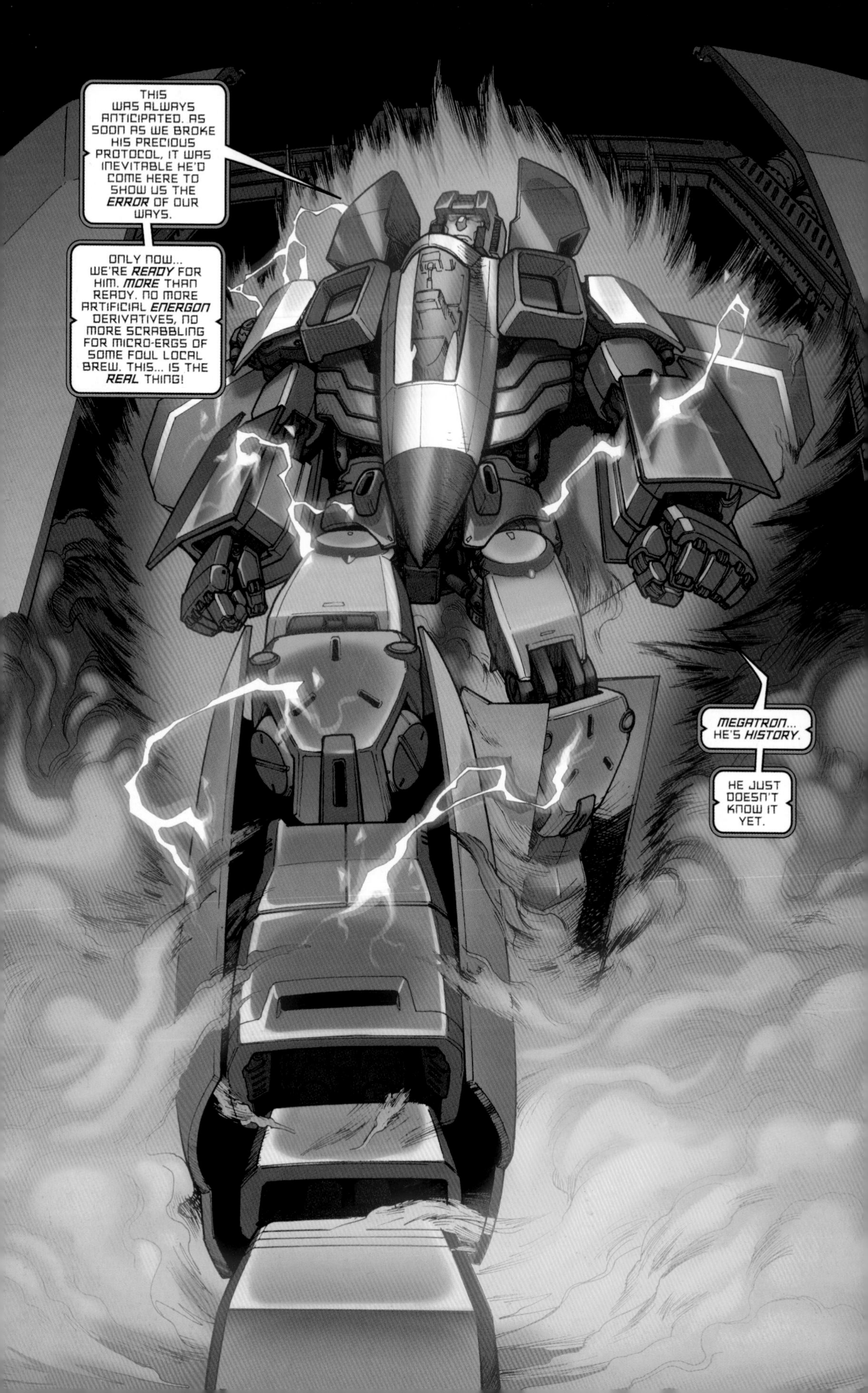
THIS WAS ALWAYS ANTICIPATED. AS SOON AS WE BROKE HIS PRECIOUS PROTOCOL, IT WAS INEVITABLE HE'D COME HERE TO SHOW US THE ERROR OF OUR WAYS.
ONLY NOW... WE'RE READY FOR HIM. MORE THAN READY. NO MORE ARTIFICIAL ENERGON DERIVATIVES, NO MORE SCRABBLING FOR MICRO-ERGS OF SOME FOUL LOCAL BREW. THIS... IS THE REAL THING!
MEGATRON... HE'S HISTORY.
HE JUST DOESN'T KNOW IT YET.

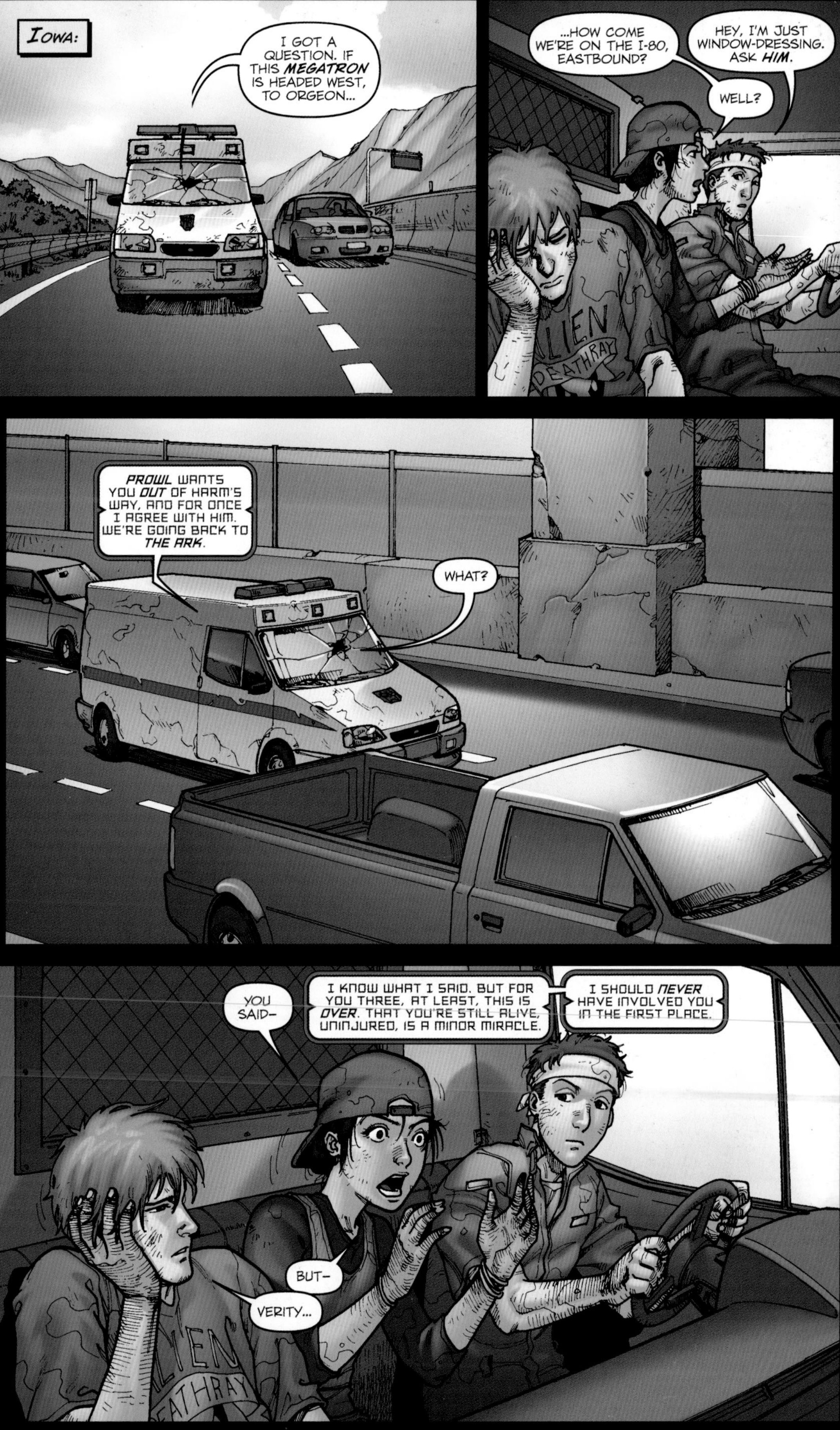
IOWA:
I GOT A QUESTION. IF THIS MEGATRON IS HEADED WEST, TO ORGEON...
...HOW COME WE'RE ON THE I-80, EASTBOUND?
HEY, I'M JUST WINDOW-DRESSING. ASK HIM.
WELL?
PROWL WANTS YOU OUT OF HARM'S WAY, AND FOR ONCE I AGREE WITH HIM. WE'RE GOING BACK TO THE ARK.
WHAT?
YOU SAID-
I KNOW WHAT I SAID. BUT FOR YOU THREE, AT LEAST, THIS IS OVER. THAT YOU'RE STILL ALIVE, UNINJURED, IS A MINOR MIRACLE.
I SHOULD NEVER HAVE INVOLVED YOU IN THE FIRST PLACE.
BUT-
VERITY...

...LET IT GO.

THIS... IS TOO *BIG*, EVEN FOR US. I-I'VE SEEN THINGS TODAY I CAN BARELY COMPREHEND, AND I FOR ONE NEED A VERY LONG MOMENT HERE.

JIMMY?

I'M WITH HUNTER. I'M ACTUALLY GLAD WE'VE BEEN SIDELINED. WE... COULD HAVE DIED BACK THERE.

LOOK, VERITY...

...IT'S *OKAY* TO BE SCARED.

KH—

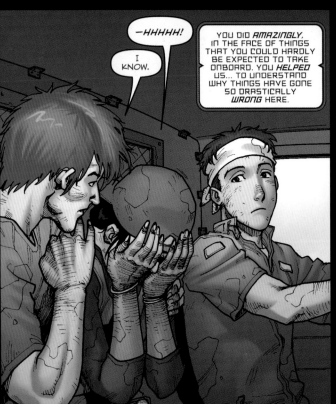

—HHHHH!

I KNOW.

YOU DID *AMAZINGLY*, IN THE FACE OF THINGS THAT YOU COULD HARDLY BE EXPECTED TO TAKE ONBOARD. YOU *HELPED* US... TO UNDERSTAND WHY THINGS HAVE GONE SO DRASTICALLY *WRONG* HERE.

LET THE *OTHERS* HANDLE IT NOW. TRUST ME...

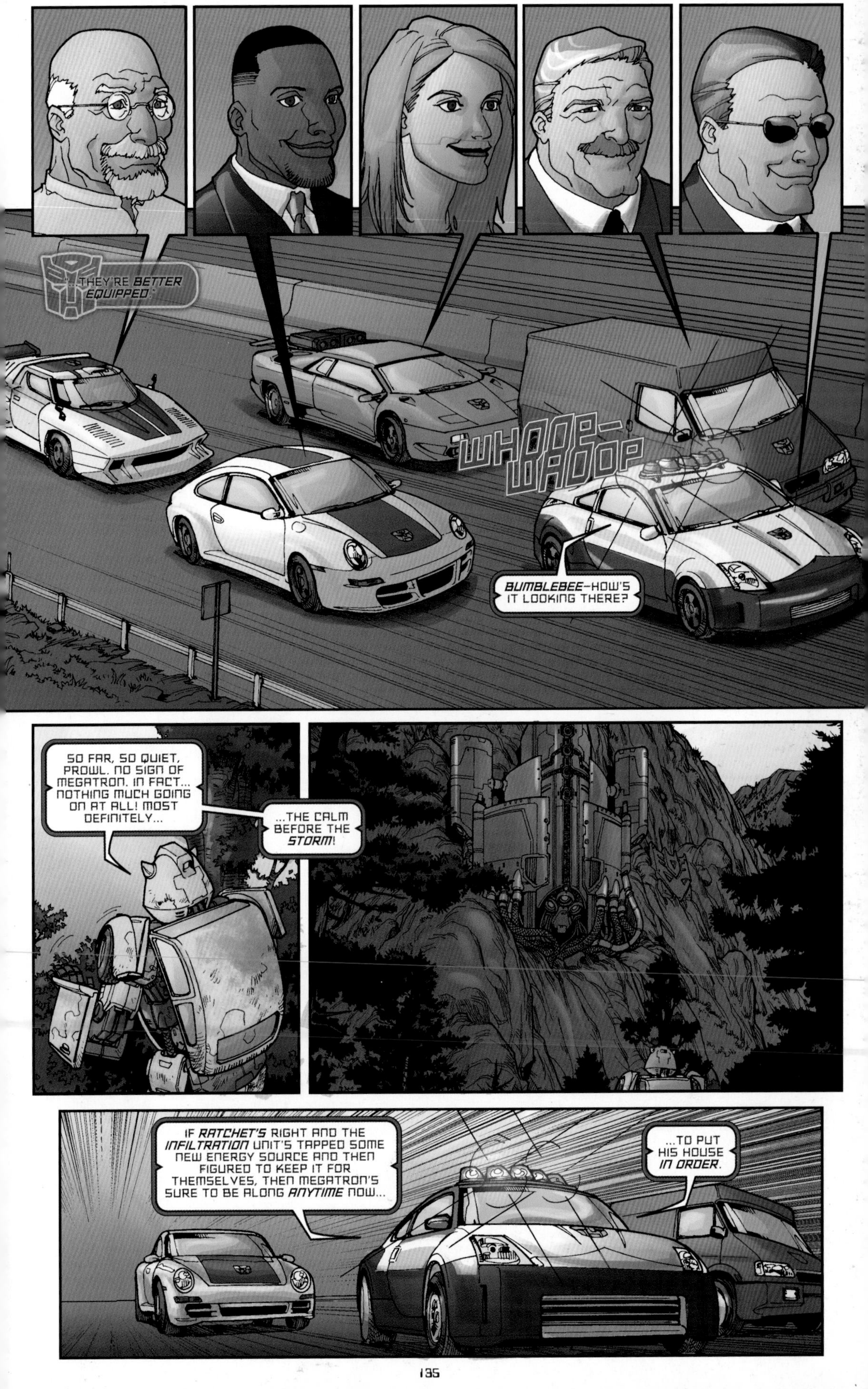
"...THEY'RE BETTER EQUIPPED."
WHOOP-WAOOP
BUMBLEBEE—HOW'S IT LOOKING THERE?
SO FAR, SO QUIET, PROWL. NO SIGN OF MEGATRON. IN FACT... NOTHING MUCH GOING ON AT ALL! MOST DEFINITELY...
...THE CALM BEFORE THE STORM!
IF RATCHET'S RIGHT AND THE INFILTRATION UNIT'S TAPPED SOME NEW ENERGY SOURCE AND THEN FIGURED TO KEEP IT FOR THEMSELVES, THEN MEGATRON'S SURE TO BE ALONG ANYTIME NOW...
...TO PUT HIS HOUSE IN ORDER.

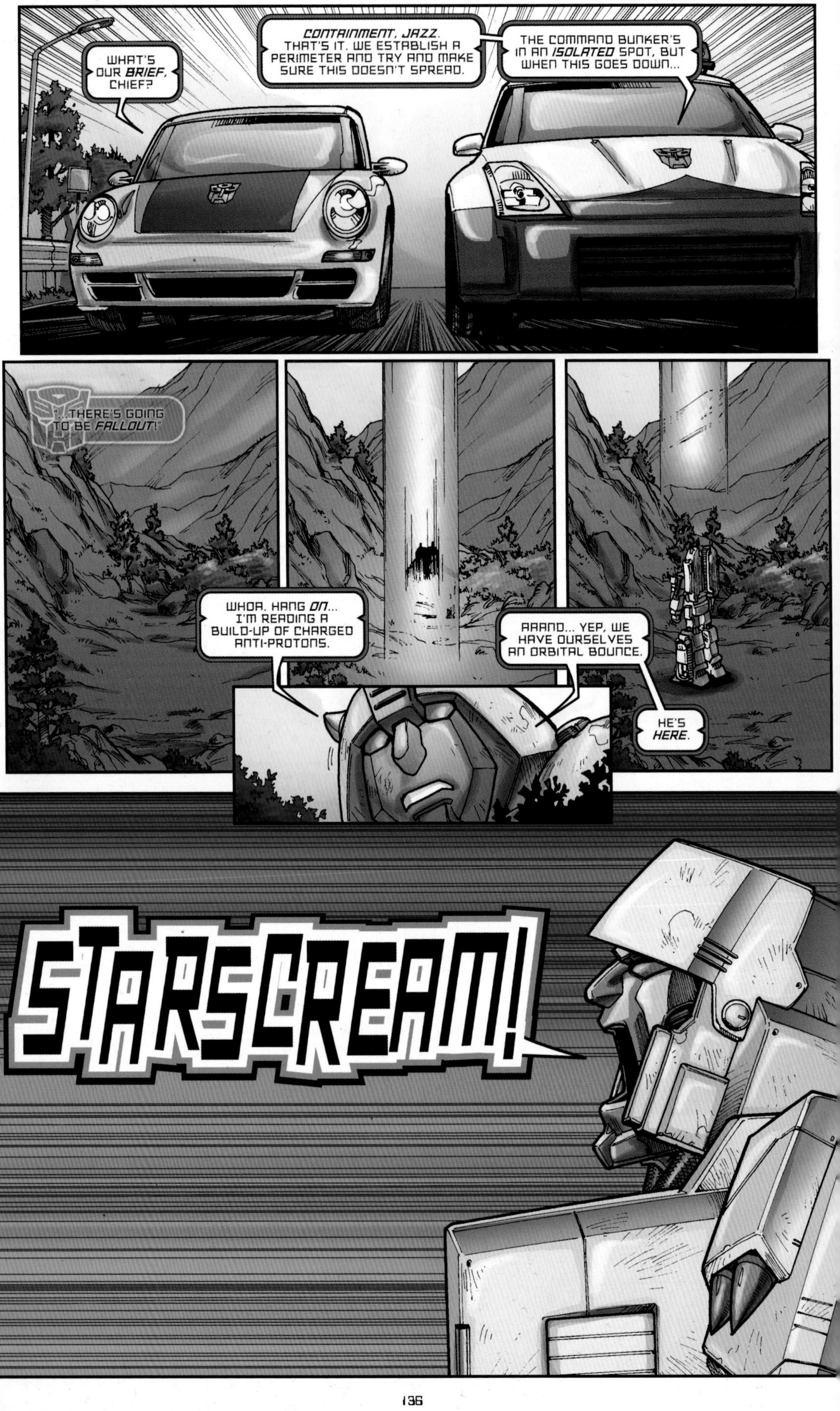

WHAT'S OUR BRIEF, CHIEF?
CONTAINMENT, JAZZ. THAT'S IT. WE ESTABLISH A PERIMETER AND TRY AND MAKE SURE THIS DOESN'T SPREAD.
THE COMMAND BUNKER'S IN AN ISOLATED SPOT, BUT WHEN THIS GOES DOWN...
"...THERE'S GOING TO BE FALLOUT!"
WHOA. HANG ON... I'M READING A BUILD-UP OF CHARGED ANTI-PROTONS.
AAAND... YEP, WE HAVE OURSELVES AN ORBITAL BOUNCE.
HE'S HERE.
STARSCREAM!

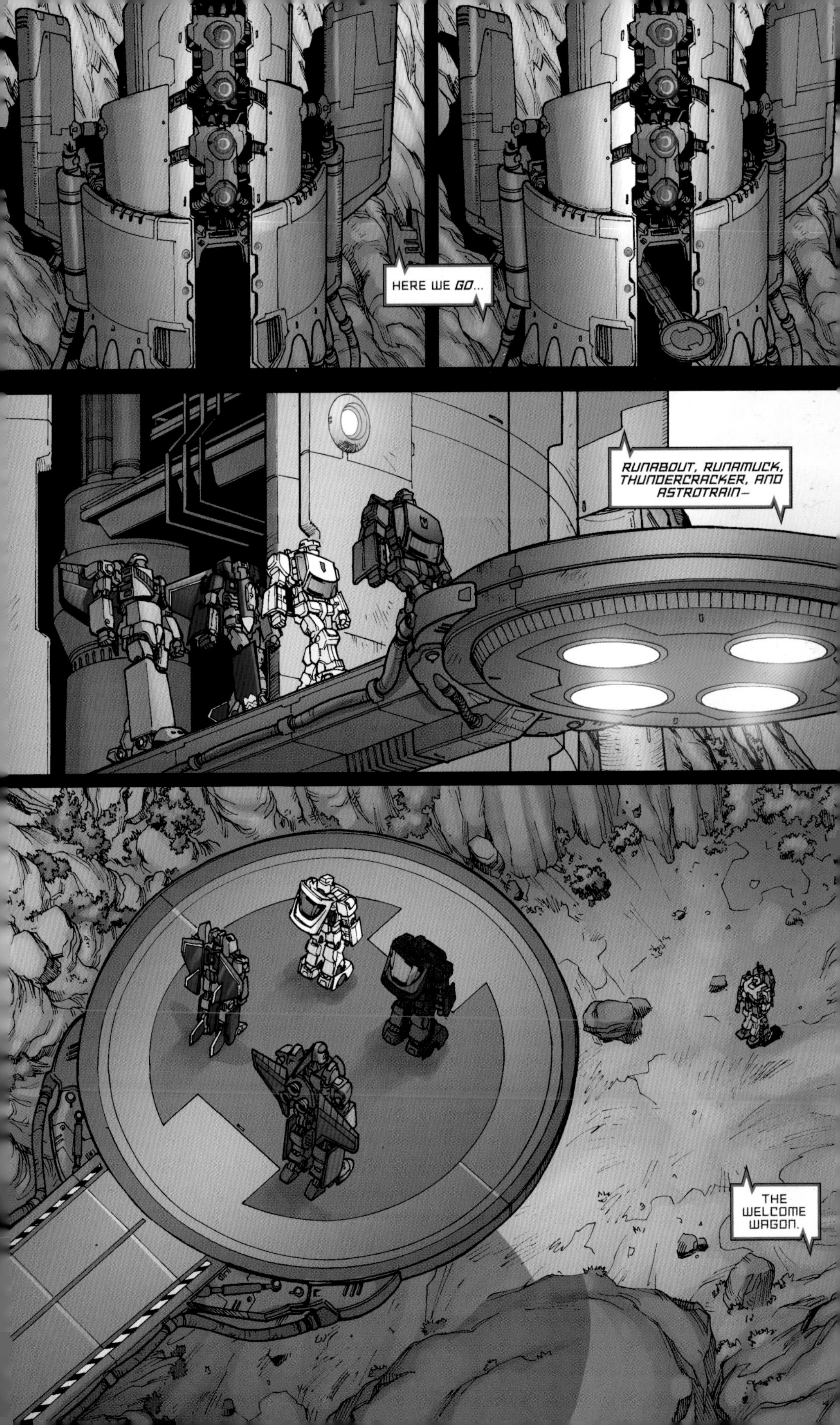
HERE WE GO...
RUNABOUT, RUNAMUCK, THUNDERCRACKER, AND ASTROTRAIN—
THE WELCOME WAGON.

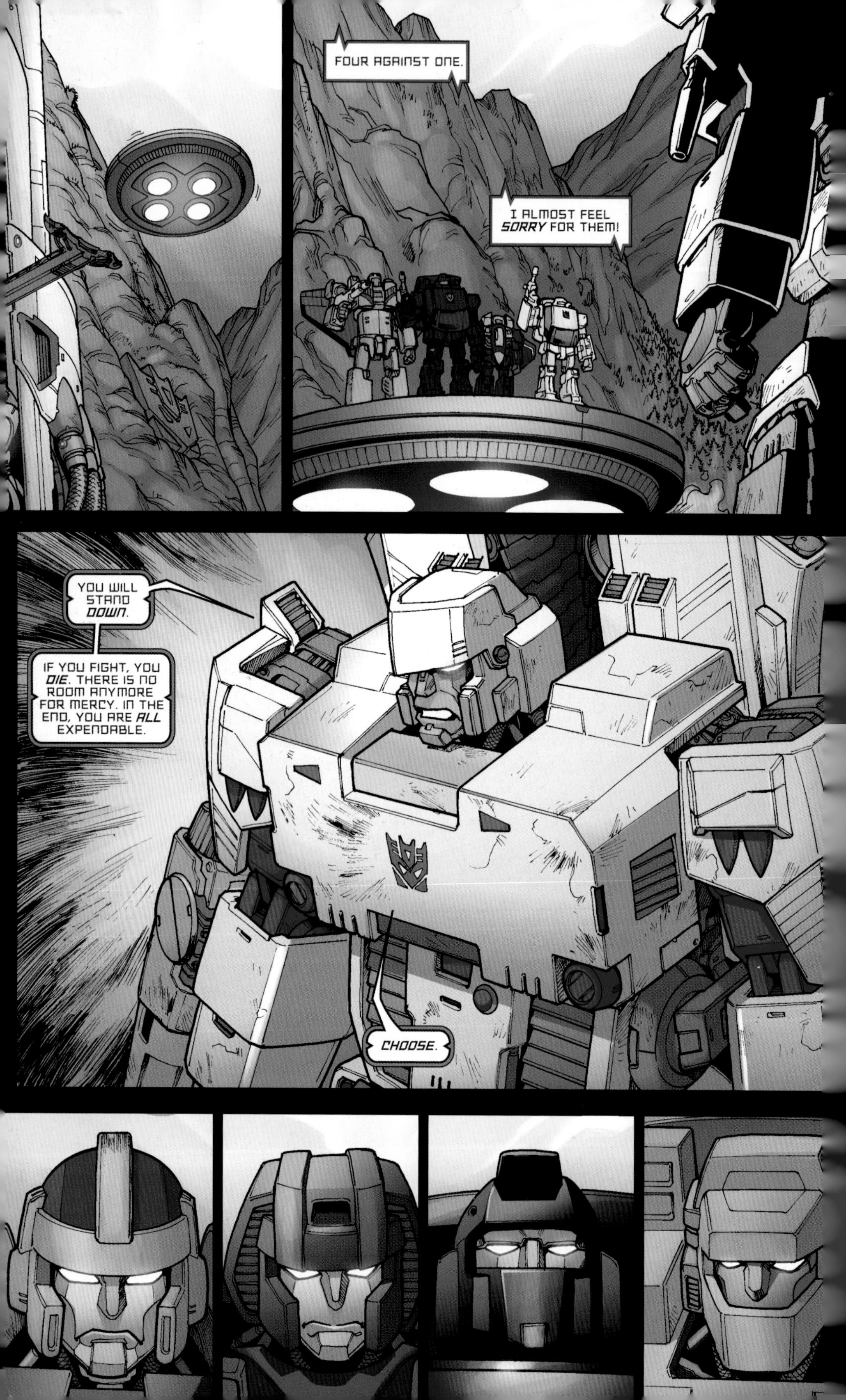
FOUR AGAINST ONE.
I ALMOST FEEL SORRY FOR THEM!
YOU WILL STAND DOWN.
IF YOU FIGHT, YOU DIE. THERE IS NO ROOM ANYMORE FOR MERCY. IN THE END, YOU ARE ALL EXPENDABLE.
CHOOSE.

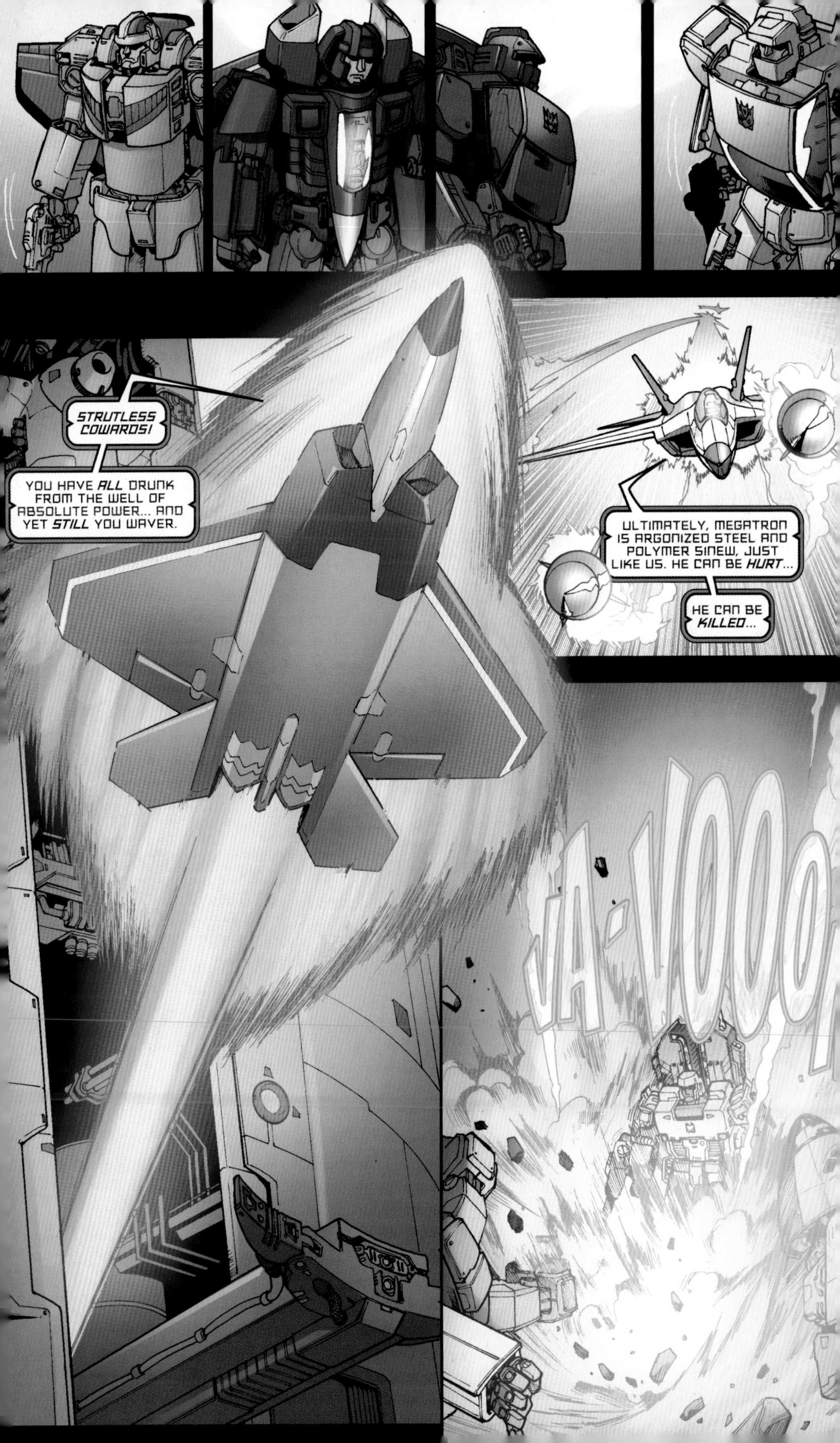
STRUTLESS COWARDS!
YOU HAVE ALL DRUNK FROM THE WELL OF ABSOLUTE POWER... AND YET STILL YOU WAVER.
ULTIMATELY, MEGATRON IS ARGONIZED STEEL AND POLYMER SINEW, JUST LIKE US. HE CAN BE HURT...
HE CAN BE KILLED...

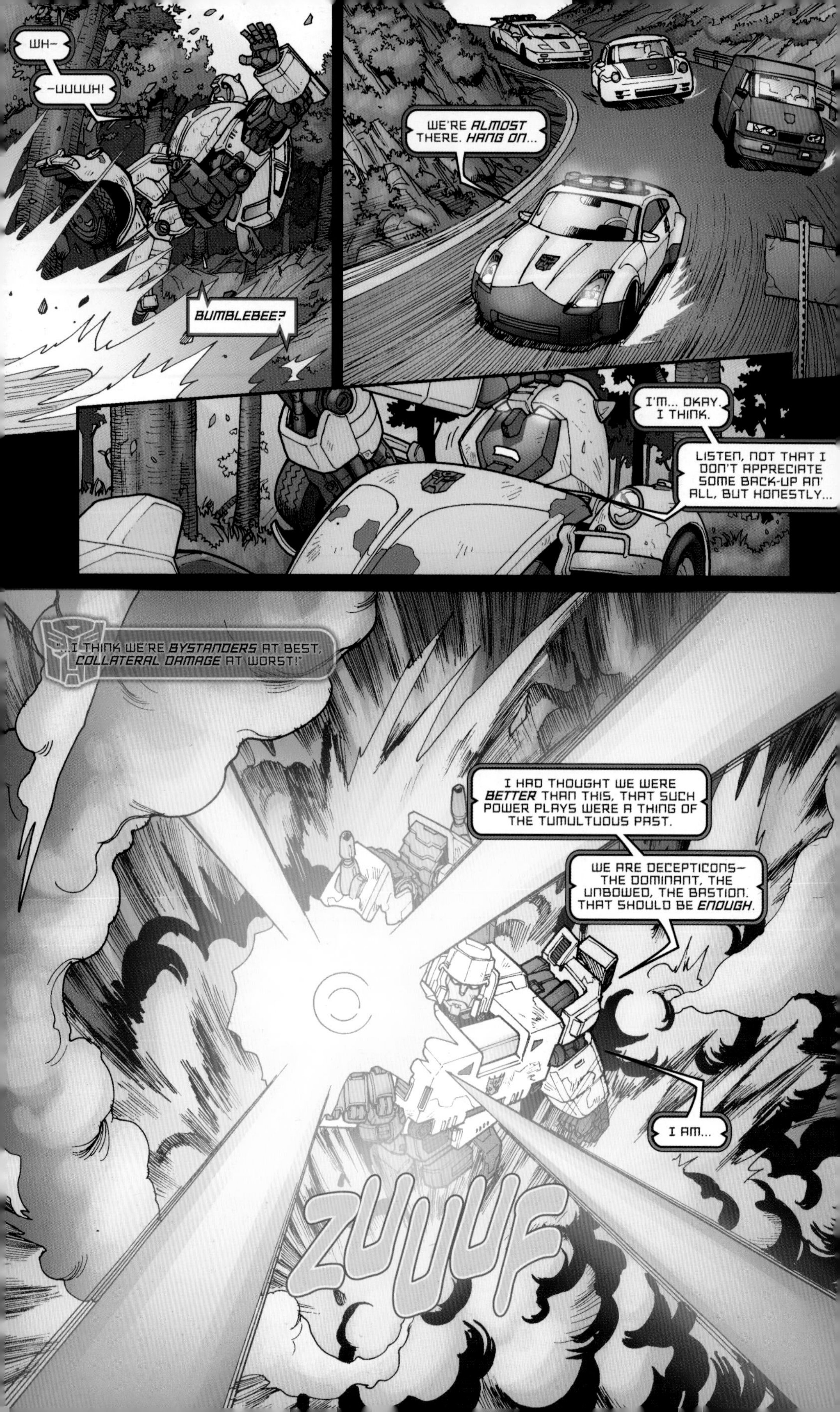
WH–
–UUUUH!
WE'RE *ALMOST* THERE. *HANG ON*...
BUMBLEBEE?
I'M... OKAY. I THINK.
LISTEN, NOT THAT I DON'T APPRECIATE SOME BACK-UP AN' ALL, BUT HONESTLY...
"...I THINK WE'RE *BYSTANDERS* AT BEST, *COLLATERAL DAMAGE* AT WORST!"
I HAD THOUGHT WE WERE *BETTER* THAN THIS, THAT SUCH POWER PLAYS WERE A THING OF THE TUMULTUOUS PAST.
WE ARE DECEPTICONS— THE DOMINANT, THE UNBOWED, THE BASTION. THAT SHOULD BE *ENOUGH*.
I AM...
ZUUUF

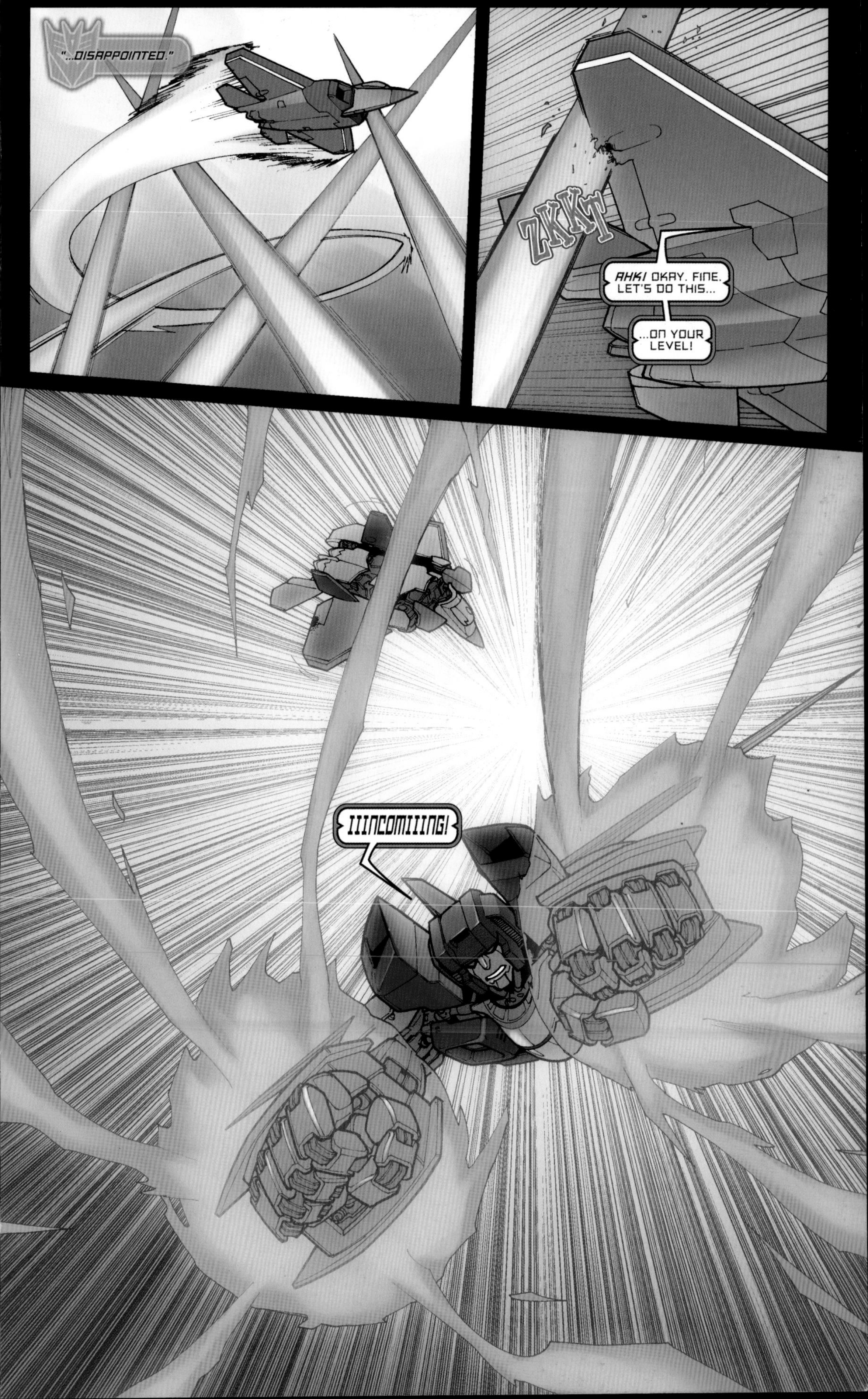
"...DISAPPOINTED."
ZKKT
AHK! OKAY. FINE. LET'S DO THIS...
...ON YOUR LEVEL!
IIINCOMIIING!

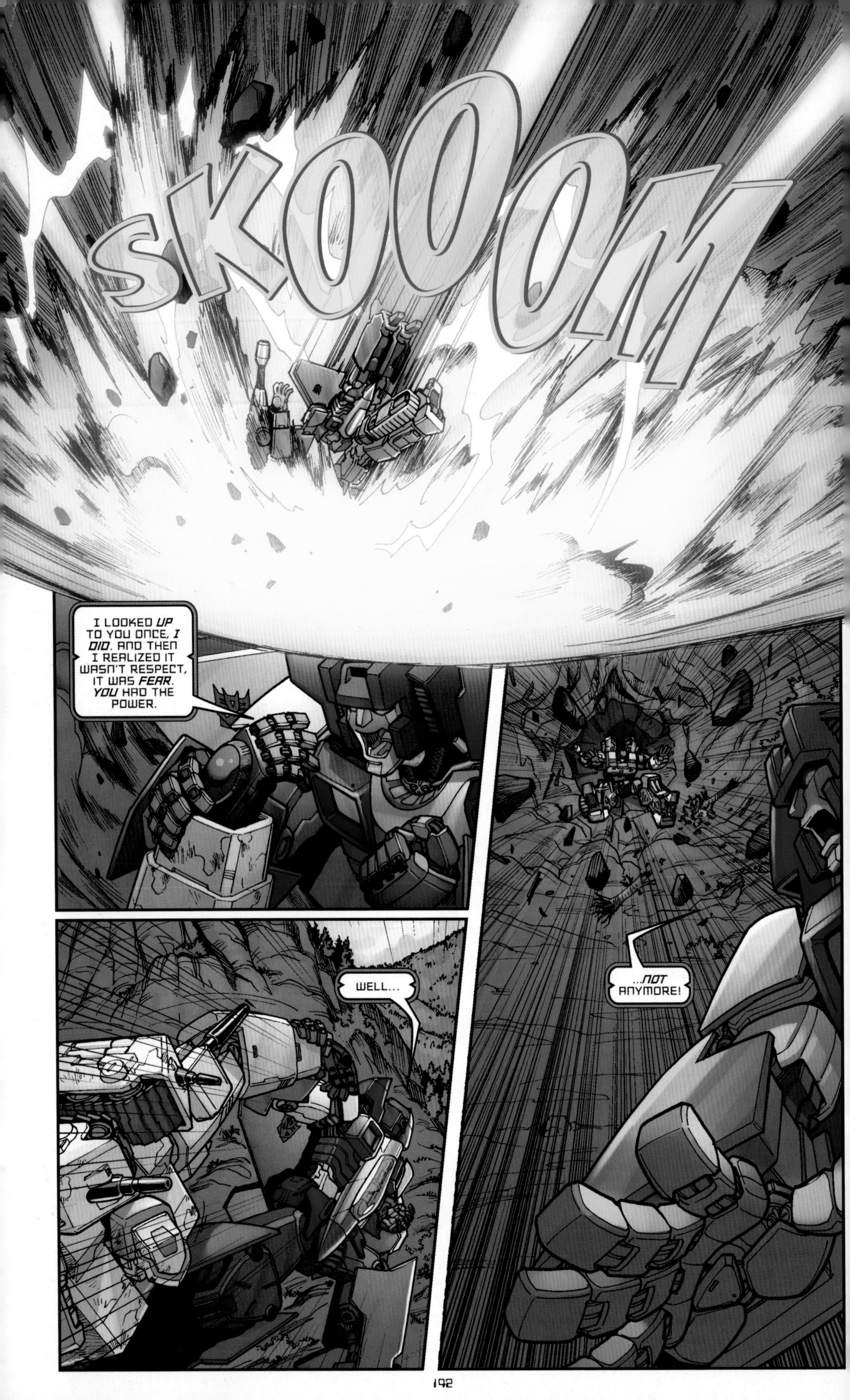

SKOOOM
I LOOKED UP TO YOU ONCE, I DID. AND THEN I REALIZED IT WASN'T RESPECT, IT WAS FEAR. YOU HAD THE POWER.
WELL...
...NOT ANYMORE!

THANKS TO ORE-13, MEGATRON, I HAVE EVOLVED... *BEYOND* YOU! I AM THE *FUTURE.* WHEN YOU POSTED ME TO THIS BACKWATER ROCK IN SPACE...

...YOU WERE SEWING THE SEEDS OF YOUR *OWN* DESTRUCTION! NOW...

...REAP THE WHIRLWIND!

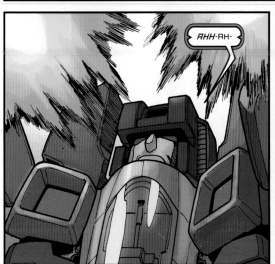

AHH-AH-

-AH-HUH.

THAT... FELT... *GOOD.* REALLY, I CAN'T TELL HOW LONG I'VE—

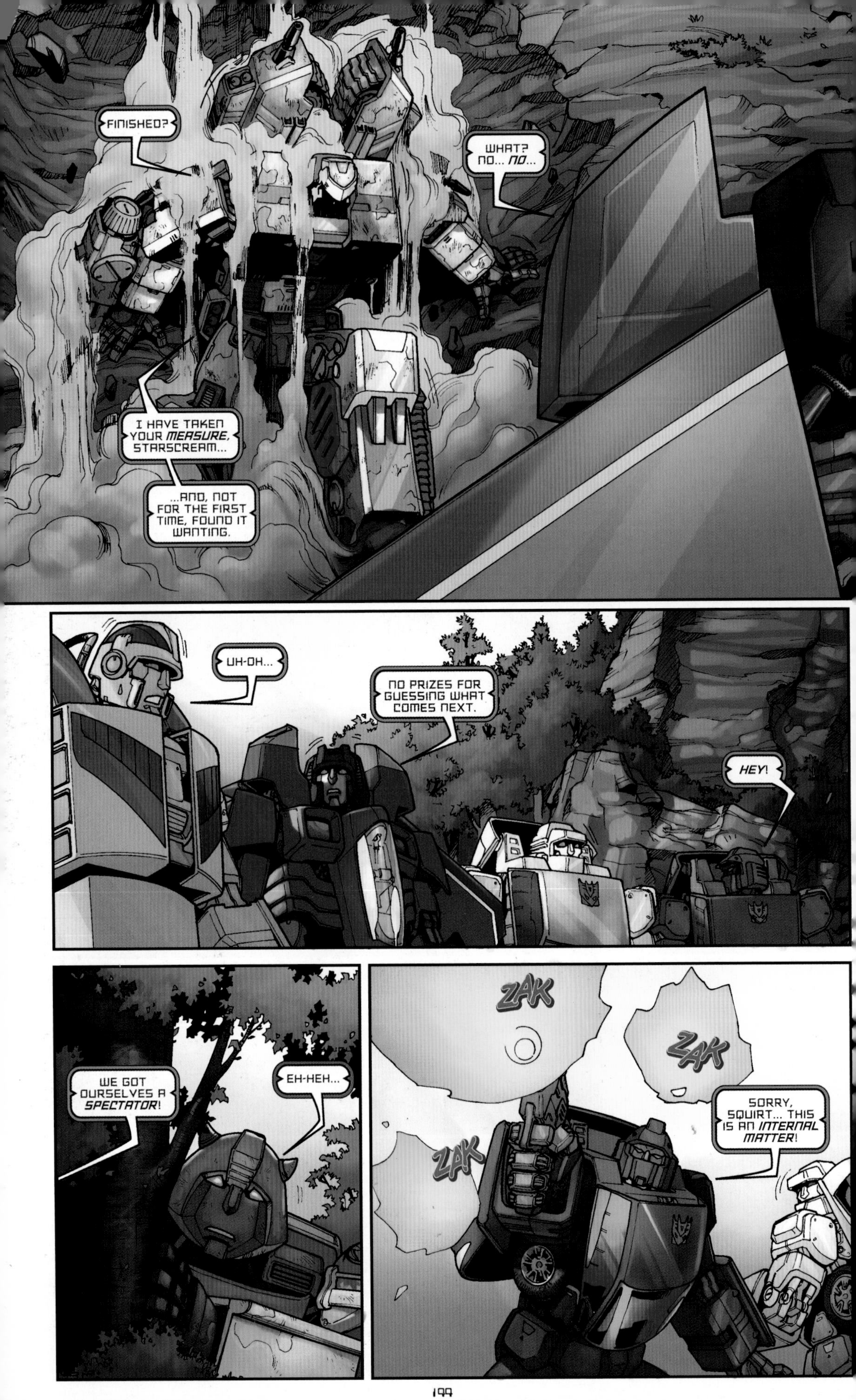
FINISHED?
WHAT? NO... NO...
I HAVE TAKEN YOUR MEASURE, STARSCREAM...
...AND, NOT FOR THE FIRST TIME, FOUND IT WANTING.
UH-OH...
NO PRIZES FOR GUESSING WHAT COMES NEXT.
HEY!
WE GOT OURSELVES A SPECTATOR!
EH-HEH...
ZAK
ZAK
ZAK
SORRY, SQUIRT... THIS IS AN INTERNAL MATTER!

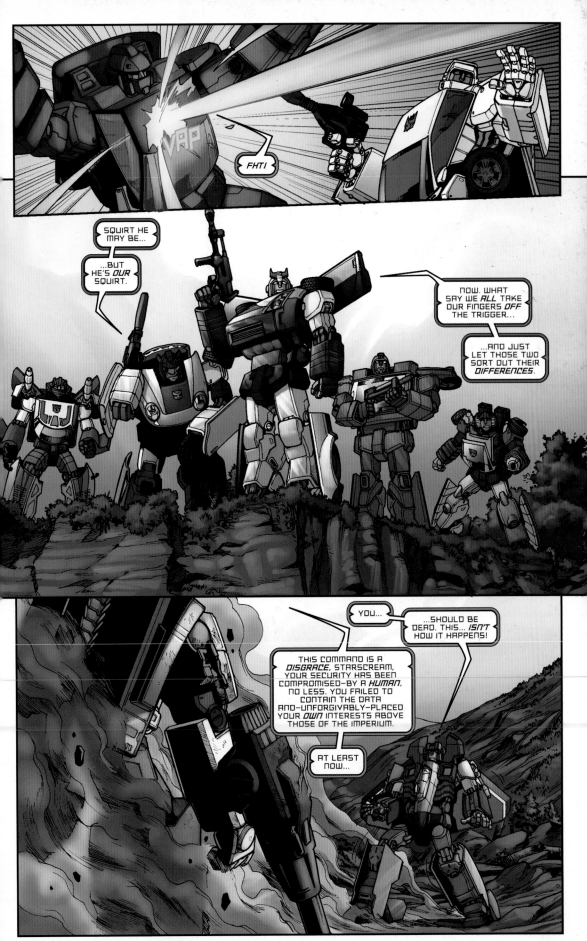

FHT!

SQUIRT HE MAY BE...

...BUT HE'S *OUR* SQUIRT.

NOW. WHAT SAY WE *ALL* TAKE OUR FINGERS *OFF* THE TRIGGER...

...AND JUST LET THOSE TWO SORT OUT THEIR *DIFFERENCES*.

YOU...

...SHOULD BE DEAD. THIS... *ISN'T* HOW IT HAPPENS!

THIS COMMAND IS A *DISGRACE*, STARSCREAM. YOUR SECURITY HAS BEEN COMPROMISED—BY A *HUMAN*, NO LESS. YOU FAILED TO CONTAIN THE DATA AND—UNFORGIVABLY—PLACED YOUR *OWN* INTERESTS ABOVE THOSE OF THE IMPERIUM.

AT LEAST NOW...

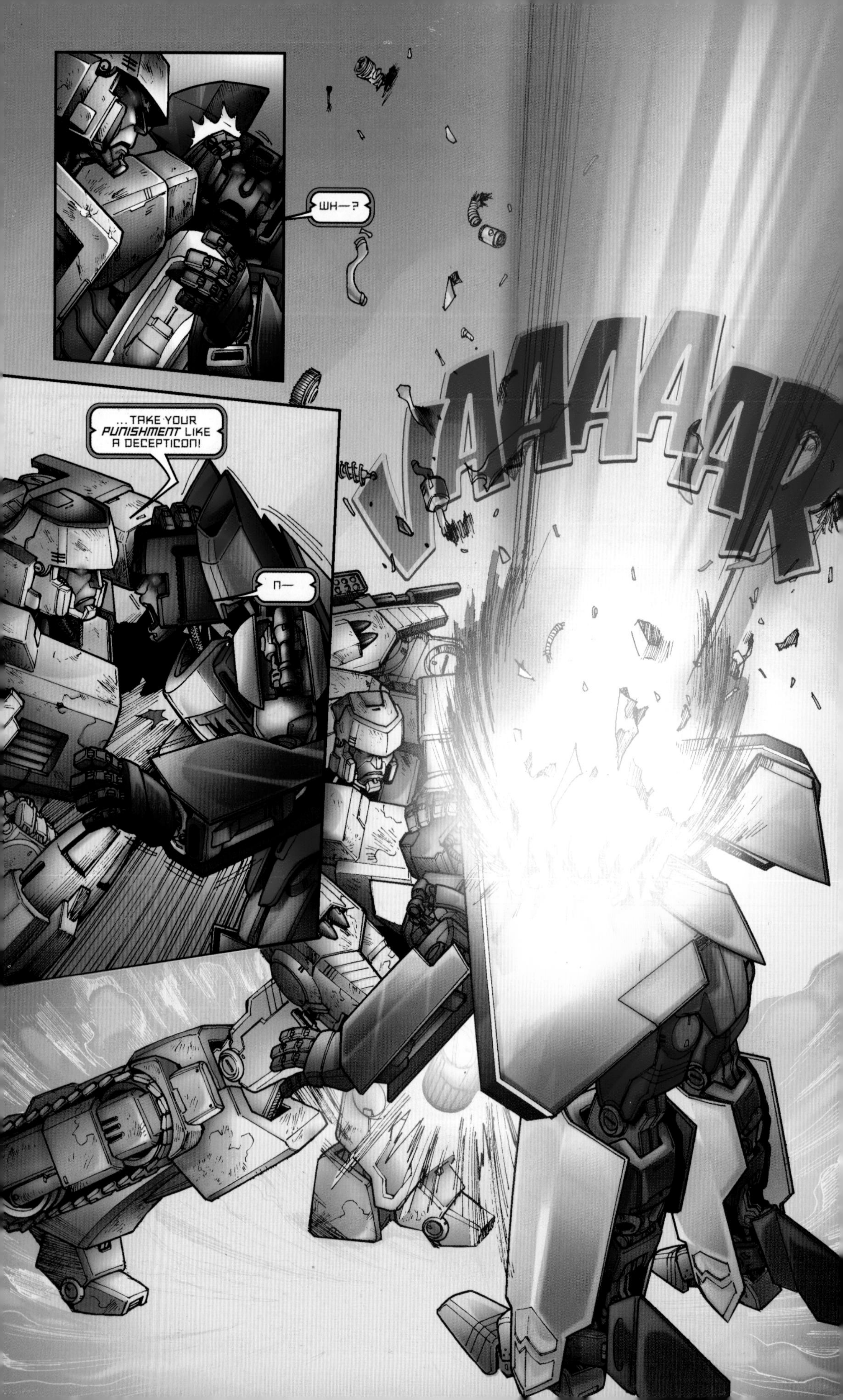
WH—?
...TAKE YOUR PUNISHMENT LIKE A DECEPTICON!
N—
VAAAAAR

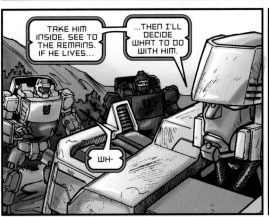

TAKE HIM INSIDE. SEE TO THE REMAINS. IF HE LIVES...

...THEN I'LL DECIDE WHAT TO DO WITH HIM.

WH-

WHAT ABOUT THEM?

PHASE...

...TWO.

PROWL?

WE JUST GOING TO LET THEM SLOPE OFF INTO THEIR COSY SIEGE BUNKER?

YEP.

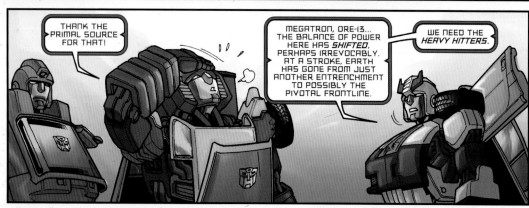

THANK THE >PRIMAL SOURCE< FOR THAT!

MEGATRON, ORE-13... THE BALANCE OF POWER HERE HAS *SHIFTED*, PERHAPS IRREVOCABLY. AT A STROKE, EARTH HAS GONE FROM JUST ANOTHER ENTRENCHMENT TO POSSIBLY THE PIVOTAL FRONTLINE.

WE NEED THE *HEAVY HITTERS*.

IRONHIDE, JAZZ, WHEELJACK, SUNSTREAKER, BUMBLEBEE?

ROLL OUT!

BUT HEY, IF YOU'RE STILL LISTENING, DECEPTICONS...

...WE'LL BE *BACK!*

LAKE MICHIGAN, LATER:

AIRTIGHT SEALS ENGAGED...

TNNG

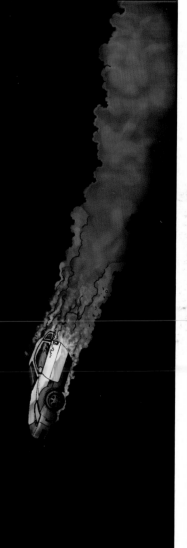

SPLASH

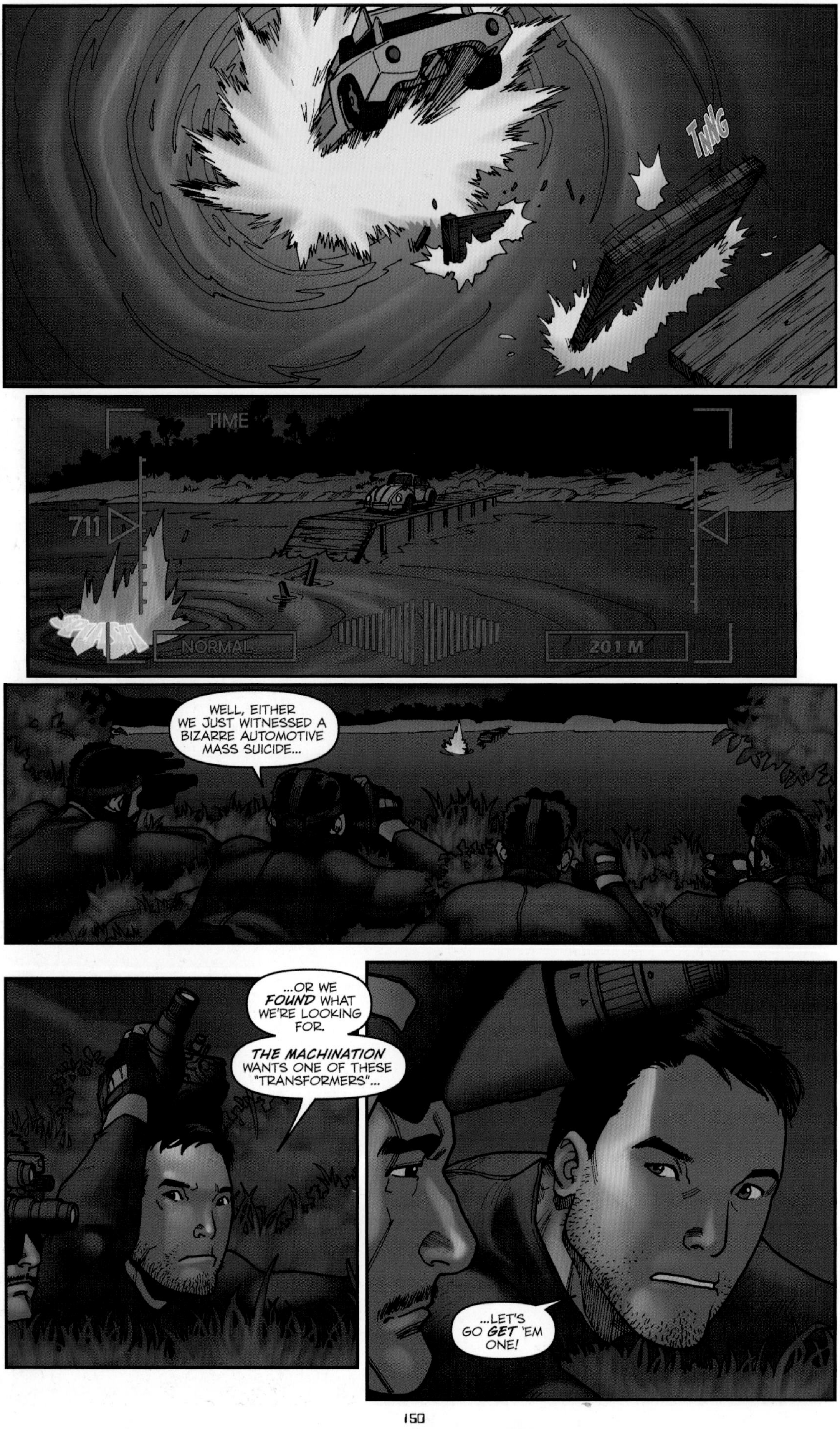
TNNG
TIME
711
SPLASH
NORMAL
201 M
WELL, EITHER WE JUST WITNESSED A BIZARRE AUTOMOTIVE MASS SUICIDE...
...OR WE FOUND WHAT WE'RE LOOKING FOR.
THE MACHINATION WANTS ONE OF THESE "TRANSFORMERS"...
...LET'S GO GET 'EM ONE!

ER, EXCUSE ME,...

...WHAT ARE THE HUMANS DOING *OUT?*

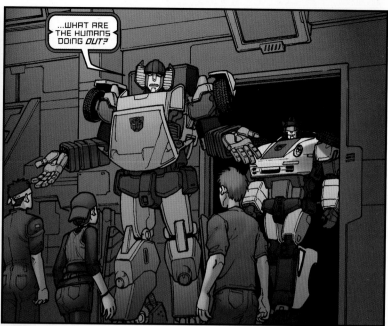

THERE'S A LOCAL EXPRESSION, SUNSTREAKER, SOMETHING ABOUT EQUINE LIFEFORMS AND THE EGRESS FROM THEIR GIVEN HABITATION.

EH?

NEVER MIND.

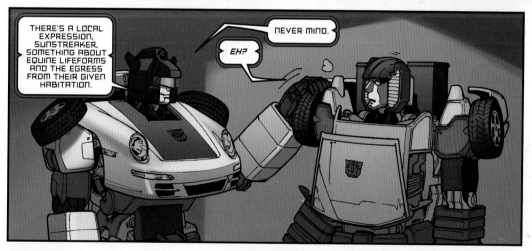

THE HUMANS ARE THE *LEAST* OF OUR CONCERNS. I HATE TO SAY IT, BUT RATCHET WAS RIGHT...

...IT'S TIME WE CALLED IN *OPTIMUS PRIME.*

ER...

...I THINK...

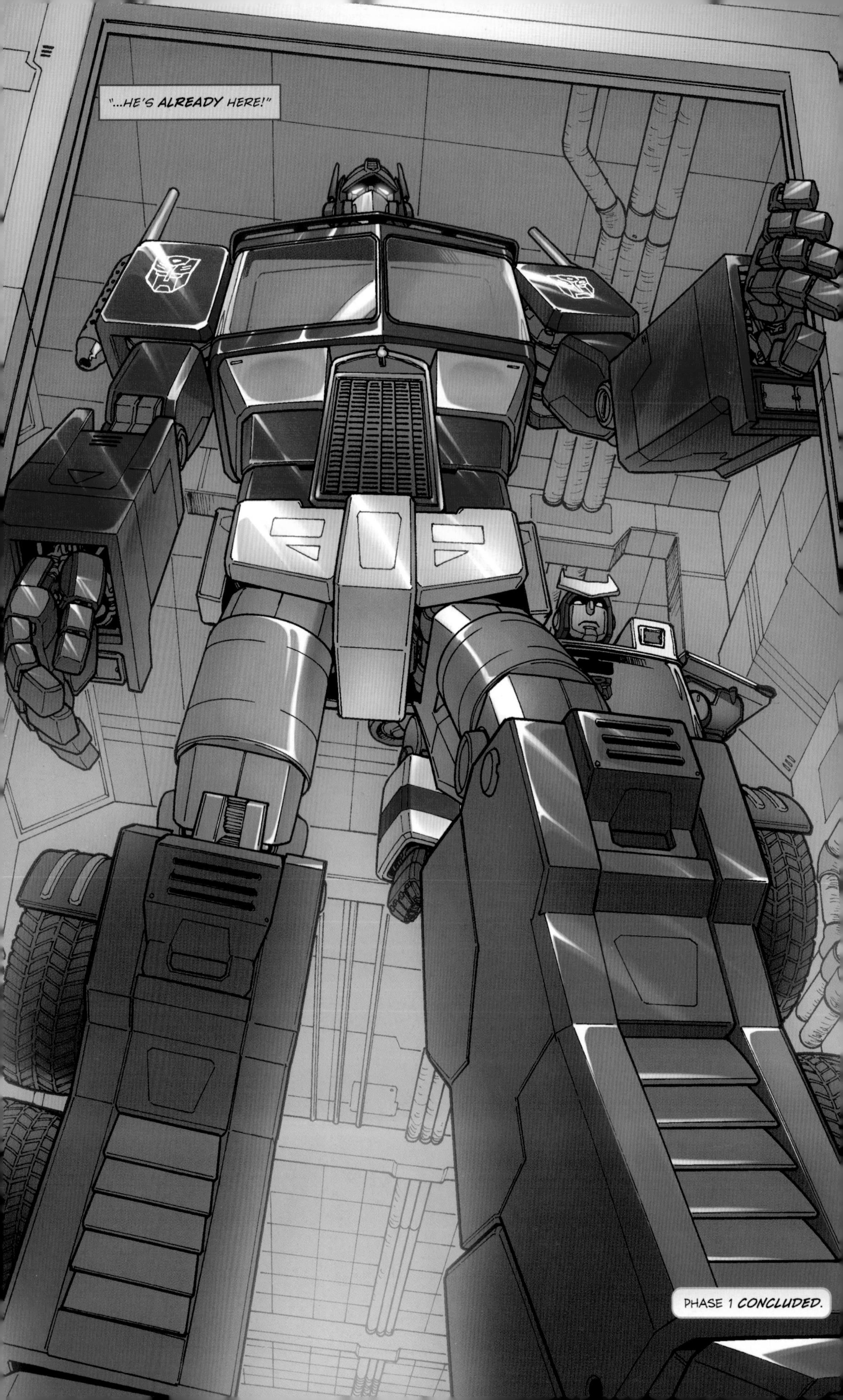
"...HE'S ALREADY HERE!"
PHASE 1 CONCLUDED.

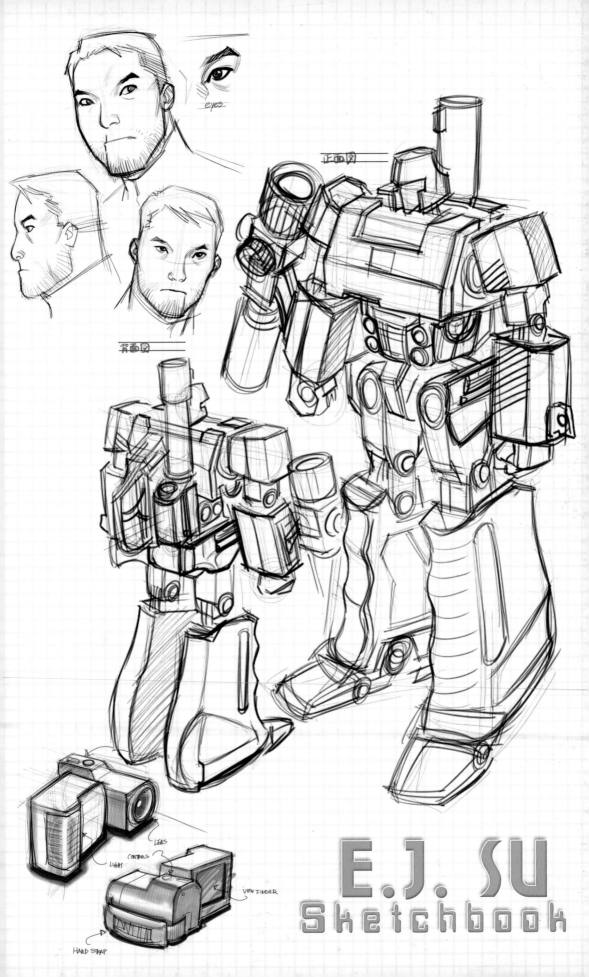

eyes

正面図

背面図

LENS

CONTROLS

LIGHT

VIEW FINDER

HAND STRAP

E.J. SU
Sketchbook

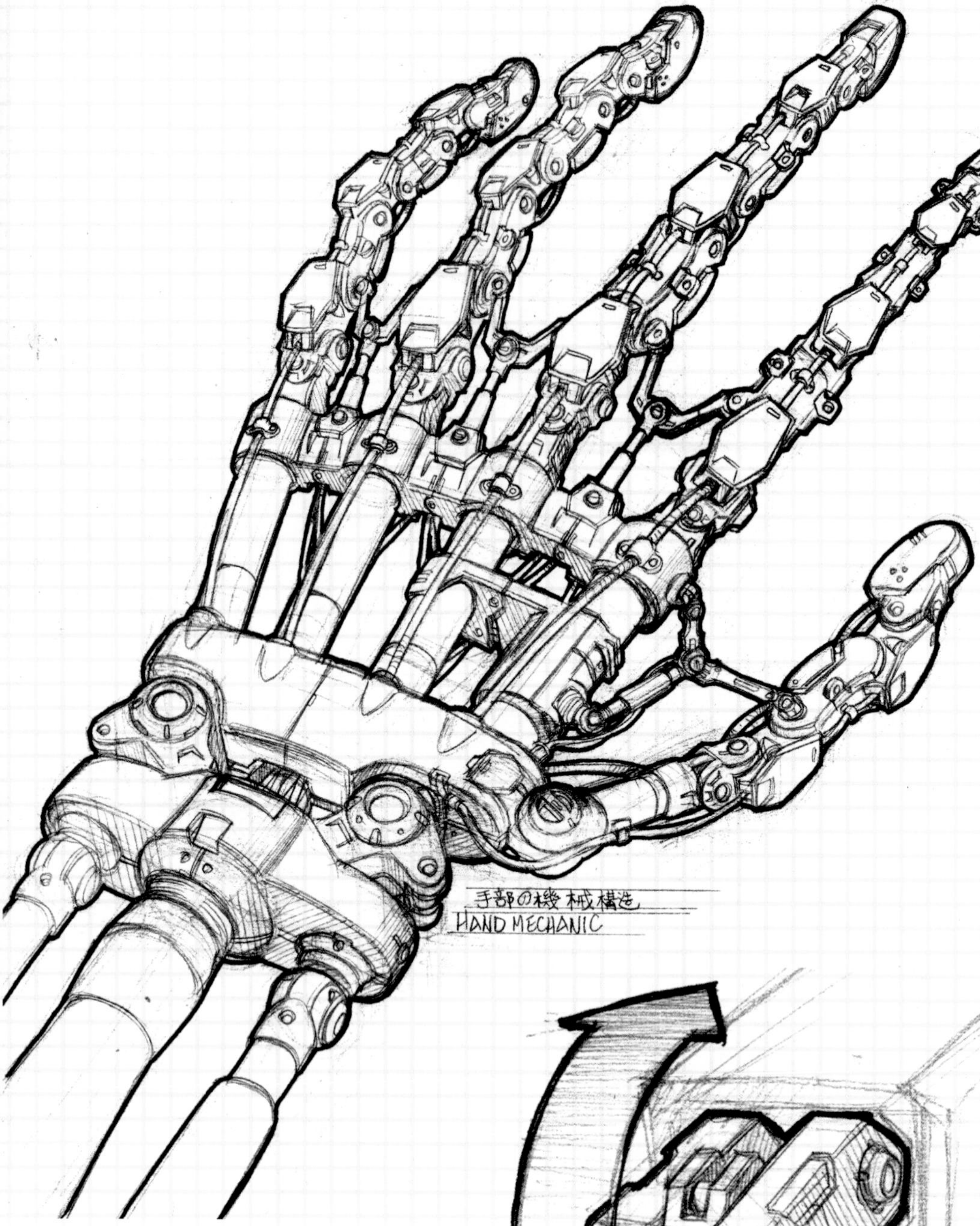
手部の機械構造
HAND MECHANIC

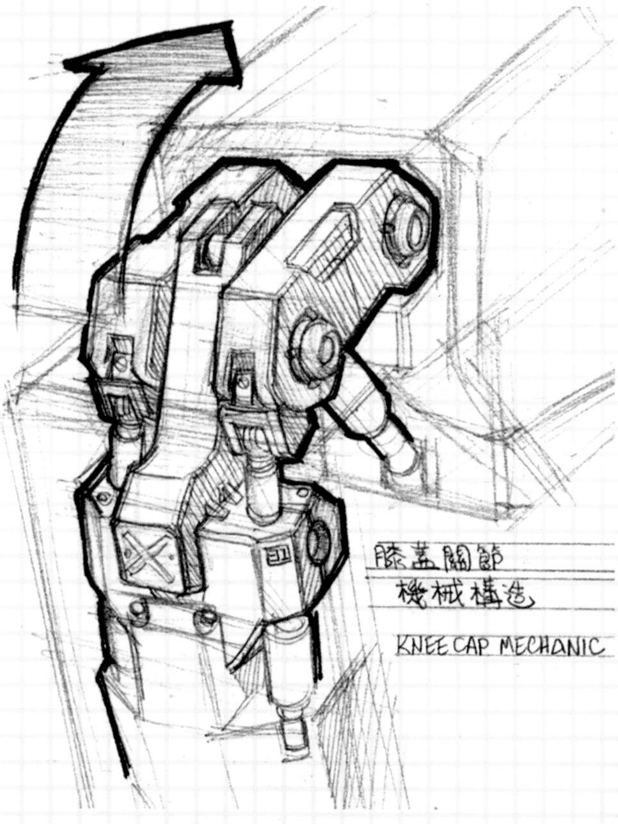
膝蓋関節
機械構造
KNEE CAP MECHANIC

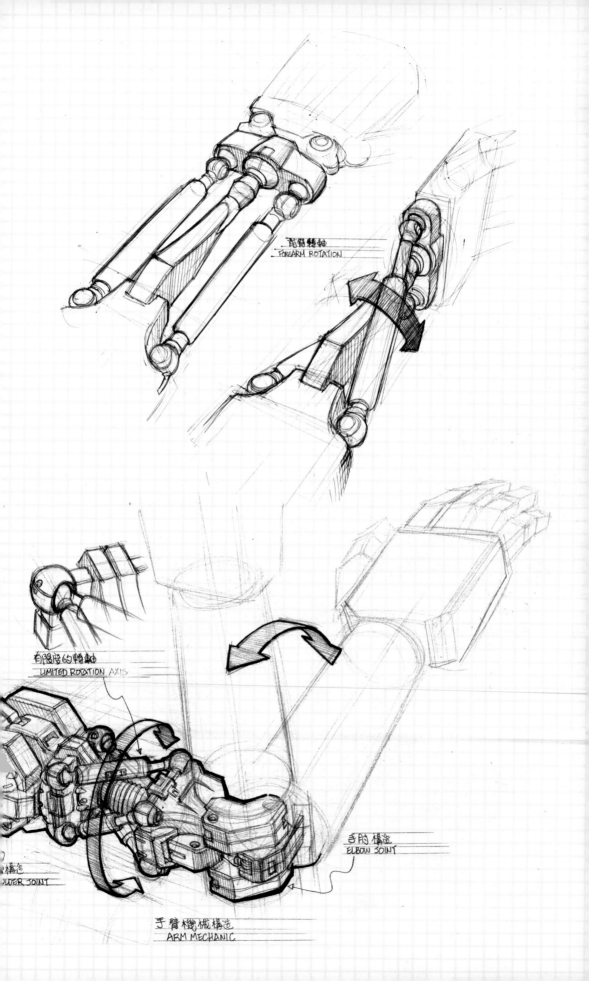

前臂轉軸
FOREARM ROTATION

有限度的轉軸
LIMITED ROTATION AXIS

手肘構造
ELBOW JOINT

構造
WER JOINT

手臂機械構造
ARM MECHANIC

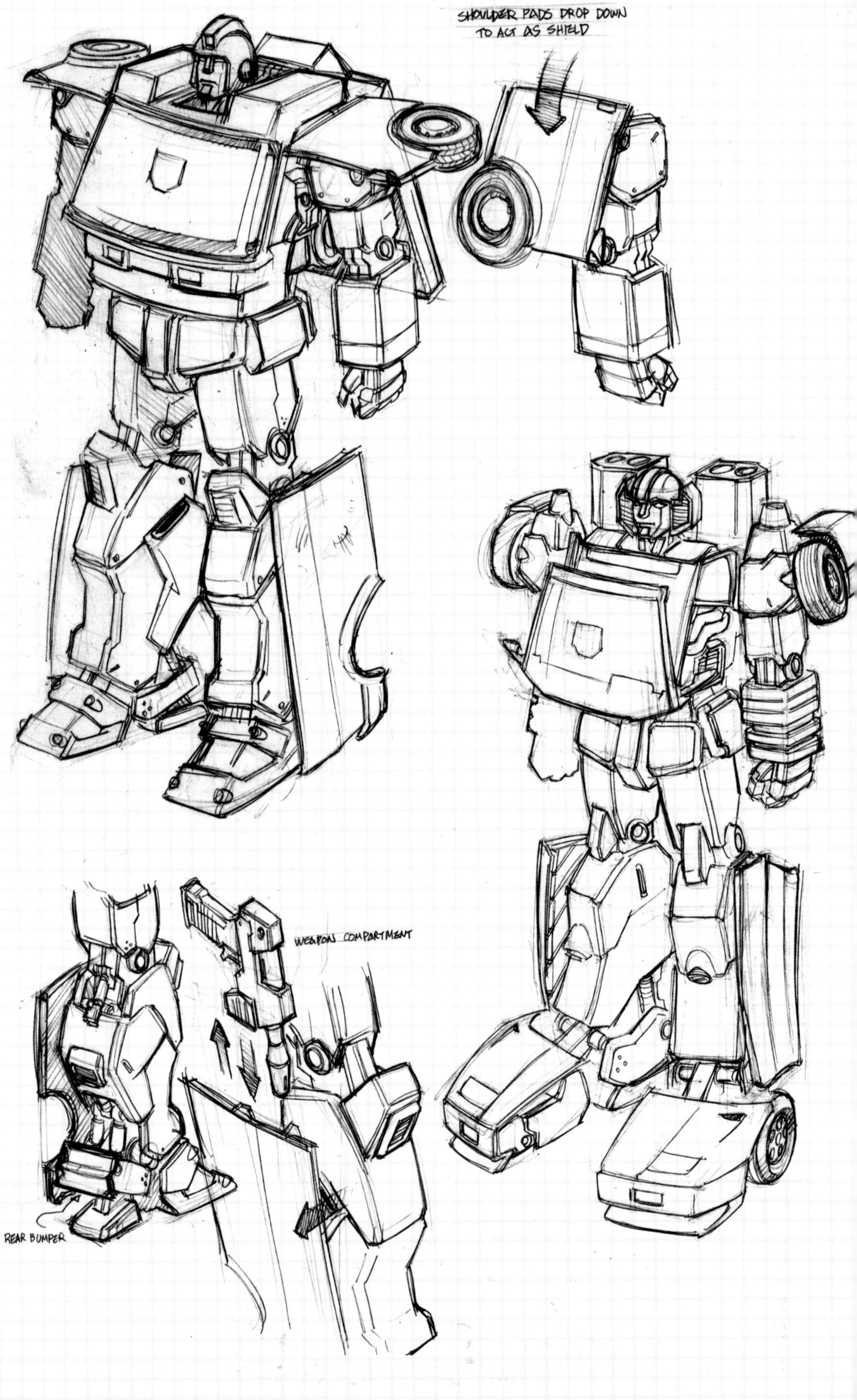
SHOULDER PADS DROP DOWN
TO ACT AS SHIELD
WEAPON COMPARTMENT
REAR BUMPER

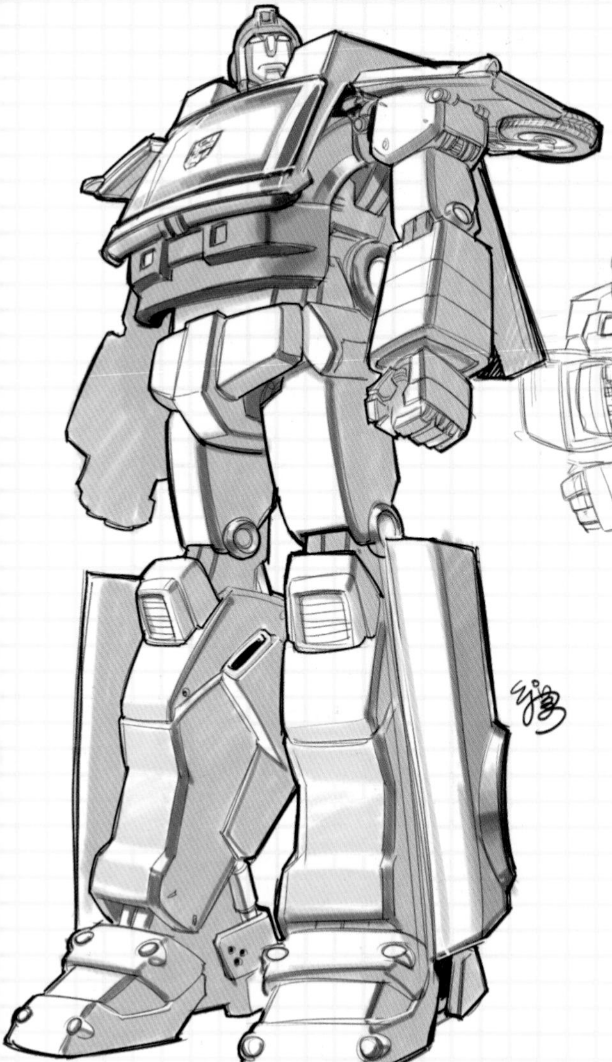

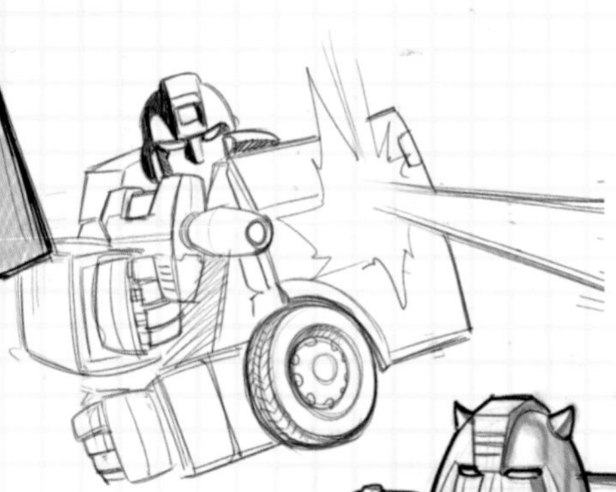

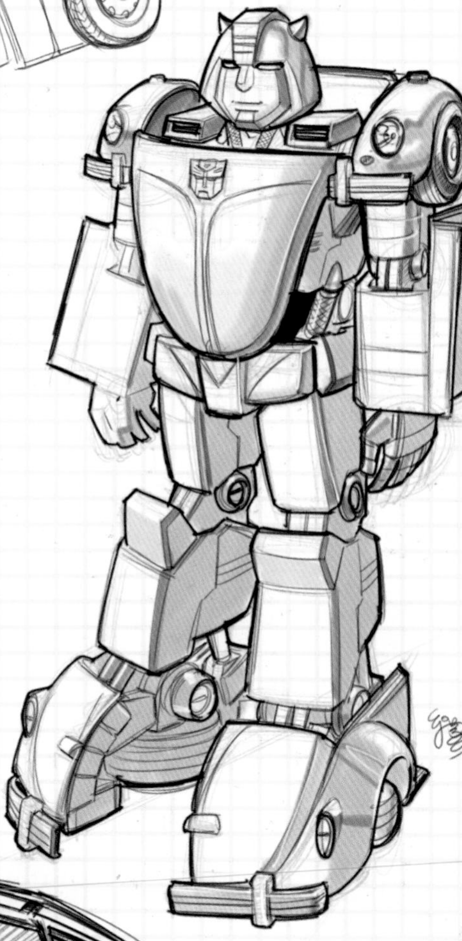

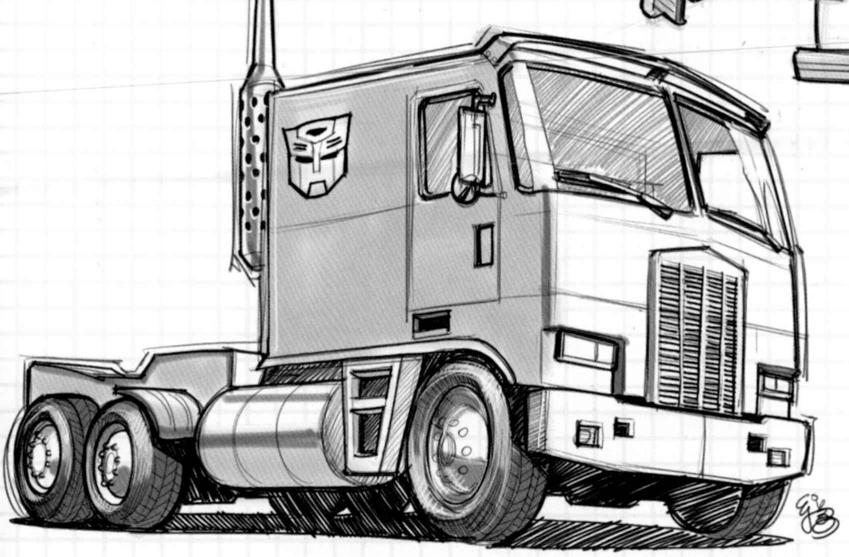

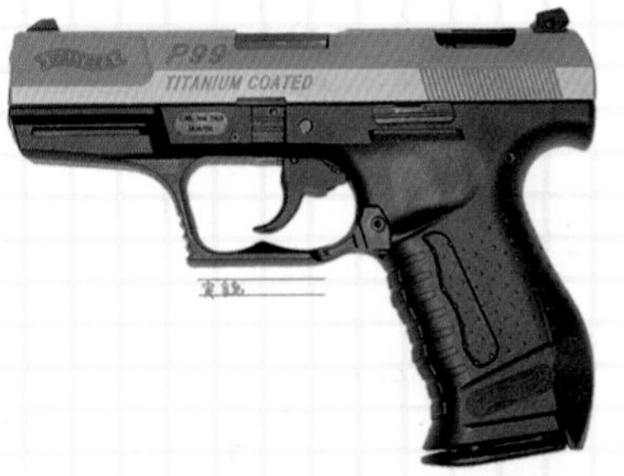
P99
TITANIUM COATED
実銃

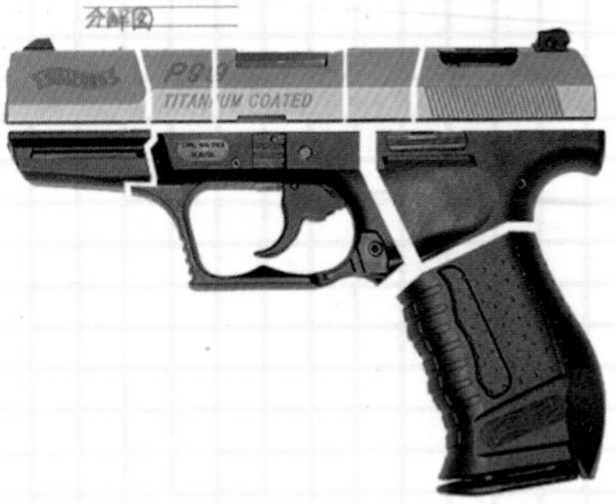
分解図
P99
TITANIUM COATED

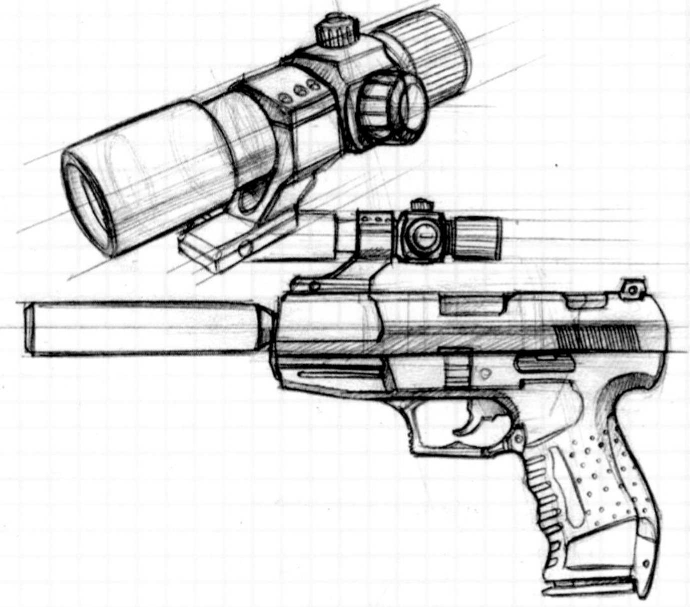

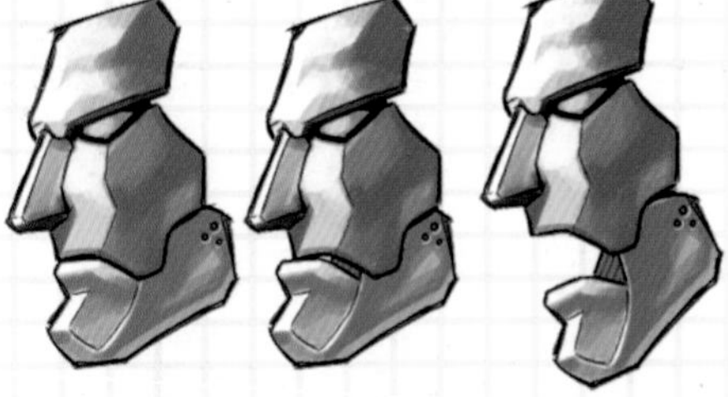

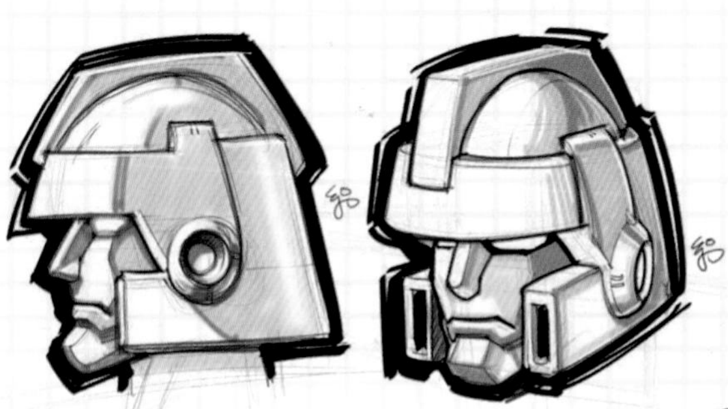

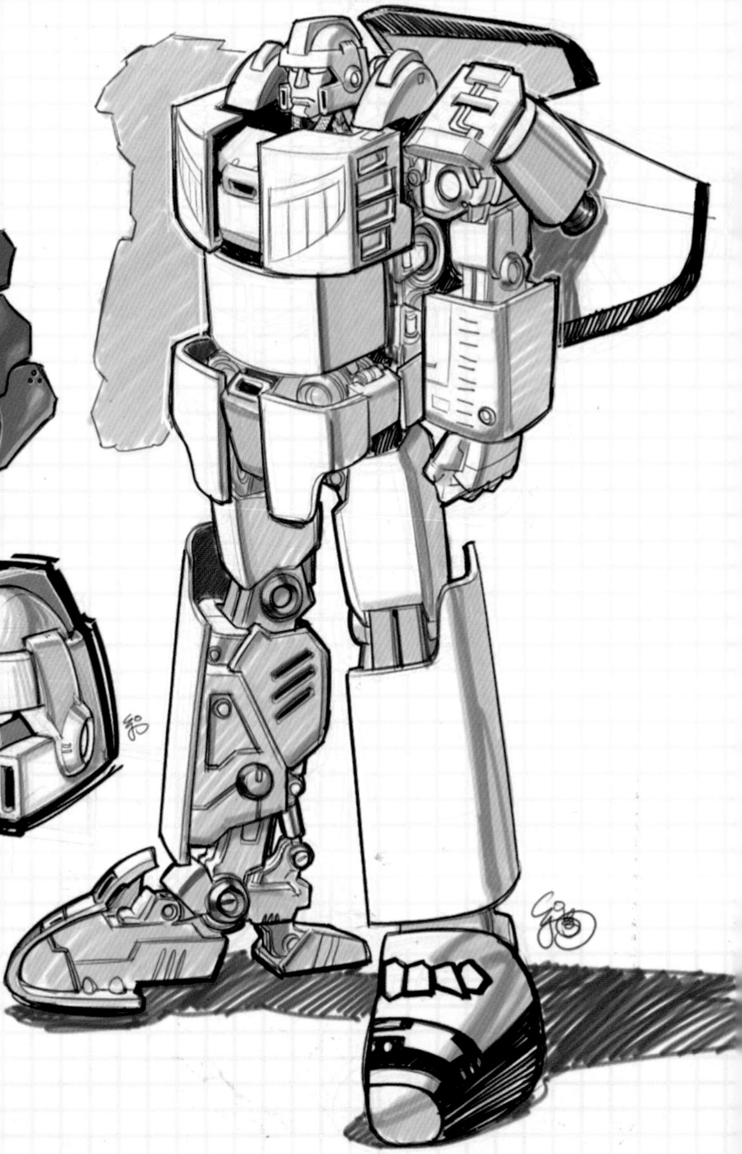

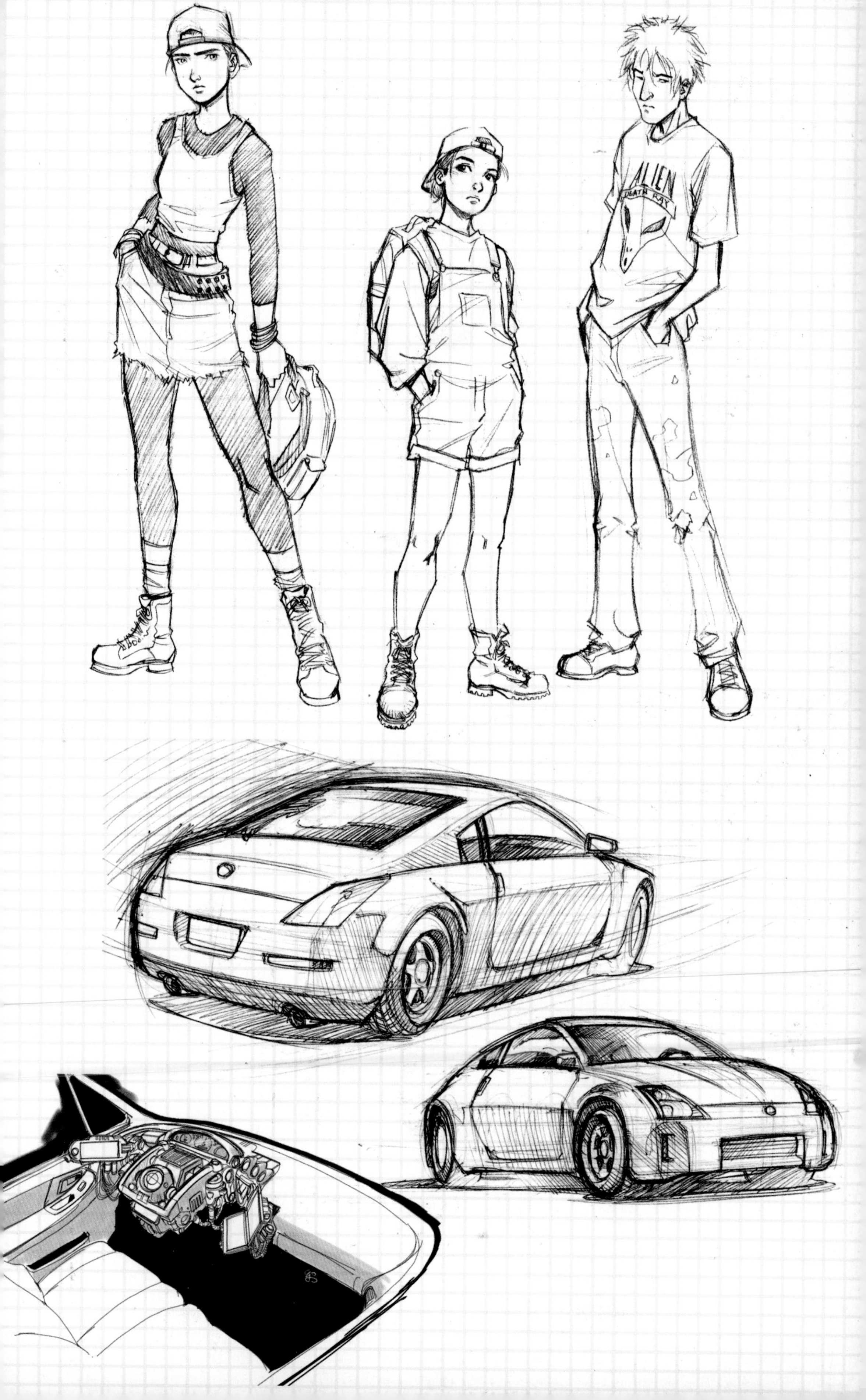
ALIEN
DEATH RAY

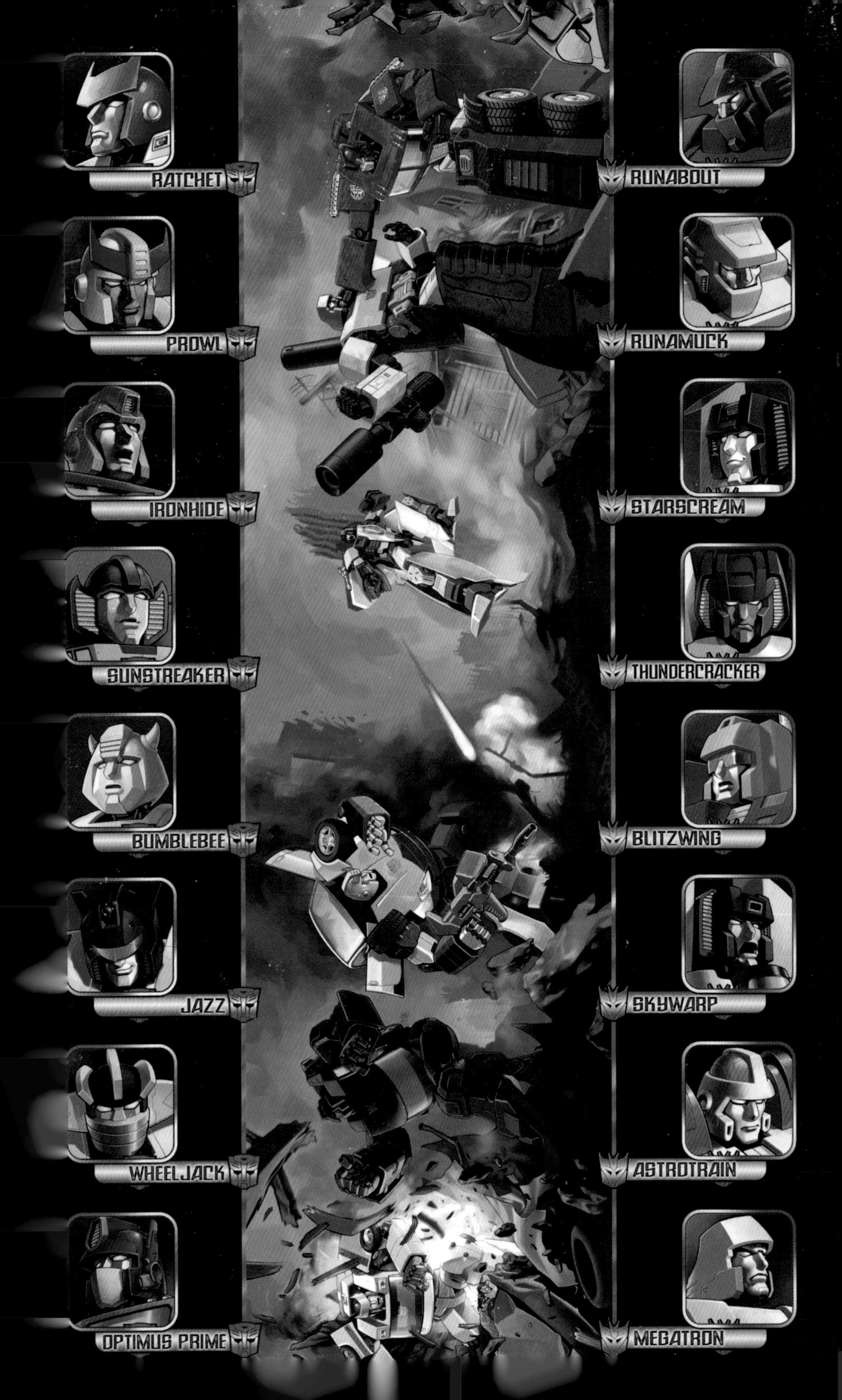
RATCHET
PROWL
IRONHIDE
SUNSTREAKER
BUMBLEBEE
JAZZ
WHEELJACK
OPTIMUS PRIME
RUNABOUT
RUNAMUCK
STARSCREAM
THUNDERCRACKER
BLITZWING
SKYWARP
ASTROTRAIN
MEGATRON